Responding to Youth Crime

Responding to Youth Crime

Towards radical criminal justice partnerships

Paul Omojo Omaji
LLM, PhD

HAWKINS PRESS
2003

Published in Sydney by

Hawkins Press
A division of The Federation Press
71 John St, Leichhardt, NSW, 2040
PO Box 45, Annandale, NSW, 2038
Ph: (02) 9552 2200 Fax: (02) 9552 1681
E-mail: info@federationpress.com.au
Website: http://www.federationpress.com.au

National Library of Australia Cataloguing-in-Publication data:
    Omaji, Paul.
        Responding to youth crime: towards radical criminal justice partnerships.

    Bibliography
    Includes index.
    ISBN 1 876067 20 9

    1. Juvenile delinquency. 2. Criminal justice, Administration of. 3. Juvenile delinquency –
    Prevention. I. Title.

364.36

Typeset by The Federation Press, Leichhardt, NSW.
    Printed by Southwood Press Pty Ltd, Marrickville, NSW.

Contents

Acknowledgments   viii

Introduction   1
    Background: the context of the book   2
    The research   9
    Content   13

1   Criminal justice thinking about youth   17
    Youth as a locus of anxiety   18
    How police think about youth   22
    How the courts think about youth   25
    How detention staff think about youth   30
    Making sense of criminal justice perceptions of youth   32
       Ideological factors   32
       Sociological factors   33
       Mass media repackaging of 'youth as problem'   34
       Reporting on minority racial and ethnic youth   37
    Conclusion   38

2   Young 'actors' in criminal justice 'imaging' of youth   40
    Youth and image construction   41
    Imaging through youth cultural expressions   42
    Fighting against being inferior or disempowered   43
    Constructing images through attitudes to criminal justice
       agencies   44
       Youth attitudes toward the police   45
       Youth attitudes toward the courts   49
       Youth attitudes toward detention   50
    It's not all perception   52
    Reality behind the reality: the broader context of youth action   54
    Conclusion   55

3   Traditional criminal justice response to youth crime   57
    A historical overview   59
    From welfare to justice model   65
    Contemporary modes of processing young offenders   69
       Policing youth crime   71
       Judicial response to youth crime   79
       Detention: 'banging up the youth'   81
    Traditional response to youth crime and international standards   82
       Juvenile justice decalogue   83
       Western juvenile justice systems breach the standards   84
    Conclusion   88

4 Trends and costs of traditional criminal justice response to youth crime   90

Trends in youth crime: demography is not destiny   91
  The tyranny of 'small numbers'   92
Trends in police arrest   93
Trends in court processing   96
Trends in detention   100
Trends in victimisation of young people   103
Reflections on trends in youth crime and victimisation   104
Costs of traditional response to youth crime   108
  Global overview   108
Conclusion   111

5 Towards partnership: changing perspectives in criminal justice   113

Failure of the reactive model, universally acknowledged   114
  Why the failing machine ticks on   121
Shifting thoughts among criminal justice agencies   122
  Police: towards a community and problem-solving model   122
  Courts: towards a therapeutic model   123
  Corrections: towards constructive custody   126
Searching for the grail: paradigm shift towards 'partnership'   127
  Conceptual debates and perceptions about the partnership
    approach   131
Conclusion   135

6 Criminal justice partnerships: selected experiences   137

Criminal justice agency-centred partnership model   138
  Baton Rouge Partnership for the Prevention of Juvenile Gun
    Violence, LA (US)   138
  Maple Ridge Youth Conference Project (Canada)   143
  Western Australian Juvenile Justice Teams (Australia)   144
  Mt Roskill Police Community Approach Project (NZ)   146
  Midtown Community Court, New York   148
Local authority-centred partnership model   151
  Safer Slough Enterprise Partnership (UK)   151
  Cairns Community Safety Project, Queensland (Australia)   157
Conclusion   164

7 The partnership benchmark for traditional criminal justice response   165

Comparing key features of the partnership projects to the
    traditional model   165
  Motivations   166
  Fundamental assumptions   168
  Types of preventative intervention   169

Structural design and administration   170
Strategies of intervention   174
Shortfalls in the existing partnership approach   175
Nature of community and youth involvement   175
No clear paradigm shift   177
Ground rules for high impact ('dinkum' and effective)
    partnerships   179
Intensity of collaboration and the autonomy question   179
Empowering structures and protocols   180
Strategically involving young people   181
Operational imperatives   183
Conclusion   185

8   **Criminal justice prevention of youth crime:**
   future directions   187

Where we have been   188
Where we should be heading   190
Moving forward with criminal justice prevention partnerships
    and youth integration   191
Towards 'youth-friendly' partnerships   192
Criminal justice agencies to get involved in all levels of
    prevention   194
Conclusion   199

References   201

Index   221

Acknowledgments

I am grateful to several individuals and organisations whose support made the writing of this book possible. I cannot name them all here, but they know themselves and the appreciation I owe to them. My special thanks are due to some, and it will be remiss of me not to mention them specifically.

Edith Cowan University funded the initial research for the book.

The Canadian Mounted Police, Canadian National Crime Prevention Council, New Zealand Police, and the Crime Prevention Unit of the New Zealand Office of the Prime Minister and Cabinet were generous towards me with some critical public, but rare, documents.

Dr Terence Love of Edith Cowan University assisted at the initial stages, when I was defining the focus for the book and determining the appropriate avenue for its publication.

My wife, Alice Omaji, helped enormously with the data collection.

Mr Charles Edwards, a former UK police officer of 20 years standing and a former colleague of mine at Edith Cowan University, read the first draft of the manuscript and made invaluable comments and suggestions.

The anonymous readers of the final manuscript drew my attention to gaps which, if not filled, could have diminished the essence of the book.

The editorial team at the Federation Press showed professional commitment to the book and offered helpful advice in relation to some aspects of the presentation in the book.

With enviable grace, my family – wife and children – bore my absences during the numerous research travels and when I had to disappear from family activities in order to work on the book.

Although the book benefited tremendously from the contributions of many, the responsibility for all the imperfections lie wholly with me.

This book is dedicated to:

To the conscientious police officers, judges, correctional officers, and other people connected with youth justice, who share the vision of working in partnership to return straying young people to productive citizenship.

To my late mother, Mrs Ataidu Omaji, who epitomised, and taught me to appreciate, productive citizenship.

To my wife and children, whose support inspires my commitment to productive citizenship.

Introduction

The intellectual's error consists in believing that it is possible to know without understanding and especially without feeling and passion ..., that the intellectual can be an intellectual ... if [s]he is distinct and detached from [subjects] without feeling the elemental passions of the [subjects], understanding them and thus explaining and justifying them in a particular historical situation, connecting them dialectically to the laws of history, to a superior conception of the world. (Antonio Gramsci, cited in Simon 1982, p 100)

This book presents a critique and a vision of the responses of criminal justice agencies to the incidence and prevention of youth crime in selected western countries. The critique examines the social and legal processes in which young lives have, with devastating consequences, become entangled with ideological constructs, political opportunism, criminal pathways, and the justice (so-called corrective) systems that are essentially one-dimensional and criminogenic. I do not suggest that the systems deliberately set out to damage their young 'clients', although this may well be the case in some instances; nor do I argue that in all cases all young people experience the systems negatively.[1] The task of the critique is to illuminate the socially grounded 'mischief' in the traditional criminal justice approaches which traps young people into, rather than turns them away from, a life of crime.

The vision, on the other hand, is about the criminal justice agencies becoming more pro-active partners in societal efforts to guide 'troubled' youth, real or imagined, into becoming happy and productive citizens. For these agencies to take on this radical role, they must exercise less of their reactive and retributive powers and more of the restorative capacities within their statutory roles in their dealings with young people. The outcome must be a reconfigured youth justice system which is youth centred, youth friendly and which protects the rights and welfare of young people, be they offenders, victims or ordinary community members (Leacock 2000, p 174). Consistent with this vision, the book validates attempts by the criminal justice agencies to break out of their traditional moulds and to refocus their crime prevention roles through partnership with community organisations. It challenges the agencies to expand rather than contract their 'reform' orientation both in philosophy and praxis towards a radical preventive partnership model which, as conceptualised in the last four chapters of this book, is a more promising way forward in the development of healthier and safer communities.

While the prevailing view is that these agencies have been needlessly and deleteriously interfering with young lives (see Chapter 4 in particular), this book expresses the hope that the lessons of the past and the more humane contemporary technologies (institutions and discourses) of justice

1

can be harnessed towards a redeeming experience for the future gene-rations of youth. In this regard, the book sympathises with the emerging research methodological tool, namely Appreciative Inquiry, which not only 'confronts the negative' but also 'accentuates the positive' in the course of any investigation. This may show a predilection for idealism over cynicism but then Appreciative Inquiry is about analysing the failings of a system, locating the sources of abiding life and energy in this system, and building on these residual 'positives'.[2]

Although grounded in dialectical sociology, this book does not attempt to compare and contrast how the socio-political and economic conditions of the selected countries affect specific practices of the criminal justice agencies across national or regional jurisdictions. Rather, it draws on some contextual commonalities among the countries in order to demonstrate, generically, the failure of the traditional approach that the agencies have taken towards youth crime and to develop an alternative approach which must stretch the role of these agencies beyond their ineffective and, indeed, counterproductive 'comfort zones'.

Admittedly, the book employs essentialising categories such as youth, traditional criminal/juvenile justice systems, negative perceptions or stereotyping, media construction, western world, race, crime, and pre-ventive partnerships. In so doing, it draws generalisations beyond the particularities of individual situations. This is justified because a conceptual cross-national and multi-factorial analysis, such as underpins this book, requires a willingness 'to essentialise certain relationships as objects of knowledge which are not reducible to each other' or to individual subjects without unduly fragmenting understanding (Snider 1998, p 4). A major risk in this approach is that significant differences can be understated or ignored.

While efforts have been made to minimise such a risk, the priority here is to provide a coherent knowledge and understanding about criminal justice responses to youth crime, using experiences of several countries and materials from disparate sources. Deriving from perspectives that embody my programmatic convictions about justice and the place of young people in society, the presentation of the knowledge and understanding has tried to avoid the *intellectual's error* that Antonio Gramsci warns about. Thus, I have sought not only to know and understand my subjects, but also to present relevant issues with 'feeling and passion' while observing appropriate canons of social scientific research.

Background: the context of the book

At core, my research has led me to the view that crime is not our problem, much less the problem we had to have. Crime is fundamentally sympto-matic of a complex set of social structures and processes within which law breaking or criminal identities are constructed, imposed, adopted and/or earned. Beside the predisposing influences which are themselves largely a product of public policies, the dyadic relationship between the apparatuses of official social control and the members of the population that end up bearing criminal identities plays an incontrovertible role in the creation of this symptom. The position that this book develops, therefore, is that it is highly suspect to continue to concentrate resources disproportionately on the symptom when the underlying causes (influences and relationships) are within our intellectual grasp and amenable to constructive and more effective criminal justice responses.

Over the years, several politicians and the mainstream media have endeavoured jointly or severally to justify and maintain the illogical traditional approach to crime control which lavishes attention on the symptomatic manifestations of crime. The biggest football in their game plan is youth crime. Politicians of various ideological persuasions have inflated this football largely with their election-driven whims and caprices. Discussion has been characterised too frequently by ill-informed and misleading assertions and political posturing. Conservatives and liberals compete for the title of the 'tougher party' on crime.[3] In all of this, the media has generally played an inflammatory role – sensationalising what is uncharacteristic of youth crime or problems in juvenile justice administration, 'beating up' images of young offenders and of young people generally, and reinforcing myths about what does or doesn't work in relation to youth offending. Thus, the dominant criminal justice approach has largely remained captive to 'ideological and political considerations fuelled by populist concerns and impulses' (Hood 2001, p 1).

For these players, the demonisation of our youth has become a pastime. By and large, the society as a whole is drawn into this demonising mode. One of Australia's foremost writers, Phillip Adams, captures this quite vividly when he says:

> Despite the immense difficulties of [post]modern times and the immense provocations of [post]modern society, children are doing their best to cope. But that does not stop us demonising them. If it's a poor workman that blames his tool, it's an appalling society that hates its children.[4]

Of particular significance in this book is the extent to which the criminal justice system has lost its potential edge in effective crime prevention because it participates in this demonisation and, in the process, has become shackled to the reactive and incarceral mentalities towards young people, as if 'imprisoned by prejudices' of the demonisation. Thus, as Phillip Adams further observes, we enter this century with western societies infatuated with prisons or detention centres and with policy-makers seeing mandatory sentencing as an extension of social policy. Adams uses the US – 'land of the free, home of the brave' – to illustrate how societies have turned to prisons as the means of 'taking the angry, the alienated and the dispossessed from the streets so that the middle class could feel safer in their beds'. Despite the atheistic stance which he always claims, Adams shows his disgust with such happenings 'in a society that trumpets its passionate belief in Christianity where the Saviour's followers overwhelmingly ignore his instructions to love their enemy, to suffer [little children to come unto me], to turn the other cheek'.

Like many a critical criminologist, Adams expresses sadness that 'the richest nation on earth can find no other way of tackling glaring social problems than to incarcerate an unprecedented percentage of its population, particularly the black, particularly the young'. As if this is not bad enough, the nation 'rejoices in what it sees as the triumphs of zero-tolerance policing and "three strikes and you're in" – sending more to jail for the rest of their lives for crimes of breathtaking inconsequence, all too often involving some of the most cynical and stupid laws in human history'. This is not the swipe of the uninformed. For it echoes Barbara Hudson,[5] who once said 'we need to discover why England and Wales and the US are apparently so addicted to responding to various forms of deviance by the use of imprisonment' (Hudson 1987, p 181). It also echoes Professor Robert Shepherd (1999) who states: 'we increasingly are demonising our children out of our fear, and that demonisation is driving public policy [especially incarceration policy] to a significant degree'. Australia, Canada and New Zealand of the 1980s and 1990s were in good company with the prison-addicted and youth-demonising UK and US.

That most of these societies do talk about the vital role of young people in the destiny of their nations cannot be gainsaid. Nor is it unusual for these same societies to simultaneously express paranoia about their youth. For instance, at the 1999 hearing before the Subcommittee on Crime of the Committee on the Judiciary (US House Of Representatives), the Chairman, Mr Gekas, introduced the subject – Reforming Juvenile Justice in America – by acknowledging that 'the future of our youth' is 'near and dear to the hearts of every American':

> Everyone knows that with 50 million youngsters in school, that that is a potential gold mine for the future of our country. But embedded in that very same body of youngsters is the potential for harm and danger, and the commission of crime and anguish, and the victimization of themselves and others while in the course of their growing up.

Thus, often, several nations in the western world acknowledge that 'children and youth are our most treasured asset'. By the same token, these nations have maintained a morbid fear of the 'young' and an emphasis on retribution, incarceration and inappropriate residential care and treatment models towards this 'treasured asset'. Their governments construct the social reality that underpins this ambivalence, especially since the last quarter of the 20th century, mainly in terms of the youth representing the 'risks and dangers involved in everyday life' in very contemporary, mundane, ordinary and, indeed, 'respectable' settings (Taylor 1999, p 1). The political and media reaction to the abduction and killing of two-year-old Jamie Bulger from a shopping mall in Bootle, Merseyside, in February 1993 by two 11-year-old boys on a nearby railway line is a UK gripping example of this point.

Scholarly works that capture this social reality have been unashamedly 'forensic' and 'socio-biological' in their account of crime and their prescription for its cure. Samuel Yochelson and Stanton Samenow produced *The Criminal Personality* in 1976 in which they not only explained all criminal violence as psychopathic but also made such construction 'a general paradigm' for analysis of this crime. Strangely, they went on to insist that such crime is 'a voluntary and freely willed act for which all perpetrators should be held personally responsible' (ibid, p 2). Their work became a significant part of the bedrock to the emerging neo-classical approach to crime control in general and the prevention of youth crime in particular.

James Wilson and Richard Hernstein's (1985) *Crime and Human Nature* reinforced this explanatory framework with a strong bent on socio-biology. This work gave a major boost to the neo-conservative politics of law and order that paraded as panacea for crime deterrence through selective targeting and incapacitation in the UK, US and Australasia in the 1980s and early 1990s. The responses of the state agencies to crime in the 1990s were guided by the same framework, bolstered by such works as Gottfredson and Hirshi (1990) *A General Theory of Crime*, and Canter and Alison (1997) *Criminal detection and the psychology of crime*. These works inspired the 'new penological project that is concerned with the identification and incapacitation of the "dangerous offender", particularly the young, as well as with new ways of surveillance – social insurance, the minimisation of personal risk arising from the sudden emergence of dangerous individuals in the broader society' (Taylor 1999, p 2). In a more panoramic view that will emerge from this book, 'the offender as-object-of-knowledge generally emerges as young, impoverished, often black, usually male and marginalised' (Hudson 2000, p 168).

There is no arguing the fact that, no matter what has caused young people's offending or 'how damaged they are by the society that has produced them' (Kucera 1993, p 237), society is entitled to protection, and every child must at least realise the consequence of his or her actions. Where most societies and their criminal justice agencies have failed, and it is here that the key issue for this book lies, is how to make sense of offending behaviour as a necessary prelude to designing appropriate responses and, more strategically, making young people realise redemptively the consequences of offending.

This book confirms the view that (1) politicians, the media and especially the criminal justice system have all badly handled this issue for a long time, choosing largely to be draconian, reactive and retributive; and (2) it is about time those players learnt their lessons. In Professor Harding's (1993, p 155) words:

> Nations should learn from experience – about the venality of political 'quick fixes', about the malevolence of parts of the media, and most of all about the nature of youth crime and the opportunities [that criminal justice has] for making a much better task of managing it than has previously been the case.

The result of these players' poor performance, even by the standard *raison d'etre* of the traditional criminal justice approach to crime control, has been an unmitigated failure in genuinely tackling youth crime for the benefit of all. The more draconian the approach became, the more traditional youth crimes played a top-heavy part in the headlines, the more frequently arrests were made for the familiar youth crimes against property and the more these incidents showed attendant violence.

The emphasis on the failure of the criminal justice system may sound like setting up a 'straw person'. After all, there is a significant body of literature that seriously questions whether the criminal justice system has any direct role in crime prevention. Van Dijk (1990, p 205) illustrates the genre of this literature when he defines crime prevention as:

> the total of all policies, measures and techniques, outside the boundaries of the criminal justice system, aiming at the reduction of the various kinds of damage caused by acts defined as criminal by the state.

The main import of this definition is that it excludes the criminal justice agencies from a critical crime prevention discourse. In that regard, I consider it inadequate and misleading. Crawford (1998, p 10) is correct in saying that van Dijk 'unnecessarily and falsely rigidifies the distinction between what is "inside' and "outside" the boundaries of the criminal justice system'. He is particularly perceptive in his view that 'much of what takes place within, or at the boundaries of the criminal justice system is concerned with the prevention of future crimes'.

Gordon Hughes's (1998) interpretation of Massimo Pavarini's (1997) work is another example of works that cast doubts on criminal justice agencies as bona fide subjects for a crime prevention discourse. Pavarini had argued that the crime question must be confronted in terms of political and economic democracy. Hughes takes this to mean that preventive or 'solution' interventions 'necessarily lie outside the criminal justice system and by implication beyond criminology' (p 151). This interpretation of Pavarini is somewhat overdrawn. Like van Dijk, the separation between the criminal justice system and the political economy that his interpretation implies amounts to a sociological fallacy.

It is argued that the separation between prevention and criminal justice (policing, adjudication and punishment) 'which is the way our policy choices are always framed' (Travis 1998) is a false separation. Criminal justice agencies can and do prevent crime. In fact, the 'Peelian' vision of policing had 'crime prevention' at its centre (Crawford 1998, p 30). Following the founding of the Metropolitan Police in London in 1829 by Sir Robert Peel, one of two joint Commissioners, Sir Richard Mayne, clearly underlined crime prevention as the primary object of the police:

> It should be understood at the outset that the principal object to be attained is the prevention of crime. To this great end every effort of the police is to be directed. The security of person and property, the preservation of the public tranquillity and all other objects of a police establishment will thus be better effected than by detection and punishment of an offender after he has succeeded in committing the crime. (quoted in Edwards 1999)

The judiciary demonstrates its connection to youth crime prevention (controlling and correcting the behaviour of law-violating juveniles) by, *inter alia*, holding detention, intake, transfer, adjudicatory, and dispositional hearings (Bartollas 1996). Close observers of the juvenile courts would notice that some of these courts use informal and flexible procedures to diagnose the causes of and prescribe the cures for delinquency (Feld 1992). In fact, several laws in the UK, North America and Australasia since the 1960s did stipulate that the court with children jurisdiction would be a place of investigation and inquiry to find a course of action which would resolve the problems thought to have led to the child's offending.[6] For instance, having reviewed Tasmania's *Youth Justice Act* 1997 and *Children, Young People and Their Families Act* 1997, Szramka (2001) remarks:

> Once an offender is prosecuted for an offence before the court, the court is able to more effectively address the interests of the offender and the community. The court is able to effect, as much as practicable, the reformation of the offender and the protection of the community, and the families from future wrong doing, by the application of a wider range of sentencing options, *as well as providing a greater flexibility of response by the court*. (emphasis, added)

Similarly, the expectations on the corrections system to deliver 'rehabilitation' of convicted offenders even under a 'justice' model have always been articulated within a crime prevention discourse (Pitts 1999). As Laurie Myers, who had worked in youth detention for about two decades in New South Wales, put it, detention is one medium where 'positive and realistic programs for young people who are incarcerated [are provided] to help them break the cycle of offending and return to the community as responsible citizens'(Myers 1993, p 105).

Common to all the views that exclude criminal justice agencies from the crime prevention discourse is the traditional argument that crime prevention efforts are directed toward those who are not yet involved in crime. This in itself shows a relatively narrow conception of crime prevention. Using the now widely accepted tripartite typology of crime prevention (primary, secondary and tertiary), such an argument seems to ignore the tertiary type which involves measures designed to enable police and other agencies of criminal justice to deal with those who have offended, with a view to stopping or controlling reoffending. Targeting 'recidivism' is no less preventative than strategies which, as Graham (1990, pp 9-12) puts it, attempt (1) to influence generically the 'root causes' of crime (primary prevention) or (2) to remove criminogenic situations and thus stop at-risk people from committing crime (secondary prevention).

I have considered it more persuasive and fruitful to adopt, as Sherman, Gottfredson, Mackenzie, Eck, Reuter, and Bushway (1998) did, a broader definition of crime prevention which includes any setting or activity that reduces the remote possibility, potential or actual recurrence of crime. Conventional thinking about criminal justice agencies excludes them from primary and, to a lesser extent, secondary crime prevention. In fact, the Sherman study which states that 'by definition, therefore, we include as crime prevention, programs in the courts and corrections that focus on reducing the criminal activities of offenders', identifies strategies for interventions that fit more into the tertiary crime prevention (see Table 0.1).

Table 0.1 Different strategies for preventing crime by the courts and corrections showing the anticipated mechanisms for impact

CRIME PREVENTION IN THE COURTS AND CORRECTIONS	
STRATEGIES	**MECHANISM FOR IMPACT**
Incapacitation	Imprisonment removes offenders capacity to commit crimes in community (General)
	Small number of high rate offenders can be identified and imprisoned during their active criminal career (Specific)
	General and Specific deterrence
Dotorrence	General: Punitive punishment will keep those in the community from committing crimes
	Specific: Punitive punishment will keep punished individuals from committing more crimes
Rehabilitation	Change aspects of offenders that are changeable and associated with criminal behaviour
	Intensive, adequately implemented programs (with treatment integrity) of sufficient duration (dosage)
	Target higher risk cases
	Cognitive, skill oriented and behavioural treatment methods
Community Restraints	Increased surveillance and control in the community will decrease offenders capacity to commit crimes
	Increased surveillance and control in the community will decrease offenders opportunity to commit crimes
	Specific deterrence

Source: Sherman et al (1998)

With imagination, it is not difficult to see criminal justice agencies as active players in the primary crime prevention domain. This book develops this point of view, showing how it is possible for criminal justice agencies to achieve the 'prevention of future crimes' through a socially oriented, pro-active and collaborative participation in legal and community safety projects.

The research

Once I took the view that criminal justice agencies do have a role in all types of crime prevention, the legitimacy of casting a research spotlight on the question of how well and with what modality they have performed this role was taken as a settled issue. Given my conviction about the crucial place that young people occupy in the 'destiny' of any nation, and confronted by the relentless sensationalist media construction of youth crime in somewhat fatalistic and aversive terms, I became particularly interested in the activities of criminal justice agencies who ultimately must respond to this crime. Compared to other segments of the society, these agencies occupy an unparalleled power position in terms of 'knowledge' about crime and the mantle of authority or coercion that they possess. In the words of Shepherd (1999), 'those who work every day in living out the fundamental premises of the juvenile justice system are the ones who know where the children hurt. They are the ones to whom society must listen'. They are therefore uniquely placed to play a leading role in crime prevention.

As previously indicated, my preliminary investigation had confirmed what by now should be trite knowledge that the heavy-handed approach adopted predominantly by the criminal justice agencies has failed to curb youth crime. More significantly, the investigation found that, since the late 1980s, two phenomena in the crime prevention field have become self-evident. One is the resurgence in the fear and concern about perceived rise in youth crime, especially crime of violence. The other is, having realised that reliance solely on the traditional criminal justice system and its one-dimensional approach to prevent youth crime leads to a dead end, criminal justice agencies (police, courts and corrections) in several western countries have turned to partnership with various community groups to 'fight' youth crime.

In relation to the resurgence of fear of the perceived increase in juvenile crime, Jackson (1995, p1) stated at the *First National Outlook Symposium on Crime in Australia,* that 'no doubt the public, the press, and the politicians – interacting as always – know that juvenile crime is always rising and out of control'. This is historically untrue: the history of the ideas and cycle of juvenile justice suggests that the perception of a rising 'juvenile crime wave' has little basis in fact (Bernard 1992; Krisberg and Austin 1993; Wundersitz 1993). Yet, this populist 'knowledge' has always generated a highly charged debate among politicians, juvenile justice officials, academics and public interest groups about what is to be done (Omaji 1997; Brown 1998). The ensuing consensus about the need to 'crack down' on the growing number of juveniles committing crimes is equally matched by the increasing public despair with the juvenile justice system's apparent inability to deal effectively with the offending behaviour of these young people (Alder and Wundersitz 1994).

Intriguingly, the perceived impotence of the system has run parallel to the burgeoning of the crime control budget. It nonetheless became even more obvious that increasing police, prosecution and prisons alone was neither sufficient nor adequately effective in stemming the perceived rising tide of youth violence and crime.

Out of this situation emerged a consciousness that prevention efforts must go beyond the narrow confines of the criminal justice agencies. In essence, the traditional view that 'if the police detect crime, the courts sentence offenders and the prison and probation service discharge those sentences, crime will be prevented' fell into disrepute (Bright 1991, p 63). Then began a somewhat paradigmatic shift towards the view that a dedicated community coalition of citizens, private businesses and public agencies, directing a collaborative effort which draws on public, private and volunteer resources for crime prevention, was the way forward (Omaji 1993; Sterner 1994).

Since Dennis Rosenbaum, a leading American criminologist, stated in 1988 that 'we are entering the heyday of community crime prevention' and that 'never before have the notions of citizen involvement in crime prevention received such widespread support' (quoted in Hughes 1998, p 78), it became clear that 'partnership' or coalition was a phenomenon whose time had come. Considering the view of the United Nations, declared in the *Beijing Rules* 25.1, that cooperation with the community is indispensable if the directives of the competent authority are to be carried out effectively, the arrival of partnership was destined to claim the global stage. The UN had stated that 'volunteers, voluntary organisations, local institutions and other community resources shall be called upon to contribute effectively to the rehabilitation of the juvenile in a community setting'. The rehabilitative orientation of the statement is remarkable, but it is the subtle endorsement of a 'coalition' beyond the traditional criminal justice approach, for all who work with young offenders, that is significant.

This position was reinforced in the UN 8th Congress in Havana on the Prevention of Crime and the Treatment of Offenders (1990) where the UN declared crime prevention not simply to be a matter for the police but must involve the contributions of other groups. In fact, the Congress went on to resolve to 'bring together those with responsibility for planning and development, for family, health, employment and training, housing and social services, leisure activities, schools, police, and the justice system, in order to deal with the conditions that generate crime'. Clearly, a multi-agency or 'partnership' approach has become favoured because, as Crawford (1998, p 10) observes, it affords an holistic approach to crime which is problem-oriented rather than organisationally driven. Sanderson (1998, p 1) puts it graphically when he says: 'strategic partnerships are increasingly becoming the way we need to do business and *crime prevention needs to be on the partnering bus or be left flat footed*' (emphasis, added).

Evidence suggests that justice agencies in the western world, especially the law enforcement officers, were seriously inclined to this view. As Bright (1992, p 87) observes in the context of the UK experience, the multi-agency approach to crime prevention came to be seen as 'a promising and systematic way of mobilising the support of relevant agencies in the fight against crime'. Not surprisingly, the Metropolitan Police had by 1995 developed an extensive program of partnership with the community, aimed largely at addressing youth crime (Omaji 1995).

At the Australian national conference on juvenile justice in 1992, the police displayed 'a convincing interest in combining the skills of their force with those of professionals from other disciplines and [saw] benefit in working in tandem when dealing with young offenders' (Sandor 1993, p 461). Such interest became evident in the Western Australian Police mission statement which provides that the police will 'in partnership with the community, create a safer and more secure Western Australia'. Since 1994, the US Bureau of Justice Assistance has been showing how the law enforcement officers in that country would accept that working in partnership with community members and groups is an effective and productive way to address crime. Corresponding bodies in Canada and New Zealand have similarly shown the rising interests of criminal justice agencies in the coalition approach.

While the concept of partnership as a crime prevention approach seemed to have acquired wide acceptability, information regarding how and why such partnerships are formed, structured and operated to what effect, and what pitfalls exist for criminal justice agencies going down this path, had not been widely researched. The partnership process is 'not always automatic or even easy' (Bureau of Justice Assistance 1994, p 3). Cross-national understanding is a major factor for success in this non-conventional response to crime by criminal justice agencies. As observed in the *South Australian Crime Prevention Strategy*, 'while it cannot be assumed that techniques successful in one jurisdiction can be applied in another, to ignore their work would be to neglect opportunities for invaluable lessons' (Government of South Australia 1989, p 7).

It was the need to extend existing knowledge about the activities of criminal justice agencies in this area from a cross-national research perspective, among other things, that motivated the investigation that has resulted in this book. The study aimed to undertake a cross-national analysis of partnership projects designed for the prevention of youth crime in Australia, New Zealand, Canada, the UK and the US. While notably different in some aspects of their economy and society, these countries (especially the first three) are 'kindred settler societies, sharing a common imperial history' (Broadhurst 1999, p 105) and have tended to move in a similar direction, generally speaking and at different times, in their juvenile justice policies and programs. And, as Zimring (2001, p 213) rightly observes, technology and normative standards, among other things, have been exerting 'pressure toward a greater similarity in criminal justice practice among developed nations'. Their experience in partnerships between justice agencies and community organisations in response to youth crime would no doubt exert a significant influence on the direction of youth crime prevention in other parts of the world.

Experience has shown that the real choice in responding to youth crime has come down to whether the agencies should continue to pursue crime control aggressively, or they should, in partnership with other groups, promote the development of functioning institutions in the community that have the net effect of reducing the amount of crime in the community (Wiatrowski 1996, p 118). It was obvious that the first part of the question leads invariably to a dead end. Thus, the real challenge was how the agencies could, in conjunction with the formal treatment of young offenders, work to improve schools, housing, employment, economic opportunities, and health and human services for young people or, simply put, deal with the conditions that contribute to youth crime in the first place. In other words, agencies are being called upon not only to be good at weeding young criminal elements, but to sow the seeds that create the sense of community that increases levels of commitment which in turn lowers the propensity to commit crime.

The study focused on those partnerships in which justice agencies have played a leading role as initiators or as major operators and which aimed to tackle youth crime in ways other than the ineffective conventional response. Using an eclectic methodology, the study adopted a two-stage approach in addressing the stated aim.

- It used an 'inventory' approach in the first stage to document information about partnership projects that are led or operated by the justice agencies in the selected countries. After an extensive documentary search in paper-based and electronic domains, an inventory schema or instrument was prepared comprising the main generic elements of partnerships. The inventory instrument was then sent on a pilot scale to selected relevant agencies in Australia, New Zealand and Canada. More extensive (or in some cases sup-plementary) information was collected during research and conference visits to all the countries studied including the UK and the US.

- At the second stage, the study applied an analytic approach which used the 'inventory' information as a basis for contextual expla-nation of the operation and effect of the projects on crime prevention. This approach allowed information not only to be turned into a database, but also to be analysed and interpreted so as to understand the history and philosophy of the partnership projects, the locus and structure of leadership, role definition for partnership groups, methods of service delivery, methods of dealing with organisational conflicts of interest, resource allocation strategies and project outcomes.

On the whole, the research was designed to shed some light on: (a) the processes that have brought the traditional criminal justice approach into disrepute, including the process of constructing and reacting to misleading images about youth offending; (b) how criminal justice agencies are changing their strategies to youth crime behind the veneer of the law and order rhetoric; and (c) the factors that are conducive not only to the development of high impact partnerships but also to criminal justice agencies penetrating deeper into the primary level of crime prevention to become manifestly pro-active in society's effort to 'correct' young people. In tackling the task, I have drawn liberally on the traditions of inter-disciplinary and critical discourses in sociology, criminology and law.

Content

Two fundamental 'truths' in criminal justice responses to youth crime are explained: (1) that 'image and perceptions matter'; and (2) that innovative ideas, policies and practices have a past. Both are poignantly addressed in Rawlings' (1999) *Crime and Power: A History of Criminal Justice 1688-1998*, a tour de force and an insightful analysis of the English criminal justice and crime control policies since the 17th century. Images have as their referent at least the 'moral character' of the processor, the motive imputed to the behaviour of the person processed, the background characteristics of this person and the modus operandi of the act in question. During this typification of the actor and the action, the image processor removes the unique background characteristics and specific contextual factors of the case so that 'essential features of socially recognised familiar' scenes may be detected and abstracted. In relation to youth crime, therefore, the abstracted familiar features become the basis for the criminal justice agencies' attitudes and behaviour vis-à-vis the typified youth or youth action (Akers and Hawkins 1975).

Chapters 1 and 2 discuss how mutual construction of negative images about each other has significantly defined the largely uncomplimentary relationship between the criminal justice agencies and young people. Chapter 1 argues particularly that the images that agencies have of them-selves and of their roles interact with the general ambivalence in society about young people, pushing this relationship towards the toxic end of the continuum. Although the training and occupational cultures of the agencies affect their self-image and interaction with societal ambivalence, it is the media that are responsible for much of the negativity that characterises youth-criminal justice relations. All of this, in turn, reflects a much deeper struggle over different forms of power (administrative, civil, political economic, etc) in society. Last, I show how the manifestation of these power relations becomes more remarkable in the dealings of these agencies with minority racial and ethnic youth.

Chapter 2 challenges the conventional wisdom that young people passively experience stereotyping and control by the criminal justice agencies. Lessons from dialectics were drawn upon to demonstrate how young people use different subcultural expressions to mediate some of the images that are constructed about them. I argue that in so doing, young people also become significantly caught up in struggles over cultural hegemony. Where young people feel compelled to fight against inferiority and disempowerment, as in the case of most marginalised indigenous youth, the artefacts of their resistance complicate the relationship with agencies and confer on them further criminal labels.

Chapter 3 demonstrates the reality of the influence of socially constructed images on the traditional modes of processing young offenders. It argues that the traditions and ideologies that define the traditional criminal justice response to youth crime have turned the juvenile justice system into a political enterprise. Further, the chapter argues that 'reaction' and 'retribution' which characterise this response have driven a crippling wedge between the apparatuses of the state and their capacity to appreciate the special needs and rights of young people. From the undifferentiated treatment for young offenders during the period up to the 18th century, through the emergence of the 'welfare' model in which a separate system of response to youth crime was devised, to the contemporary 'justice' model that purports to apply to young offenders all the rights of a fair trial, the dominant attitude towards young people has remained ambivalent and punitive. An assessment of the activities of the criminal justice agencies against international (UN) standards shows that most of the countries are in breach of universal protections for children and young offenders.

Much has been written about the fiscal implications of the traditional response to crime. Chapter 4 argues that the response to youth crime is a costly business in more ways than one. Trends in the rate of youth crime are as tied to the activities of the criminal justice agencies as they are related to the actual criminality of young people. The chapter shows that despite the generally simple nature of youth offending, which in fact has also been in decline since the late 1990s, the approach to policing, judging and correcting the youth that come in contact with the system has kept the monetary outlay ever increasing. With the exception of the 'gun' and 'gang' factors which have escalated the level of violence in some youth crime, especially in the USA, there is hardly any justification for the media-driven moral panic about youth offending and for the political infatuation with draconian responses as illustrated at the beginning of this Introductory Chapter and later discussed in Chapter 3.

Chapter 5 examines the policy dynamics of the context in which youth crime has been addressed at the political and agency-operation levels. The chapter documents various views about the important questions regarding the 'health' of the traditional criminal justice system. Is the system working well? This question focuses on effectiveness or purpose and accountability issues. Commentators question what the system is supposed to be doing and whether it is doing it properly. As to whether the system is providing justice, preventing crime or, indeed, causing crime, the verdict weighs more towards the crime-generating performance of the system. The chapter discusses how huge swings of ideology and policy underscore the crisis in the system: the rhetoric of 'rights' being replaced by 'responsibility', and security and punishment replacing diversion and rehabilitation. All along the chapter demonstrates how juvenile justice has been politicised, leading to confusion in the community, crisis of confidence among the justice staff, and alienation or abuse among the clients of the system.

More significantly, the chapter examines the eventual preparedness of the criminal justice agencies to shift their philosophies about crime control towards preventative partnerships. Even in the US criminal justice system where incapacitation remains the primary reason for intervention (see Zimring and Hawkins 1995), there is remarkable evidence of a paradigm shift. Whether there have been sufficient political and bureaucratic commitments to sustain a genuine radical shift remains to be seen and would be a good subject for another book. Any optimism might be tempered by the fact that prison building and management are a multi-billion dollar a year industry in the USA, with an important Washington lobby that would persuade the government away from substantial shift.

It became necessary to take up this question again in Chapters 6 and 7 where I focus mainly on the concrete examples of partnership projects and the fundamental characteristics of these projects. Using a case study approach, I discuss in Chapter 6 details of selected relevant projects from Australia, Canada, New Zealand, UK and the US. Samples of two models of partnership (criminal justice-centred and local authority-centred) were selected for this exercise. In Chapter 7, I examine key features of the partnership projects and compared their preventive capabilities with those of the traditional criminal justice approach. The examination revealed a far superior potential of the partnership approach for understanding and responding functionally to youth crime.

Notwithstanding this superiority, the analysis finds certain shortfalls of the partnership approach that criminal justice agencies have adopted. Based on the identified strengths and shortfalls, I then construct some ground rules for high impact (or 'best practice') partnerships. Good faith about how much independence agencies are willing to 'sacrifice', establishment of empowering structures and protocols, and constructive thinking towards young people emerge as the core principles in these ground rules. When supported by appropriate operational imperatives that I outline toward the end of Chapter 7, these principles represent a major advancement in criminal justice agencies' role as youth crime preventers.

Invariably, future directions must be developed by involving and encompassing all those concerned with societal response to youth crime. Giving stakeholders a voice and establishing dialogue with the broader social processes which underpin youth offending is a major challenge for criminal justice agencies. The partnership approach provides a relatively fruitful opportunity for the machinery for youth crime prevention to involve the experiences and perspectives of the stakeholders of the system – young offenders, their families, victims, community workers, staff and members of the public – in a systematic way (Family and Children Services 1990).

In the concluding chapter, I reiterate the debilitating effect of the traditional criminal justice response to youth crime and the sorry state in which it has left several western societies and their 'treasured asset', the young. Holding up a multi-agency, family preservation, home-based and intensive wrap-around model as the beacon for effective youth crime prevention, I then make a case for criminal justice agencies to form not just any partnership, but youth-friendly ones,[7] to incorporate developmental perspectives of crime into their policy and operational activities, and to become more directly involved in the primary level of crime prevention.

The agencies must view all young people as a valuable resource in the context of an integrated social and economic policy, and base their response to youth crime on a paradigm that prioritises restoration of victim losses, reconciliation between the victim and the offender, reintegration of the offender back into his or her family and community networks, and reharmonisation of the entire community through healing of the rift caused by the offence (Owen and Carroll 1997, p 451). They must become active players in the quest for:

> a safe and secure [society, a society] organised in such a way that every individual or group [especially young people] is afforded maximum opportunity to earn for themselves … a decent livelihood, the esteem that goes with that capacity and an equitable chance to fulfil their lawful aspirations of self-development. (Omaji 2001, p 170)

This is a call for a 'radical engagement' (Giddens 1990). Anything less than this will intensify the already dim view of the criminal justice agencies on the radar screen of youth crime prevention, well into the 21st century.

Notes

1   Duncan (1996) argues that for some prisoners/detainees, contrary to Erving Goffman's classic thesis that people experience 'total institutions' negatively, the experience of incarceration is both positive and gratifying. Some see custody as a place for 'spiritual rebirth' and a refuge from the uncertainties and dangers of 'freedom'. See Hadfield (2000) for a review of this work as 'a contribution to the scientific explanation of psycho-social phenomena'.

2   See Liebling, Elliot and Arnold 2001 for a useful application of this tool.

3   Compare the law and order policies of the Reagan and Clinton governments in the US; the Thatcher and Blair governments in the UK; the Lawrence and Court governments in Western Australia, etc. The two different political persuasions converge remarkably in their achievement over tougher political 'crime-talk', crime policies and legislation, and the rising rate of juvenile incarceration.

4   *The Weekend Australian*, 21-22 October 2000, p 32. The theme of 'hating young people' in Western societies is discussed in more detail in Chapter 1.

5   A renowned researcher in criminal justice and a professor of sociology.

6   For example, see the UK *Children and Young Persons Act* 1969; Canada's *Young Offenders Act* 1982; New Zealand's *Children and Young Persons and their Families Act* 1989; and Western Australia's *Young Offenders Act* 1994.

7   Criminal justice and community committees may not have been successful or constructive in addressing youth crime. This is because, frequently, these committees have targeted young people rather than involved them. When appropriately constructed and applied, partnerships can significantly increase the preventive potentials of these agencies.

1

Criminal justice thinking about youth

The criminalisation of young people begins with manufacturing the image of menacing, out-of-control, armed-and-dangerous youth who are not responsible to society [and] not respectful of any authority. A society that is scared to death of itself requires a villain, and is unlikely to look to the heart of its own dominant institutions to find one. (Against the Current 2000)

What criminal justice agencies think or what images they hold about 'youth' is fundamental to how they respond to the activities of young people in the context of policing, judging or correcting. The argument that these agencies are merely servants of the law, acting within the law at all times and thus not open to extra-legal influences such as preconceived notions or 'imaging', stereotypical biases or socio-political imperatives,[1] has no basis in fact.

Criminal justice agencies, composed of human beings, must actively construct their own perceptual world. In their traditional orientation to crime, this world is always at least one step away from the world 'as it really is'. The distance between perception and reality in this orientation widens because the agencies most often respond to events that have already happened which they do not in most cases actually observe. This is the 'reactive mode' of justice par excellence. Here, they 'must depend on interpretations, stereotypes, definitions and accounts at least one step removed from the actual events' that they address (LaFree 1989, p 236). If, as Wallace Stevens rightly observes in his *Opus Posthumous* (1957, p 135), 'reality is an activity of the most august imagination', it begs the question as to how reaction-based negative imagination influences criminal justice agencies' response to their 'clients'.

As this chapter will show, when the 'clients' are young people, the imagination takes on a heightened significance in the crime prevention enterprise of the state through the agencies in question. It is, therefore, critical to examine the character of stereotypes about youth and the 'gullibility' or sheer malevolence with which elements within criminal justice agencies employ them (Lippmann 1992) against the backdrop of a broader perception of youth as a locus of societal anxiety in general. Thus, the chapter discusses how the police, courts and corrections think about young people. While the criminal justice imagination is diverse, diffuse, shifting and amorphous, this chapter concentrates on those common and long-standing or enduring perceptions of youth held by its agencies. As I shall show, these perceptions happen to be generally negative.

The chapter then attempts to explain these perceptions by highlighting the role of ideological or idiosyncratic factors, sociological factors (such as community defence, organisational life, socialisation, danger, authority and conception of normality) and the media factor. What this attempt seeks to illustrate is that perceptions never take place in a vacuum. By locating the specific contexts of criminal justice 'imaging' of youth, the chapter would prepare readers to better appreciate a major theme in this book, namely the contingent nature of the search for a 'better way' in criminal justice response to youth crime in a number of western countries.

Youth as a locus of anxiety

All modern western societies have shown ambivalence in the way they perceive 'youth'. To the extent that a simplified dichotomy allows, these societies have either idealised or demonised youth as a stage in life course. In the main, though, these countries tend to view young people as a problem group. If young people are not spoilt home brats, they are homeless hoodlums. If they are not protesting, they are resisting. In any case, they are prone to drug and drag, to violence and vandalism. Youth 'is contemporaneously expected to be an age of deviance, disruption and wickedness ... We are bombarded with images of idle, anti-authoritarian, subversive – and inevitably criminal – teenagers' (Brown 1998, p 3). The 'folk devil' of these societies is everywhere young! S/he embodies the 'in-your-face' incivility.

Take Britain as an example. Young people seem ever and always to have been a source of anxiety and trouble. They constitute 'a metaphor for social change' and often, especially when new youth cultural styles have begun to emerge, 'an angry metaphor for changes which that comfortable, socially powerful and adult fraction of English society had generally not wanted or even positively resented' (Anderson, Kinsey, Loader, and Smith 1994, p xii).

It is not surprising that this resentment has extended to other countries with strong ties to Britain. As recently as 1997, the Executive Officer of the Youth Affairs Council of South Australia, Mr Kym Davey, observed the presence of this phenomenon in Australia: 'I think as a culture we don't like adolescents particularly much'.[2] He was referring to practices in which young people are treated as second-class citizens. Earlier in the 1990s, the European Forum for Urban Security had produced a report, *Security and Democracy, Analytical College on Urban Safety* (1993), with a chapter titled 'As if we considered Young People our Enemies'. About the same time, UNICEF published an investigation by Hewlett (1993, p 2) where it was noted that 'an anti-child spirit is loose in these [western] lands'.

Indeed, groups of lower class young men in particular have been constructed as the feared 'Other' in western societies at several points since the late 19th century. They have been viewed 'as symbols of a breakdown of community and trust, or even, in some accounts, as the source of such a breakdown'. On 15 June 1868, a Conservative Member of the British Parliament, J Hubbard who later became Lord Addington, raised with the Tory Home Secretary, Gathorne Hardy, the concern that 'the lamentable amount of juvenile criminality' was largely attributable to 'the children of the lower classes' being corrupted 'into courses of dishonesty and vice' by the spread of certain publications and theatrical representations. He warned that the government must find 'remedy for these growing and most serious evils' (Springhall 1998, p 2).

Writing in the Foreword to the *Cautionary Tales* (Anderson et al 1994, p xii), more than a century after Hubbard expressed his anti-youth concern, Ian Taylor, professor of sociology and criminology, aptly notes similar sentiments in contemporary times:

> In the post-war period, a never-ending sequence of youthful 'folk-devils' (teddy boys, mods and rockers, skinheads, football hooligans) have been paraded through the media and the popular imagination … There is a strong sense of a society … that really does not like young people very much, especially when they are the offspring of the lower orders.

In youth justice discourse, children from disadvantaged backgrounds have been ascribed particularised identities which resonate with 'otherness', 'immorality' and 'failure' and essentialised through images of evil and pathology (Goldson 1999, p 24).

Since the Victorian era in England, at least seven images of 'childhood'[3] have emerged: the romantic child, the evangelical child, the factory child, the Apollonian child, the psycho-medical child, the welfare child and the delinquent child. Of these, only the 'delinquent child' has maintained the firmest grip on adult imagination in most of the western countries, instilling fear more than mere dislike. The reason for this is not hard to find. In the delinquent child, it is believed, lies the terrifying potential for 'dangerous classes' to reproduce themselves and to spread the seeds of disorder and debauchery on the streets (Brown 1998, p 10). As in the Victorian society of the 1800s, the fear still lies in the real prospect of these classes causing manufacture to decline, agriculture to languish and commerce to disappear. Perhaps the best literary capture of the extent of this fear in the Victorian age can be found in Shakespeare's *The Winter's Tale* (Act III, scene iii):

> I would that there was no age between sixteen and [twenty-three], or that youth would sleep out the rest; for there is nothing in the between, but getting wenches with child, wronging the ancientry, stealing, fighting.

Fear, they say, precedes the bad object – the negative stereotype. In turn, 'the stereotype perpetuates that fear' (Sibley 1995, p 15). When the idea of 'adolescence' emerged in the 1800s, referring to the teenage years, it was applied to the children of the working and lower classes. These children had become dislocated and unattached – they rapidly lost economic independence as a result of the changes brought by industrialisation and urbanisation. Feared that the only avenue of survival for them was to steal property from wealthier people, they were constructed as delinquents who, unlike the children of capitalists, could only be 'shaped and moulded and formed into God-fearing, law-abiding adults' by a new system – the juvenile justice system (Bernard 1992, p 55).

On the whole, criminal justice agencies have come to share with the wider society the constructionist processes of life course images, ranging from the 'innocent' childhood, through the 'deviant' youth, and the 'sanitised' mid-life, to 'infantalised' old age. While some people might be amused by these images, research shows that those who are responsible for public law and order or criminal justice, namely the police, courts and custodial corrections,[4] are particularly obsessed with, and averse to, the perceived 'deviant' dispositions of youth.

To these agencies, young people are largely a pain: delinquent, maladjusted and pathological (Jamrozik 1991; Stratton 1992; and Omaji 1997). With very few exceptions, the 'long hair-equals-hippy-equals-psychedelic drug taker' formula of the late 1960s has not completely vanished from the images that these agencies hold about youth. By and large they traditionally respond to these young people as a threat to be neutralised or put away. In 1835, six years after Robert Peel created the London Metropolitan police, nearly 7000 young people were in prison. In under two decades, this number nearly doubled to 12,000 in 1853 (Muncie 1984). Today, the numbers are down to a few thousands but the underlying aversive response to youth endures.

Impressions may be wrong, but their consequences are real in the operations of those who hold such impressions. Perceptions about young people 'significantly determine the youth policy response of both governments and of the figuration of agencies [towards] young people' (Bessant 1993, p 2). Clearly, a successful imaging or labelling of young people as offenders, aided by the media construction, would not engender a more humanitarian attitude towards them. Rather, it would justify an increased surveillance not only of them but their families as 'offenders'. Consider the event that became the subject of Stanley Cohen's (1973) classic *Folk Devils and Moral Panic: the Creation of the Mods and Rockers*. Groups of young people had an altercation over a bank holiday weekend in small seaside towns in the south and south-east of England in 1964. As Cohen found, the disturbances were largely based on regional rivalries among unskilled and semi-unskilled young workers who did not appear to be particularly affluent. Most of them did not own scooters or motorcycles, and the resulting criminal damage or violence was limited.

When the *Daily Express* of 19 May 1964 had finished reconstructing these same facts, what emerged was an imagery of unfettered, undisciplined young people with too much time and money, corrupted by popular music and the values of consumption. According to the newspaper, 'there was Dad asleep in a deckchair and Mum making sandcastles with the children, when the 1964 boys took over the beaches at

Margate and Brighton ... and smeared the traditional postcard scene with blood and violence' (ibid).

Having excited the public to perceive that they were being caught between the 'mods and rockers' subcultural gang warfare, there was a clarion call for something to be done about it. The result 'was increased police surveillance and arrests, perceptions by the courts dealing with cases that they were facing a "new" threat' (Brown 1998, p 40). It is not far-fetched to suggest that those 'boys' would have received a jaundiced 'redemptive' welcome from detention staff and, in those days, a short back and sides army-style haircut.

Since the time of industrial revolution, the terms 'hooligan' and, in the case of Australia, 'larrikin' entered the English vocabulary to describe young people who, having been dislodged from villages and families, were 'thrown idle into the teeming streets of the new cities' (Polk 1997, p 490). They were Irish terms for what was seen as an unprecedented eruption of youthful disorder on Britain's streets. More significantly, post-1914:

> [They] provided a crystallising focus for any number of overlapping anxieties associated with imperial decline, material incapacity, the erosion of social discipline and moral authority, the eclipse of family life and what was feared to be the death rattle of "Old England". (Pearson 1983, p 107)

As Lynette Finch (1993) clearly demonstrates, the social outrage of larrikinism in the 19th century was of middle class design. The construction of working class youth culture as the youth subculture of the 'larrikin' was the way that key middle class commentators came to describe forms of behaviour which they noticed and perceived to be threatening. In post-Fordist societies,[5] one of the most obvious areas of discontent is the ever-intrusive fear and reality of youth crime (Taylor 1999).

Whenever sharp social and economic conditions heighten endemic youth-adult tensions, resulting in a sense of crisis as reflected in massive changes in both developmental organisations such as schools and employ-ment, and social control organisations such as criminal justice agencies (see Polk 1997, p 491), a role is created for young people as 'enduring scapegoat (and contingently a whipping post) for the collective neurosis of a society' (Brown 1998, p 12).

In these circumstances, criminal justice practitioners are particularly susceptible to the stereotyping and labelling that strongly affect the exercise of their discretionary powers. Seymour's (1997) analysis of how the role of the courts is defined by the way in which childhood is socially constructed illustrates the fact that 'imaging' age-appropriate behaviour presents a debilitating threshold for criminal justice agencies to cross. The next three sub-sections discuss specific processes of 'imaging' in the police, courts and corrections arenas.

How police think about youth

In most modern western societies, police are the gatekeepers to the criminal justice system. Indeed, they are 'usually the first representative of societal authority and the criminal justice system to come in contact with a youthful offender' (Territo, Halsted and Bromley 1992, p 538). As the US President's Commission on Law Enforcement and the Administration of Justice put it, 'contacts with police are the gateway into the system of delinquency and criminal justice' (quoted in Hess and Wrobleski 1993, p 360). In this position, they maintain a high level of contact with young people especially in malls, shopping centres and other public spaces (Cunneen and White 1995).

More significantly, it is the particular image that police have of themselves that has played a major role in the way they think of youth and how they react when they come in contact with young people. While not all police in all jurisdictions think or behave in one or the same way, the essence of their traditional orientation towards young people has at least three elements. First, they see themselves as 'the "thin blue line" protecting upright respectable citizens from the tidal wave of criminality' (Box 1987, p 148). The New South Wales Commissioner of Police, Mr Peter Ryan, echoed this attitude when he said: 'let's get on and catch the criminals who are making life such a misery for large sections of the community' (quoted in Chan 2001, p 130).

Second, the police view themselves as the 'guardians of public morality' (Box 1987, p 148). Finally, they see themselves as 'front line troops in a war against certain types of dissidents – marginalised, alienated and alien youth, terrorists, football hooligans, industrial agitators, and militant trade-unionists – all of whom, so it appears to those suffering from cultural amnesia, have crawled out of the woodwork only recently' (Box 1987, p 148). In relation to minority youth in particular, the interface of images and roles comes across as 'police racism':

> whereby police authorities stigmatise, harass, criminalise or otherwise discriminate against certain social groups 'on the basis of phenotypical or cultural markers, or national origin' through the use of their special powers. (Chan 1997, p 17)

Through training and general operations, the police who think traditionally tend to develop a cultural common sense of offenders as a pathological, almost subhuman, species. Within such a cultural framework, offenders are perceived to have brain, chromosome, glandular, psychological or personality disorders; they are, in a word, *flawed* and are up to no good. Specifically in relation to youth, these traditionally oriented police perceive young offenders in these terms: difficult children, street kids, gangs, indigenous or Aboriginal, disrespectful, trouble-makers, 'smart arses', and rough speakers in 'guttural' adult voices. As Blagg and Wilkie (1997) put it, 'the police ... have a highly developed sense of the potential for youth to be violent and cause trouble'.

Selective deployment patterns adopted by the police result in officers and especially new recruits 'on the beat' coming into direct and personal contact with a limited slice of 'deviant' or 'criminal' life. These deployment policies, determined by higher management, interact with and reinforce media images of the typical criminal and politicians' warnings of our escalating crime problem. Frequently, this keeps young people, especially the unemployed and racially different males, in the sights of the police – being noted for 'street crimes'. Conversely, the police would rarely meet upper-class criminals deeply involved in corporate violations of state regulations, government malfeasance, professional malpractice, embezzlement or security/insurance fraud.

The way modern policing evolved, being assumed to be a rational and successful response to the burgeoning need for more effective means of crime control following the Industrial Revolution, largely defines the manner in which police have continued to encounter young people. Simply put, the business was to police the dangerous class! Like the logic of *Realpolitik*, not to do so is 'to face meaninglessness' (see Omaji 2001b, p 237).

Youthful life, evolving around friendship groupings or large networks of similarly inclined conglomerates of young people who are likely to drift in the public spaces together, presents all the trappings of 'dangerousness'. Whether they coalesce in 'loose groupings' or engage with life in some orderly fashion, the police see them as 'gangs'. It is immaterial that 'they are not likely to have the territorial base, the uniforms and colours, or the formalised hierarchies of American street gangs'. The perception deepens if they happen to have 'distinctive clothing and hairstyles' that are in stark contrast to older residents (Polk 1997, p 492).

Later in this chapter, I show that police are reinforced in their perception by the media's portraits of young people as thugs, bully-boys, granny bashers, louts and hooligans. How this gets them, wittingly or unwittingly, to draw a cloak of 'protecting the public' over their professional conscience and thereby make them feel able to practise a little 'vigilante' justice will be discussed in Chapter 3 among other themes. It suffices to note here that by negatively imaging youth and aggressively approaching their work in consequence, the police set in train a dynamic of fear, lack of respect and resistance on the part of many young people.

The dynamic assumes a remarkable character especially in relation to those young people – the migrant youth – who had experienced police brutality or misbehaviour in their countries of origin. With these 'ethnic minority youth', another aspect of police imaging becomes manifest. Research shows that, with a police subculture that continues to be 'notoriously ethnocentric with strong insider-outsider boundaries' (Easteal 1997, p 159), police frequently form stereotypical images of the outsider (usually the ethnic groups) and then harass them accordingly.

'Troublemaking' and 'gangsterism' are the two most typical stereotypes noticeable in police attitudes to ethnic minority youth. For instance, police regard Australia's Aboriginal youth suspiciously and believe instinctively that young Aborigines are 'up to no good'. They carry the social prejudices of the wider community from which they are drawn that racial and ethnic minorities are inferior and not to be trusted. They regard all Aboriginal youth as 'constant offenders' and that 'most black fellas pinch cars' (Beresford and Omaji 1996, pp 70-76). That this police perception not only extends to all indigenous Australians but also resonates with police practices has been aptly captured by Cunneen (2001, p 152) when he states that 'the view of Indigenous people as not law-abiding, as hostile and unco-operative, as drunken, is a view which redefines them as a criminal class, and corresponds with particular policing practices'.

In a US study, one highly placed official in the police department was said to have made the following statement:

> If you know that the bulk of your delinquent problem comes from kids who, say, are from 12 to 14 years of age, when you're out on patrol you are much more likely to be sensitive to the activities of juveniles in this age bracket than older or younger groups. This would be good law enforcement practice. The logic in our case is the same except that our delinquency problem is largely found in the Negro community and it is these youths toward whom we are sensitised. (Piliavin and Briar 1991, p 435)

In the UK racial prejudice manifests itself in some police officers who, faced with what they see as the inexorably rising tide of street crime, 'lapse into an unthinking assumption that all young black people are potential criminals' (Lord Scarman report 1981). In July 1995, the UK Metropolitan Police commenced Operation Eagle Eye on the grounds that they thought that 80 per cent of street crime in Inner London was carried out by young blacks. In 1998, another report finds that the situation remains:

> For their part, the police sometimes view members of ethnic minority groups, and black people in particular, as 'problematic'. They tend to perceive them as being disproportionately involved in certain types of crime and, correspondingly, have heightened notions about the 'suspiciousness' of their behaviour. (Home Office 1998)

The Australian Law Reform Commission (1992) had found that ethnic young people, who gathered together because they were related, were family friends, went to school together or lived near each other, would be assumed by the police to be involved in illegal gang activities simply due to their different appearance. Simply by dressing in tracksuits and Reebok shoes, they were identified as 'colour gangs' instead of groups of kids.

Since the 1970s, New Zealand police had begun to change their perception of ethnic youth groups such as the Stormtroopers in South Auckland from that of 'a juvenile problem to a major threat to law and order, and a social problem of dangerous proportions' (Meek 1992, p 255). In a submission to the Committee of Inquiry into Violence in 1986, police attitudes to these groups had been made manifest:

> Gangs have been a problem for the last 20 years but in the last few years a noticeable change in their attitudes towards authority and their involvement in criminal offending has occurred ... Their members are now hardened ... This reflects the arrogant attitude ... in pursuit of its [sic] goals and objectives.

> Gang members have opted out of society; they do not wish to be like normal citizens or dress like them; that is why they are eager to perform shocking and disgusting acts. (NZ Police 1986, pp 80-83)

The 1990s witnessed some slight change in New Zealand police attitude mainly because police officers were legislatively compelled to 'adopt low-key responses to juvenile offending whenever possible' (Morris and Maxwell 1998).

In America, 'the land of youth gangs', most police officers who get attracted to young people who look 'suspicious, funny or out of place', define suspicious as 'black kids in white neighbourhoods' (Wordes and Bynum 1995). The following incident illustrates the operation of this stereotyping: One officer, observing a youth walking along the street, commented that the youth 'looks suspicious' and promptly stopped and questioned him. Asked later to explain what aroused his suspicion, the officer explained, 'He was a Negro wearing dark glasses at midnight' (Piliavin and Briar 1991, p 435).

As regards prejudice per se, 18 of 27 officers interviewed by Piliavin and Briar during their research openly admitted a dislike for Negroes. However, they attributed their dislike to experiences they had as policemen with youths from this minority group. The officers reported that Negro boys were much more likely than non-Negroes to 'give us a hard time', be uncooperative, and show no remorse for their transgressions. Recurrent exposure to such attitudes among Negro youth, the officers claimed, generated their antipathy toward Negroes. The following excerpt is typical of the views expressed by these officers:

> They [Negroes] have no regard for the law or for the police. They just don't seem to give a damn. Few of them are interested in school or getting ahead. The girls start having illegitimate kids before they are 16 years old and the boys are always 'out for kicks'. Furthermore, many of these kids try to run you down. They say the damnedest things to you and they seem to have absolutely no respect for you as an adult. I admit I am prejudiced now, but frankly I don't think I was when I began police work. (Piliavin and Briar 1991, p 435)

Undergirding all these negative perceptions is the police view that 'disorderly' behaviour of these youth denies police their status as holders of authority. In any case, it is rhetorical to wonder whether officers who harbour such perceptions could successfully handle perceived youth crime or insubordination in ways other than through an aggressive and punitive response.

How the courts think about youth

A 75-year-old man, Maurice Berger, who assaulted his 81-year-old brother, was convicted in a British court in 1996. While delivering a 30-month suspended sentence, Judge Timothy Pontius told the man: 'I am rather more used to dealing with young thugs and drunken hooligans for offences such as this, not respectable and law abiding pensioners [like you]' (*Daily Telegraph* 24 February 1996, quoted in Brown 1998, p 4). The age-specific stereotype evident in this comment is not just widespread. It generally exerts a decisive influence on the way courts respond to young offenders.

It is a common thinking among traditionally oriented judiciary that 'youth' and 'crime' are inextricably linked. More to the point, in the eyes of the generality, especially of the lower court magistrates or judges, criminality is youth's specialty! Any attempt by young people to distinguish themselves – for example, through symbols of subcultural identity such as dress – fortifies this criminal image among these judges. When the Teddy Boys, a group of working class youth adopted the Edwardian suit – a postwar dress style prevalent among young English men of higher social status – in the 1950s, they were seen not only separated subculturally from the larger society since the middle and upper class youth abandoned the style immediately. They were also viewed as a criminal gang. The chairman of the Dartford Juvenile Court was quoted in 1954 as saying that the Edwardian suits were 'flashy, cheap and nasty, and stamp the wearer as a particularly undesirable type'.[6] There is no reason to doubt that visible difference has continued to sponsor a criminal stereotype both from the public and the agencies of criminal justice, well into the present time.

Combine this sort of difference with ethnicity and the young ethnic male is doubly vulnerable to this stereotype. Perceptions of judges about youth, and especially ethnic youth who have adopted some subcultural identity, are that these youth suffer from lax supervision; they are unresponsive, culturally deprived, cognitively deficient and are anything contrary to conceptions of social normality.

From the moment a young accused steps into the courts, some judges misconstrue several nuances of body language, including differences by age, generation, race, gender, ethnicity and other indicators of identity. Combined with this stereotyping is the adherence in most western societies to white middle-class standards which the courts perceive to be far removed from the constructed reality of most young people. Thus by the turn of the 20th century, for instance, some English judges had young people firmly in their view when they wanted the 1908 *Anglo-Welsh Prevention of Crime Act* extended beyond the professional criminals for which the law was enacted to include those people (mostly young) 'whose abstinence from crime is so infrequent that society is justified in requiring special protection from their habits of depredation' (Pratt 1995, p 6).

At the broad philosophical level, the factor which seems of greatest importance in shaping the 'judicial attitude' is anxiety about growing 'social permissiveness'. Rightly or wrongly, judges, more than any other justice practitioners, feel that 'the erosion of moral constraints ... would in the end precipitate a weakening in the authority of the Law itself' (Hall, Critcher, Jefferson, Clarks and Roberts 1978, p 34). At the courtroom level, they tend to rely on pre-sentence reports and other 'tip-offs' for their views about young offenders as perpetrators of this moral decay or harbingers of trouble. Both the reports and tip-offs are fundamentally ideological in nature and rest on their presenters' particular assumptions about the offenders and the causes of their offending (for example, see Cunneen and White 1995, p 225). In describing his orientation about how he conducts his court hearings, a judge made this point:

> We look for tip-offs that *something is really wrong*. We get some tip-offs just from the fact-sheet; truancy, school attendance, conduct, and effort marks ... *If you get something wrong there, you know there's trouble*. When you get truancy or bad conduct plus the delinquency, there's definitely something wrong. (Emerson 1969, p 84)

Imaging youth filters into this process as the courts usually try to sort out cases involving 'trouble' by making judgements about the nature of the 'criminal' youthful actor: 'what kind of youth are we dealing with here?' In answering this question, the courts venture beyond the presenting offending behaviour to look at the youth's *moral character*. As Emerson (1969, p 90) observes, as soon as 'trouble is located, ... character is rendered *problematic*. This initiates more intensive court involvement with the case, as well as more intensive concern with accounting for the youth's behaviour'.

> Court staff distinguish three general kinds of juvenile moral character. First, a youth may be *normal*, ie, basically like most children, acting for basically normal and conventional reasons, despite some delinquent behavior. Second, a youth may be regarded as a *hard-core* or *criminal-like* delinquent, maliciously or hostilely motivated, consciously pursuing illegal ends. Third, a youth may be *disturbed*, driven to acting in senseless and irrational ways by obscure motives or inner compulsions ... To explain such behaviour by fitting the individual case into one of these categories both suggests and justifies particular court actions to deal with it. (ibid)

Of the three elements in this moral typology, research shows that the courts have been prepared to perceive accused young offenders more readily as criminal-like or disturbed than normal. Against this background, it is easier to understand the portrait of a typical young offender that Sir Leo Page, a chairman of a bench of magistrates in Britain, presented in 1950 and which seems to linger on till today. He saw this offender to be below the ordinary standard of intelligence and knowledge who wags school. To the offender, he said, schooling gives no wholesome interests or hobbies. Sex, the cinema, the street corner, betting and the public house together give him all the pleasure he knows or asks of life. He has literacy problems. Going by false standards, he measures his life, not as something contemptible, but as something bold and glamorous. He aims to be tough, a wide guy, a wise guy, whatever his current expression may be to indicate what by his own sorry standards he imagines to be a man of the world. As a spoilt young man, he is utterly selfish, resents all discipline and authority, and is quite indifferent to the rights of others (Page 1950, pp 270-271).

Half a century later, in 2000, Judge Eugene A Moore, Chief Judge, Probate Court, Oakland County, Michigan and past president of the National Council of Juvenile and Family Court Judges, in an article titled 'How the Courts Can Help Fight Delinquency and Neglect',[7] provides a similar portrait of young offenders. Judge Moore identifies five common denominators present in the backgrounds of most youth who appear in juvenile court:

- Most youth come from problem homes that fail to provide attention, love and discipline. Society must focus on the issue of family and re-establish the importance of proper parenting. This includes the obligation that all parents must set as their number one priority: love, discipline and encouraging moral growth for their children.

- The youngster is impeded in school achievement. The delinquent 10th grader who reads on a fourth- or fifth-grade level soon begins to drop out and eventually is either pushed or drops out of school.

- Most of these youngsters have never participated in any community activities. Community agencies seldom reach out and go into the community with a program to meet the needs of the neglected, underprivileged or pre-delinquent child.

- Most of these youngsters have never been involved with any church or synagogue of their choice. Most have never had any on-going religious training involving the Judeo-Christian ethic.

- The typical delinquent has low self-esteem and does not like others and cares very little about being caught because it is merely one more failure.

Add to the class assumptions inherent in the above portrait the deeply racist assumptions, and it is easy to understand, as studies of the unequal use of capital punishment have shown dramatically, the nature of the responses of the American courts to 'black young criminals' (Taylor 1999, p 31). Some English courts have consistently displayed discriminatory responses to 'black crime' that only stereotypical imaging can explain. According to several studies, the chances of a black offender in England receiving a custodial sentence in broad terms are about 8 per cent higher, on average, than for whites. Across Europe as a whole in the late 1990s, there was widespread evidence of increased involvement by racial minorities in the criminal justice system (see, for example, Leonard, Pope and Feyerherm 1995). The Australian, New Zealand and North American experiences are amply illustrated by the overrepresentation of indigenous youth at all levels of their criminal justice systems (Beresford and Omaji 1996; Cunneen, Fraser and Tomens1997; Cunneen and McDonald 1997; Samuelson 1993).

In all of these jurisdictions, judges cherish the convenience of having a 'visible' minority available as the 'obvious scapegoat for ongoing public anxieties in respect of crime and social dislocation' (Taylor 1999).

The belief that there are millions of idle hands on the streets doubtless provokes more anxiety in judges and magistrates than any other segment of these societies. As Box (1987) observes, many believe that the unemployed are likely to help themselves to other people's property. They also believe that a major part of their judicial function is to be seen protecting private property:

> When to these beliefs is added the "knowledge" that crime is getting worse and the fear of crime is becoming a major social problem – the messages that politicians, via the media, communicate – then the judiciary are bound to become more sensitised to the dangers that lurk in high levels of unemployment. Consequently, it is very likely that their decisions, both in terms of verdicts and sentences, will be tinged with hostility and anxiety whenever they sense a deterioration in class relationships and a slackening of discipline – through-work (or school, or family) among subordinate classes. (Box 1987, p 135)

The courts perceive unemployed males as 'problematic' because, in western culture, work is not only believed to be the typical way in which males are disciplined but it is also their major source of identity and thus the process by which they build up a stake in conformity. The unemployed will be seen to develop various anarchistic responses among which criminal behaviour is likely to feature quite strongly. Thus, young unemployed males will be perceived as potentially or actually more dangerous than older males simply 'because their resistance to adversity will have been less worn away by barren years of accommodative strategies to inequalities in the distribution of income and life chances ... their physical prowess and energy, attributes often considered prerequisites for conventional crime, will still be in prime condition' (Box 1987). With such a perception, it is not hard to see why the 'jurisprudence of the vulnerable', in which the courts are said to consider themselves as defenders of the 'vulnerable' – persons most exposed to the decisions of people with power hardly identifies young people (whether victims or offenders) in the list of priority (for example, see Finn 1996). This is despite the recognition (or the rhetoric?) within the judiciary that 'protecting the young and otherwise vulnerable', as Justice Kirby (1995, p 22) once declared, should be one of three aims for criminal justice.

Generally, judges develop a subculture of sentencing based around the 'law and order' views to which they subscribe. Racialised or class-based views have tended to dominate the manner in with western judges perceive and respond to 'problematic' male youth. Thus, for instance, some base their judgements 'on social characteristics that indirectly mirror race, rather than on legal variables, [and] their decisions frequently result in differential processing and more severe sentencing of minority youths relative to whites' (Feld 1995, p 70; see also Walker, Spohn and DeLone 1996).

However, from time to time, some enlightened views emerge from within the judiciary about the reality of young people's involvement with crime. For instance, in an address to the Youth Affairs Council of Western Australia in 1999, the Chief Justice of Western Australia, David Malcolm, discussed among other things the representation of juvenile crime in the media and the relationship between young people's use of public space and juvenile crime. He concluded with a recommendation of the establishment of a dedicated youth facility in the centre of the city of Perth, 'where young people can meet and "hang out" – their own space, safe, with inexpensive food and entertainment available' (Malcolm 1999). Such views are distinguished more by their rarity than by their deviation from the traditional orientation.

How detention staff think about youth

Like the other parts of the criminal justice system, detention staff bring several assumptions and perceptions to bear on their charges behind the walls. Prominent among these perceptions are the 'wards in chancery' and 'convicted criminals' images.[8] One of the most classic studies of the way custodial staff think about the young inmates is by Barry Feld (1977). This study focuses on Dr Jerome Miller's attempt to create a humanised and therapeutic climate within the existing institutions, during the period of some of the most sweeping reforms of youth corrections (the Massachusetts experiment) in the US.[9] Specifically, it examines 'a storm of protest from old-line staff' who resented what they considered to be attacks on their absolute control over the inmates.

By means of interviews and questionnaires, Feld investigated staff perceptions of the 'kinds of kids' they were treating. His findings bear significantly on the theme of this chapter and will be summarised below in some detail.

Custody staff perceive their charges as 'rejected children who need help' and as suffering from emotional or psychological problems. As delinquents, these charges are incapable of normal relationships, for example they 'cannot be friends among themselves'. Further inmates are incompetent to 'make decisions even about everyday living problems'. Further still, as a prison officer sums up the perception about young inmates in Plymouth youth custody centre, 'they are prolific liars in here' (Little 1990, p 122).

On the extreme side of negative perception, inmates are 'hard-core' posing 'serious control and management problems'. Staff believe that 'most of the kids sent here are capable of flying off the handle … We used to be able to categorise them as mean or vicious or sick, but now, with the drug problem, they can be charming and disarming one minute and vicious the next'. 'Some are just full of the devil'. 'Clusters of boys' are conspiracy groups and they must be denied the opportunity to connive (Feld 1977, pp 46-50).

On the whole, the staff displayed strong elements of authoritarianism, as reflected in an emphasis on obedience, respect for authority, reliance on external controls and a preference for the status quo. Obedience, conformity and deference make a 'good kid', as opposed to inmates gaining insight and self-awareness, participation and involvement in the change process, and acting responsibly towards others (p 49). Their views of the charges are those of inmates as 'dangerous' and 'untrustworthy'. They operated causation and prevention models in which they see individual exercise of free will as the source of deviance and can be deterred by a simple pleasure-pain mechanism. Within such frameworks, partnership approach to solving the crime problem of the inmates was remote in their thinking.

The staff hardly think that 'the expectations and treatment strategies in the custody programs may actually create or exacerbate' the observed tendencies in the inmates rather than an independent characteristic of the inmates. Because of their general perception of inmates and their apprehensions about inmate collusion against staff, the staff frown on informal inmate association, preferring inmate self-isolation.

By any criterion of judgement, it is clear that perceptions of inmates as 'mad' or 'riotous' – because they kick and scream, lead to very poor staff-inmate relations. Chapter 3 discusses the relationship between this ideological backdrop and the relative emphasis the staff place on controlling inmates' anti-social behaviours as opposed to addressing their socio-emotional problems.

The issue of negative perceptions is compounded by the fact that, in most of the countries, custodial staff do not reflect the ethnic and racial mix of the detained clientele. For example, the staff of NSW detention centres during 1991-93 were nearly all Anglo-Saxon, while the young people in these centres 'come from over 60 ethnic and cultural backgrounds' (Graham 1993). As the New Zealand example shows, this produces some detriment to the detained youth (Atkinson 1997, p 412). Despite the fact that in the 1980s, the majority of the prison population in New Zealand were of Maori descent, staff's management strategies for custodial gang activities, namely 'neutral turf', was founded upon an individualistic philosophy of inmates to 'do their own lag' which has a greater applicability to Pakeha (white) inmates than Maori and Polynesian prisoners (Meek 1992, p 270).

Officers use isolation cells as a managing tool (with highly damaging consequences); they see no need to equip young inmates for life after release. Few staff are trained in the language, culture and traditions of youth category. The behavioural and social value differences of ethnic minority youth are not only misjudged by those in authority to be apparent displays of insolence, lack of cooperation or excitability, but frequently anger these authority figures, putting further strain on an already unhealthy cultural construction of minority youth (Hazlehurst 1987, p 114).

As will be shown later in this book, a shift has been occurring, especially in the past 10 years, in the formal criminal justice system towards preventive partnerships – some based on a restorative justice paradigm which promotes rather than abolishes 'self-responsibility' as signalled by the enactment of *Children, Young Persons and their Families Act* 1989 (Consedine 1995). It is expected that this would result in changed perceptions of youth among detention staff and the way these staff manage the detainees.

Making sense of criminal justice perceptions of youth

Ideological factors

With the exception of perhaps the highest courts in the land,[10] all state agencies of criminal justice perceive themselves traditionally as defenders of law and order, not guardians of human rights. At this ideological or idiosyncratic level, these agencies' imaging of the subjects with whom they deal is heavily influenced by authoritarianism, fear of subversion of authority or the law, some masculinist orientation and the characteristics of the subjects. I will use the police to illustrate this point.

Police, on the standard personality measurements and in their traditional mode, show a high level of authoritarianism which manifests in conservatism, aggression, power or toughness, destructiveness, cynicism and stereotypy (James and Warren 1995, p 5). As the Fitzgerald Inquiry in Australia found, the Queensland Police Force in the late 1980s perceived that they were combatants in an unequal fight with criminals whose legal rights needed to be subverted for the sake of achieving the kinds of effective justice believed to be expected by the community. The tactics they employed in this imagined combat embodied all the hallmarks of authoritarianism (Queensland Commission of Inquiry 1989).

Jerome Skolnick's analysis, which found that the most salient factors in policing attitudes are danger and authority, is consistent with this understanding. The exposure of police to danger in their working environment forges a strong sense of suspiciousness and a tendency to be constantly alert to signs of violence and offending. Ironically, this sense tends to weaken police commitment to procedural regularity or abiding by the rule of law. Further, police suspiciousness of the conditions for dangerous or threatening situations foster a preference for predictable, conventional and stable events and people and a dislike and intolerance of unpredictable, erratic and deviant events and people (James and Warren 1995, p 7).

Also, perceived challenges to their status as legitimate holders and wielders of authority are a trigger for police abuse of power and force. Beside the tendency to exercise more coercive authority and force against people who match stereotypes of deviance and dangerousness, police react aggressively to people who defy or deny their authority. When the question of authority remains unresolved, police responses (especially from some male officers) are more likely to be violent (Reiss 1970). Consider this story from a field diary of a Vice Section of Licensing, Gaming and Vice Squad shift in Victoria, Australia:

> A kid of eighteen or nineteen cruises past in a high-powered sedan; apparently he has connected the microphone of his citizen-band radio to a loudspeaker concealed beneath the bonnet of the car. As we clamber into our car he pulls alongside and barks through the loudspeaker – at a volume which could be heard fro several hundred metres. 'Did youse have a good fuck, fellers?' ... Katie, the policewoman, chuckles. 'No such luck, mate!'.

> However the young Detective Senior Constable is agitated; he revs the car and demands that we pursue the sedan and charge the driver with offensive behaviour ... [He] drives at high speed until we intercept the sedan at a set of traffic lights and he leaps out to confront the driver. (Settle 1990, p 18)

An element of the police culture which sustains antagonism towards youth is the powerful masculinist orientation that privileges or rewards strength and glamorises violence (Sutton 1992). This has meant that the youth have remained most vulnerable to police coercion and aggression. Confirming the argument that Rob White made about the way policing of community space affects the youth, James and Warren (1995, p 9) note that 'young people are ... particularly vulnerable to the application by police of culturally-determined practices such as the prediction of dangerousness and the invocation of delinquent stereotypes'.

Other research works have shown that 'subject characteristics', especially those exhibited by young people, interact with various conceptions of normality and legitimacy that criminal justice agencies bring to their encounters with the public.

Sociological factors

In his celebrated taxonomy of police behaviours, Wilson (1968) shows not only that there are continuities and divergencies in policing ideological constructs but that substantial variations are a product of particular structural (social and political) factors. For instance, the conflict between young people and the police is, in essence, a reflection of a much deeper struggle over economic resources and the uses to which community or public spaces are, or should be, put (White 1997, p 258). Illustrating what can be termed essentially as 'policing in the interest of business', White recounts the story of three Aboriginal youth who were picked up by police and taken from a central mall area and driven to the outskirts of Brisbane:

> When they reached there, the boys were taken out of the vehicles. They were told they must keep away from the Valley mall, and that they weren't welcome there. They showed them a flat piece of timber, told them to place their hands on the timber so that they'd have their fingers cut off. The police then told them to remove their shoes. The boys refused to do that, so the police pulled their shoes off, threw their shoes into the bushes, told them to keep out of the Valley or they'd end up in the river, and then the police vehicles drove off. (White 1997, p 259)

Illuminating as the ideological and sociological perspectives may be, readers should be aware that this approach, taken to the extreme, can result in cultural or sociological determinism. Yet a careful analysis of the complexities in the construction of reality shows that criminal justice personnel are not cultural dupes, blindly following internalised rules, or haplessly obeying structural imperatives. Rather, they are active participants in the construction of action (see Shearing and Ericson 1991). It is with this more sophisticated framework that one can understand why is it that certain representations are popular, powerful and influential; why certain types of content and images are selected over and above others; and why certain kinds of representation are fashionable at any given time (Brown 1998, p 39).

Mass media repackaging of 'youth as problem'

The most powerful tools in the criminal justice imagining of youth are the mass media. It is now common knowledge that the way the media construct the popular imagery of youth filters directly into the views that criminal justice agencies hold about youth. As will be shown later, the relationship between the media and the agencies as primary definers of crime (through which the dominant ideology of crime is filtered into the public arena) is also very complex (Welch, Fenwick and Roberts 1997).

Two bodies of research underpin an understanding of the complex media-criminal justice perception or policy relationships. These are the communication and journalism research and the social construction of reality research. The former links the media with public opinion formation and the emergence of attitudes and perceptions concerning crime and justice (Stroman and Seltzer 1985; Page, Shapiro and Dempsey 1987). The latter examines the media's role in the creation and promulgation of social knowledge (Surette 1996). Most of our worldly knowledge is, in fact, gained not from reality as we experience it but from symbolic reality largely constructed by the mass media. The 'experienced and symbolic realities are combined by each individual to create a model subjective reality' (Surette 1996, p 183)

The media represent young people as perpetrators of 'predator crime' defined as interpersonal, stranger-to-stranger, injury-causing crime in which usually innocent, helpless victims are randomly chosen. Media representation of youth behaviour conjures up images of youth as demonic. Taylor (1999, p 8) graphically illustrates the contemporary context in which these images are conveyed:

> In most western societies at the end of the 20th century, the mass of audiences for newspapers, television and cinema are bombarded by the day with an essentially theological, medieval criminology, with a gallery of insane or evil individuals, devils and witches and a range of theories of individual possession, through which they are asked to make sense of a fast-breaking story about "crime".

Without ignoring the fact that young people, from time to time, feature in the media as 'noble and wonderful', it is fair to say that the attention they get presents them preponderantly as 'deviant and dangerous'. With such a content, the media influence official action by reinforcing the distorted stereotypes of crime and criminals. In the media, crime is almost universally attributed to individual characteristics rather than social conditions, and the causes of crime are rooted in individual failings rather than social ills (Surette 1996, p 185). This construction of dangerous fugitives let loose in the violent and uncertain world encourages ever-broader social controls.

Research on the coverage of children and youth by the national news media in the US reveals that in the mid 1990s:

- television news devoted more than 47 per cent of all its news coverage of youth to crime and violence and only about 15 per cent of its stories to education issues;
- newspapers devoted about 40 per cent of their youth stories to crime and violence and 25 per cent of its coverage to schools.

During the same period, child poverty, childcare and child welfare occupied only about 4 per cent of the attention of the media, both electronic and print. Very little space in either medium was devoted to policy discussions about possible solutions to youth problems (Shepherd 1997).

The following story by the National Director of the US National Crime Prevention Council, John Calhoun, and the two Tables below show that media coverage not only projects the news about youth crime news in terms of 'if it bleeds, it leads' (Table 1.1), but that the coverage also attempts to reinforce public impressions by raising the violent crime news very high on the order of social issues (Table 1.2).

Table 1.1: Select media coverage of violent youth crime in America, 1992-97

Date	Media source	Sensationalist title
9 March 1992	Cover story, *Newsweek*	'Kids and Guns: A Report from America's Classroom Killing Grounds'
26 October 1992	*Time*	'Children Without Pity'
August 1993	Cover Story, *Time*	'Big Shots: An Inside Look at the Deadly Love Affair Between America's Kids and Their Guns'
August 1993	Cover story, Newsweek	'Teen Violence: Wild in the Streets'
8 November 1993	*U.S. News & World Report*	'Guns in the Schools: When Killers Come to Class. Even Suburban Parents Now Fear the Rising Tide of Violence'
1996	*U.S. News & World Report*	'Teenage Time Bombs'
June 1997	*People Weekly*	'Heartbreaking Crimes: Kids Without a Conscience'

Source: Constructed from Shepherd (1997), using figures from the Center for Media and Public Affairs in Washington.

Table 1.2: Ranking of Crime Stories in America, 1990-96

Year	Rank of Crime stories
1990	5th
1991	6th
1992	3rd
1993	1st
1994	1st
1995	1st
1996	2nd (overtaken by the presidential campaign)

Source: Constructed from Shepherd (1997), using figures from the Centre for Media and Public Affairs in Washington.

Mr Calhoun was once asked to speak on *The Larry King Live Show*. The show had two segments, the first which was supposed to go for 30 minutes described the release from jail of a young person who had been convicted of killing. King interviewed the victim's wife, family, the arresting officer, psychologist and assorted others for over 50 minutes. The second segment in which Mr Calhoun was supposed to discuss prevention of such a horrific crime was also planned to go for half an hour, but he was not invited on until nine minutes before the close of the show. When he came on, the following exchange ensued:

> Larry King: OK, Mr Calhoun. Given this what's wrong?
>
> John Calhoun: This show. My heart goes out to the victim's family and all those connected with this horrible crime, but just look at what you've done. Over fifty minutes devoted to the crime and its aftermath and *only nine minutes* on how we can prevent such awful events from occurring.
>
> Larry King: It's time for a commercial. (Calhoun 1998, p 3)

The effect of media reporting has a great bearing on the construction of social attitudes and the framing of political responses to youth crime. For instance, the way they report conventional or street crime clearly affects criminal justice agencies' perception of their own roles. In relation to the police,

> fictional and non-fictional accounts of police work provided on television and through the press and books may stimulate or feed into ideas that policing is primarily about 'crime fighting' and that violence is part and parcel of the way in which you actually do policing. (White 1997, p 255)

The parochial interest that underlies the media's creation of 'moral panics', a turbulent, excited or exaggerated response to deviance or social problem', should by now be obvious to attentive scholars of criminology and criminal justice. Perceptions of the state of society, and of crime and drug abuse, illegal immigration and youth gangs, are mostly exaggerated by the media, which, in order to survive, need to create a good story by over-dramatising these issues (Lumby 2000).

The media's alarmist treatment of the 'youth underclass' in the western world is particularly noteworthy. From their accounts, these young people are disengaged from integrative institutions in the society (for example, employment, education, and families) and do constitute a major threat to order and civility. They are 'explosives', 'brewing ferment', roaming through the suburbs as 'breeds of outlaw children'. They are 'armies of young people', 'ticking like time bombs'. They are wild, predatory, untamed, feral, urban tribes and under-socialised young people (Bessant, Sercombe and Watts 1998, p 198).

For these young people to fit into the 'rule of relevancy' with which the media deal with crime news, they must be constructed as 'folk devils' and 'lords of misrule' (Cohen 1979). Within these castings or designations, their deeds satisfy the criteria for 'crime news' which must focus on:

- visible and spectacular acts;
- sexual and political connotations;
- graphic presentation;
- individual pathology;
- deterrence and repression (Chibnall 1977).

The most fundamental aspect of the representation of young people is that it constructs them as 'Other' (Bessant, Sercombe and Watts 1998, p 134). The exclusionary bias of this construction ultimately defines how the young people are governed, policed, judged and controlled in detention.

In the period leading to the explosive growth of juvenile shock incarceration programs in several western countries, but especially the US, the media portrayed juvenile delinquents simply as younger versions of irredeemable, adult predatory criminals (Surette 1996, p 186). In this context, the media showed how they could fan a disquiet into a rage, an ebb into a wave, a trickle into a tide. A punch-up among a group of teenagers would come out in the media as rival gang fighting with weapons. These teenagers might be no more than a group of 'bored and lonely youths gravitating to street corners in the absence of structured recreational support' (Easteal 1997, p 155).

Reporting on minority racial and ethnic youth

In relation to minority groups, such as Aboriginal youth in Australia, young Maori in New Zealand, African American youth in the US and the First Nations youth in Canada, the media reporting shows some momentary inclination towards 'benevolent paternalism' but, on the whole, remains focused on representing these young people 'as a threat or challenge to public order and ... property'. The media locks the image of problem youth in their respective societies into a generalised 'climate of hostility to "marginal" groups and racial minorities' (Brown 1998, p 44). As Sercombe (1995, p 78) had observed in relation to Australia, 'the news about Aboriginal young people is crime news'. Over the years, there has been 'a dramatically increased visualisation' of Aboriginal youth, by the media, 'as criminals, as major instigators of disorder' (Mickler 1998, p 19).

Populist mass media ideology attributes incivility and parasitism to the ethnic underclass (Taylor 1999, p 18). The most prevalent approach is to portray the group activities of these young people in 'gangster' terms, most of the time without supporting empirical evidence. For instance, despite a widespread media cry about ethnic gangs overrunning Australia, a study sponsored by the Australian Multicultural Foundation in 1999 which examined young people from the Vietnamese, Turkish, Pacific Islander, Somalian, Latin American and Anglo Australian communities, found that such gangs are quite rare (White, Perrone, Guera and Lampugnani 1999).

Media-driven moral panics about ethnic youth crime are firmly linked to periods of economic crisis, as the official responses to the crime of mugging in England of the 1970s show (see Omaji 1997). The 1990s, characterised by severe economic downturns, saw 'a return of the tribes' (reversion to the notion of 'blood and belonging'), 'new fortress' and 'draw-bridge' mentality in the suburbs with an accent on reaction and retribution against crime. Calls for more punitive approaches grow louder when the community is feeling economically stressed. When people feel economically safe (they have houses, jobs, holidays), they are more inclined to tolerate or support liberal social policies, more willing to be generous to others. One can see, looking back, that swings of the pendulum in juvenile justice policy are not unrelated to the economic conditions of the time.

Conclusion

All social control agencies have the capacity to construct their own roles or functions and their perceptions of the phenomena they attempt to control. With regard to perceptions, they can give particular kinds of social, political and moral meaning to what they perceive. From time to time this situation is triggered by traumatic episodes. For instance, the killing of James Bulger by two 10-year-olds (UK) and the killing of a girl classmate by a six-year-old (US) both had a profound flow-on effect on perceptions of youth by the criminal justice agencies.

The way criminal justice agencies respond to these perceptions can be criminogenic. For instance, the study by Sherman et al (1998) found that to some extent 'the police themselves create a risk factor for crime simply by using bad manners'. Thus, 'making both the style and substance of police practices more legitimate in the eyes of the public, particularly high-risk juveniles, may be one of the most effective long-term police strategies for crime prevention'. It is not idle speculation that the mannerisms of the criminal justice agencies towards young people, based on their own jaundiced perceptions, define the character of their responses and severely constrain the crime prevention potentials of their privileged positions. As a New Zealand Queen's Counsel once said, 'the evil of our [justice] system is that not only are our [systems] generating more criminality but they are promoting crime' (quoted in Consedine 1995, p 27).

Notes

1   Criminal justice agencies try to foster this image of themselves as bureaucratic bodies, doing precisely what they are mandated by law to do.
2   *Portside Messenger* 21 May 1997.
3   This is cultural artefact or construction of a stage in life. It is different from 'children' as a biological concept.
4   Criminal justice scholarship encompasses crime control agencies of police, prosecutors, trial courts, correctional facilities, probation and parole. Thus, the focus of this book on the decision processes in police, courts and custodial corrections has a narrower canvass.
5   These are established, 'developed' societies which have been so fundamentally transformed by the demise of mass manufacturing industry over the past 25 years. Great Britain and the USA are clear examples of these societies.
6   *The Times*, 25 March 1954.
7   See *A World of Prevention* at <http://www.tyc.state.tx.us/prevention/howcourt.html>.
8   Julia Lathrop, in her introduction to *The Delinquent Child and the Home*, stated that a major feature of the Illinois Juvenile Code of 1899 was that it recognised a delinquent youth as 'a ward in chancery and not as an accused or convicted criminal'.
9   A seven-year period, 1969-76, culminating in the closure of old training schools and establishment of a network of decentralised community-based services by Dr Jerome Miller who was newly appointed as the Commissioner for the Department of Youth Services.
10 For example, the High Court in Australia, House of Lords in Britain, and Supreme Courts in Canada, New Zealand and the US.

2

Young 'actors' in criminal justice 'imaging' of youth

This chapter challenges one important position which is taken for granted in several conventional works on youth, crime and justice in western societies. This position is the predominant representation of young people as passive objects upon which criminal justice agencies impose their own images and control mechanisms. To adapt Robert Waters' theatrical metaphor, the tendency in much of the debate is to depict young people as passive actors in a drama in which the script is written exclusively by criminal justice agencies, rather than to see them actually and potentially as groups that are reshaping the nature of the performance and the capacity of the theatre (Waters 1990, p 157).

This book departs from such a view by using a dialectical perspective to articulate a more complex framework in which young people and criminal justice agencies are simultaneously both producer and product. As a counterpoint to the main focus of Chapter 1, I shall analyse here young people's active participation in shaping the incidence and prevalence of images about youth held by the criminal justice agencies.

In challenging the one-dimensional view of 'imaging' young people, the chapter will foreshadow the critique of emerging partnerships that the agencies have forged as part of their 'normality' project and the development of 'best practice' models of partnership. These issues are the subjects of Chapters 6 and 7 respectively. The critique for which I shall continue to lay the groundwork in this chapter will be cast in two related questions. First, if young people are active participants in the construction of images that justice agencies hold about their activities, can any partnership project truly work without young people playing a significant part in it? Secondly, if the overwhelming majority of young people are 'normal', how can it be best practice for criminal justice partnerships to ignore their resourcefulness while pursuing the expensively ineffective goal of punishing the 'abnormal' minority? Standing astride these two questions is the issue of whether, given the generally negative view that young people hold about criminal justice agencies, they would agree to participate in agency-initiated partnerships as anticipated by the discussion of ground-rules for an appropriate crime prevention partnership model in Chapter 7.

Youth and image construction

Young people are not passive or neutral receptacles primed to receive and be shaped entirely from outside, whether by peer or adult agencies. The Hippie movement that represented a middle and upper-class youthful subculture in the 1960s clearly illustrates this argument. It 'advocated active participation rather than passive spectating, as applied to all forms of self-expression' (Richards 1991, p 376). This advocacy was a call for young people to become 'creators' of their own image.

The previous chapter has shown how young people can be *subjects* and/or *consumers* of the image construction by the criminal justice system. The task here is to examine young people as *producers* of or active participants in the images constructed about them. In this role, young people may not have a controlling influence, but they surely have a contributory influence. They are not 'helpless dupes' of the criminal justice construction machinery. As Foucault observed, subject populations themselves do take on an identity and participate in the development of discourses around their population group (see Bessant, Sercombe and Watts 1998, p 60).

Young people use subcultures as one way to forge the category of 'youth' and its attendant images. They do this by taking on, latching onto, consuming, and/or inventing artefacts that express their feelings or define their stance in relation to the world in which they live and its sub-systems, including the criminal justice system. By definition, the active nature of this expression or definition almost invariably brings them into conflict with this world or its subsystems. Where the adult members of society perceive such activities as subversion (and this is how the conflict generally emanates), the stage is set for an inter-generational 'war' of resistance or cultural hegemony.

The construction of their activities as subversion makes young people experience cultural tensions to which they respond in several ways. Some develop a false cultural being that meets with parental, group and/or societal approval but is seldom richly satisfying in terms of providing a firm sense of identity and ownership. Others rebel culturally, seeking solace in a highly subversive youth pop culture, which can lead them away from the security of local identifications into the consumerism and anonymity of international media and often into self-destructive or anti-social actions. Still others retreat into a cultural box, estranged and without commitment or purpose in relation to the mainstream society – a response that further poses a challenge to, and alienates them from, the adult's sense of normality.

By and large, the 'cultural muscles' relevant to young people are rhymes, jokes, riddles, games, taunts, songs, parodies, gestures and much more that young people operate with and amongst their peers, manipulating, creating, negotiating, absorbing and reacting within a vital, interactive cultural matrix. It is such experiences that validate their existence, make worthy their very being (rather than their becoming) and underscore their joy in living. Yet, some responsible adults seem to view such circumstances with suspicion or derision. Rather than being respected as their right to personal expression, this world of young people is frequently equated with dark or sinister behaviours, and as contributing to violence on the streets, or racial and gender stereotyping, or 'mischief' in its various aspects from sexual exploration to drug use. Sure, these behaviours may be involved, but the view that they define absolutely every youth expression is more fictional than factual. Yet this view dominates policy and legal responses to the youth category.

Further, 'hanging around' in groups which is one of the strategies young people employ to ensure their own protection, or simply because they like it, is ironically perceived by many adults as threatening. Some of these adults resort to the criminal justice system, especially the police, to 'neutralise' this threat. Naturally young people become bewildered by this and they resent the consequences of the adults' alarm about them. The result is that one of young people's means of coping with crime para-doxically brings them into conflict with patently 'concerned' adults and further adversarial contact with the criminal justice system.

Imaging through youth cultural expressions

Through dress codes, hairstyles, music, language or manner of speaking, collective action, and other indicators of identities, young people make statements that set them apart. It is a form of "Teenspeak" which, denied access to mainstream mass media, finds these alternative means to com-municate about the world and to the world in relation to their existence. The views of adults and experts that this 'proves just how deviant or delinquent young people can be' (Bessant et al 1998, p 52) accord with the construction of 'youth' as a universal psycho-biological 'stage of life' between adolescence and adulthood, characterised by 'the tension between selfhood and the existing order' (ibid). Strangely, this definition attributes selfishness or self-awareness only to young people and not to the adult portion of the social order.

While there is symbolism tied up in the clothes, music, hairstyles and language, it is important to question whether authority figures such as police, court officers and detention officers read too many counter-cultural meanings (pathologically self-conscious, aggressive and subversive identities) into youth symbols. For these agencies, 'styles favoured by young people ... carried with them the smell of delinquency' (Bessant et al 1998, p 61). Or as Springhall (1998, p 156) tersely observes, 'whatever amuses the young for a price but does not appear to elevate public taste will attract criticism'.

Talcott Parsons, an American sociologist writing in 1942, informs us that youth culture was 'irresponsible' because it values athleticism for boys and physical attractiveness (the 'glamour girl' role) for girls, often at the limits of (or beyond) parental approval and contravening mainstream values of hard work and sobriety (see Bessant et al 1998, p 54). Put tersely, it focuses on 'having a good time'. But who says the two sets of values are inherently contradictory or mutually exclusive? For instance, isn't athleticism intertwined with hard work? Ask the Olympians of all generations and other sport icons and big businesses that now dole out sponsorship money in millions.

The real issue has to do with cultural hegemony and the power to control the 'Other'. It matters little to those who are uneasy with youth subcultures that the crucial condition for the emergence of youth cultural forms is the existence of a number of 'actors' forced to mobilise by similar patterns of adjustment.

> The presence of subcultures within a society signifies a struggle for supremacy among a number of lifestyles and value systems. Although deviance can be viewed as a creative response to irrelevant, ineffectual social rules, members of society are more likely to perceive nonconformity as a potentially destructive force undermining the security of that which is familiar. Enthusiastic mass media delineation of the activities, lifestyle and appearances associated with the offending subcultures fuel a 'moral panic' and lead to an eventual perception of the deviants as 'folk devils'. (Richards 1991, p 369)

When the establishment launched a publicity campaign designed to stamp out long hair in the Hippie movement, with billboards appearing along American highway – reading 'Beautify America: Cut Your Hair', the response from the Hippies was equally staunch. They flaunted their long hair and other symbols of different-ness. In such a showing of counterpride display, one Hippie male stated: 'if you ask me why I have my hair long, I'd say, principally because I like it ... and to kick society in the bollocks ... wave my fingers at them' (Richards 1991, p 378).

Fighting against being inferior or disempowered

Some research with young people who had experienced life on the streets, known poverty and dislocation, and suffered educational and social disadvantage, tends to argue that what is usually seen as resistance to authority by young people is actually a creative response to traumatic life experiences (McFadden 1993). However, there is evidence to suggest that a significant proportion of young people who come in contact with criminal justice agencies not only detests the 'put down' by the system but actively resists the degradation ceremonies through which such system-induced 'inferiority' is imposed.

In a research into the dynamics of contact between Australia's indigenous youth and the mainstream criminal justice system, Beresford and Omaji (1996, p 86) found that these young people hated the way that their older generations were treated by the system as inferior beings. In response, they were determined not only to fight off this inferiority but also to show that their generations would not 'cop it sweet' or take it lying down. As one interviewee told the researchers, 'old black people feel inferior, but do not want to make waves, while kids want to fight against being inferior'. The result was an emerging pattern of resistance to over-policing in particular.

As part of their resistance, these young people engaged in bravado and believed that getting into trouble was a big thing – a status symbol. They did not hesitate in acknowledging that 'crime is empowering'. For instance, they saw stealing cars as a form of engagement that gave the poor black youth 'a piece of the action'. The car had become a symbol of power and freedom. To fight off the powerlessness brought about by their being denied participation in the mainstream through legitimate means, they use cars to bait or provoke authority figures into a 'power contest'. In most cases, this resulted in high-speed car chases by the police – some ending in tragedy. To the young Aborigines, the tragedy is largely inconsequential (a small price to pay) because they 'want to make society pay for what it has done to Aboriginal people or for the powerlessness of their own parents' (Select Committee 1992, p 9). Creative? Yes, but no less resistant and no less capable of generating negative images from onlookers and the authority figures alike.

Subversion is the name of the game, and Atkinson (1993, p 271) is right when she observes thus:

> Aboriginal people, so omnipresently involved with the criminal justice system, know how to subvert that system; to derive different meanings for, and experiences of the system from those originally intended. Our criminal justice system is intended to create fear, shame and conformity to mainstream norms in transgressor ... Aboriginal people have learnt how to shift the moral burden instead to those who police, try and imprison them and to re-interpret their experiences of the ... system to subvert those experiences and hence make them tolerable. By these means they gain some fleeting sense of power – however illusory and transitory this might be – over a system which is overwhelmingly stacked against them.

Through anger and frustration with the system and life in general, these young people use several means to re-construct and re-establish an identity for themselves that jettisons the image of the 'under dog'. Indigenous and other minority youth in countries such as Canada, New Zealand, the UK and the US have been noted to have also used similar means to counter their system-imposed inferiority and powerlessness (see Leonard, Pope and Feyerherm 1995).

Constructing images through attitudes to criminal justice agencies

In the next three sections, I examine the specific attitudes and behaviours of young people to the three main agencies of criminal justice. The focus is on the actual or potential influence of these attitudes and behaviours on the images that the police, courts and corrections hold about young people.

The works that have emerged to date suggest that the relevant young people's attitudes correlate largely to three main types of variables:

- Demographic: Non-whites are less satisfied with the white-dominated system and thus hold less favourable attitudes than whites. This is likely to result from minorities' negative contact with the system. Also, younger individuals often possess less positive attitudes than older citizens, the latter believing more – as they get older – that the system plays a legitimate role in protecting the status quo. In some cases, males have less positive images of the system than females. This difference becomes insignificant among minority youth.

- Crime-related: Crime victims have less favourable attitudes toward the system than those who have not experienced any criminal victimisation, directly or indirectly. Similarly, young people who perceive that their neighbourhoods are crime-infested tend to have less favourable attitudes towards the system.

- System conduct: Police-citizen encounters that are evaluated by young people as negative give rise to their negative attitudes toward the police. 'Persons knowing of police misconduct experienced by others will have less positive attitudes toward the police' (see Hurst and Frank 2000, pp 191-192).

Youth attitudes toward the police

The overwhelming majority of young people would rarely encounter police in a criminal context during their youth. Only one in 20 would ever be apprehended for crime in any given period, and no more than three in 20 would be stopped for any inquiry. While these numbers are definitely higher for minority youth, the fact remains that most of the images young people have of the police and the attitude they develop in the process are shaped by the media (both in news reports and fictional dramas) rather than direct experiences. These images may 'present a skewed picture of who the police are and what they actually do on a day-to-day basis' (Cunneen and White 1995, p 201), but they certainly serve as handles with which young people construct their actual or potential interactions with the police.

The 'common media portrayals of the police' identified by Cunneen and White (ibid) are quite instructive:

- *The Rogue Cop:* the 'Dirty Harry' type of police officer, who breaks the rules in order to get the 'bad guy' and thus protects the rest of us from predatory crime.

- *The Boy Scout:* the 'Mountie always gets his man' type, the kind who does things by the book and who speaks nicely during investigations.

- *The Crazy Cop:* this character is a bit twisted, like Riggs in the *Lethal Weapon* movies, but is essentially OK and has the special kind of craziness needed to handle serious street crimes, terrorism and drugs.

- *The Super Hero:* these police possess a whole range of special physical qualities and technological aids, as seen in the *Batman* movies and the 'Police Rescue' television series.

- *The Sleuth:* the officer who uses brains, rather than brawn, in order to outwit the criminal mind, and who generally is more sophisticated or educated than the average street cop; for example, Columbo and Inspector Morse.

Cunneen and White also observe that the idea of violence dominates the images of police that the media convey. It is as if 'violence is intrinsic and absolutely necessary to the job'. In view of what was discussed in Chapter 1, it is hardly surprising that police would subscribe to this view given that they see themselves as crime fighters.

Winfree and Griffiths conducted their survey of high school students to determine 'adolescent attitudes toward the police' in 1977. They followed up with another study in 1982, comparing the attitudes of Canadian and American adolescents to the police. More recently, Leiber, Nalla and Farmworth conducted a study of attitudes of juveniles toward the police. It was a 'rigorous assessment' of the relationship between subculture theory and the attitudes of males that 'were either accused of delinquency or adjudicated as delinquent' (Hurst and Frank 2000, p 191). All these studies found that young people tend to highlight violence and the law and order fixation of the police.

In a study of the experience-based perspectives of young offenders on the aetiology of, and intervention for, crime in seven US States, Goldstein (1990) found that several respondents believed police abuse their power. And that this, in turn, forms part of the criminogenic environmental influences on young people. As one respondent put it:

> When you walk in a store the policemen watch you like a hawk, and that makes a younger person want to steal. It's just how much they can get away with, being at the age that they are, and everything makes them want to challenge them. I know myself, I see a cop and he gonna say a certain thing to me, and I'm gonna look at him and say, "F ... you", like excuse my language, but that's what I say. You know, he looking and you gotta make your comments. I can beat the shit out of you, why don't you be a man and do this and that. I don't have to, you know, they get paid and my father works and, you know, my mother works same as everybody else. It's the taxpayers' money they get paid with, and it should be all for one, not two for two, if you know what I'm saying by that. (p 66)

In response to the question concerning what a city that had a delinquency problem could do to stop it, another respondent expressed a view on police abuse of power:

> If kids are hanging out, the police should approach them with care and concern, rather than with that authoritative stare and intimidation ... . The police should get to know the kids, so the kids will learn to trust them and turn to them if they are in trouble. (p 139)

The perceived misuse of power extends to the issue of racial bias. In the words of another respondent:

> Cops see a Black person walking and say, "Oh, God, you're about to steal". You know it's not like that in all cases. And a White person will walk in and they'll turn their eyes away. I don't like to go in stores no more 'cause every time I walk in a store they look at me ... (ibid)

Other previous research works have found a significant measure of racial bias in the western world police encounters with juveniles. In this bias-driven policing, black youth and other young people whose appearance matched the delinquent stereotype were more frequently stopped and interrogated by patrol officers, compared to white youths. 'I get stopped so regularly that I wonder if I should leave my house sometimes', says one young black man in Tottenham, London, who was interviewed in 1996 for a NACRO study on 'Policing Local Communities'.

As Piliavin and Briar found from their study in the 1960s, often this selective apprehension occurred even in the absence of evidence that an offence had been committed. Where there were offences, usually these young people were given more severe dispositions for the same violations (Piliavin and Briar 1991). Apart from the intrusion of long-held prejudices of individual police officers, these authors attribute these selective apprehension and disposition practices to police's prior experience with black youth as 'difficult clients' and as the category of youth most likely to offend:

> First, the tendency for police to give more severe dispositions to Negroes and to youths whose appearance corresponded to that which police associated with delinquents partly reflected the fact ... that these youths also were much more likely than were other types of boys to exhibit the sort of recalcitrant demeanour which police construed as a sign of the confirmed delinquent. Further, officers assumed, partly on the basis of departmental statistics, that Negroes and juveniles who 'look tough' (eg, who wear chinos, leatherjackets, boots, etc) commit crimes more frequently than do other types of youths. In this sense, the police justified their selective treatment of these youths along epidemiological lines: that is, they were concentrating their attention on those youths whom they believed were most likely to commit delinquent acts. (Piliavin and Briar 1991, p 435)

Another negative view of police seems to be born out of the contradiction between young people's 'needs as victims of crime and their experience of the police as adversaries'. Simon Anderson and his colleagues who spotted this perception in their interviews with several young people in the Lothian Regional Area of Scotland, illustrate the point by a statement from one of the female interviewees. She said the police were 'always moving us on for something, but they never do anything about all the perverts and the weidoes' (Anderson et al 1994, p 2).

47

There is a general feeling among young people that their contact with the police is largely adversarial. The way Anderson and his colleagues capture this feeling from their study is so apt and bears a detailed summary here. As they noted, many of the young people thought that merely being on the streets in groups made them readily susceptible to police attention. This is combined with the feeling that they themselves were doing no harm, and they could see no understandable motive for the police action. This is compounded if police officers offer no adequate explanation.

The impression that police attention to young people is unwarranted is exacerbated by the perception that the police do not take seriously their more serious problems of victimisation and safety. Thus, even when young people realised they were doing something wrong, they often considered their actions petty and trivial compared with the more serious things which happened to them, for which the police provide little or no protection. As a result, young people's perceptions of police behaviour centrally revolve around the idea that they are singled out for attention merely because they are young, in a group and out in a public place.

The following are some of the excerpts from what Anderson et al's (1994) respondents thought gave rise to realities of the unjustified anti-youth police actions:

- Some of them are so bored they would stop and hassle you if you're just standing around. (*14 year-old girl, Marchmont*)
- They just drive around, cos they're bored they just look for somebody to chase. (*13 year-old boy, Wester Hailes*)
- I suppose they get a bit bored and they think well we might as well have a bit of a laugh. (*14 year-old boy, Wester Hailes*)

For some young people police 'boredom' offers one reason why the police devote so much attention to them. Others account for police action simply in terms of 'stereotyping' – based on either age, the place they live or how they look:

Sometimes they dinnae do anything to help you. Everyone 15 or 16 is classed as a stereotype, all drinkin and rowdy vandalism. (*14 year-old girl, Corstorphine*)

They think we do things and we're all wee criminals. Cos of the area. (*15 year-old boy, Wester Hailes*)

The truth or falsity of such accounts is not relevant here. What counts is the way in which either side views the other and acts in consequence.

Bad policing has a far greater impact on young people's perceptions of the police than any positive contact they may have experienced. This relates to the general point made by Lord Scarman in his *Report on the Brixton Disorders* (1982), where he argues that stories – even rumours – of police deviance spread like wild fire through certain communities at enormous cost to the police and police effectiveness.

Young people display a deep ambivalence towards the police. They perceive the police as simultaneously a source of protection and of control. This leads to contradictory feelings and responses. Far from being universally anti-police, young people can and do discriminate between what they see as 'good' and 'bad' police practice.

Youth attitudes toward the courts

The attitudes of young people toward the courts are shaped by several factors. Among the most identifiable are physical discomfort, fear (reverent or pathological), lack of comprehension, delays and loss of trust in relation to judicial personnel and processes. Until recently, the physical conditions of many courthouses, especially those that were built as magistrate courts before they were converted to juvenile court buildings, did not inspire comfort in their clients. They were generally inadequate and intimidating with characteristics including:

- cold and austere atmosphere;
- small and confined;
- cramped waiting rooms (so people queue in hallways and corridors);
- lack of privacy; and
- bad acoustics (Griffiths, Heilbronn, Kovacs, Latimer and Pagone 1993, p 366).

Although special courts have been established for children in some cities of Australia, juvenile justice proceedings operate in adult courts in most country towns. In New South Wales, for instance, Local Courts do sit as children's courts. Apart from lacking a 'separate identity', 'some of the courts used, particularly in the cities, are large, have high, raised benches, are acoustically inadequate and make effective communication between magistrate, children and parents extremely difficult' (Seymour 1988, p 296).

Describing the Melbourne Children's Court, Griffiths et al (1993) state that the new building despite its modern furnishings suffers from most of the deficiencies identified above and that children on criminal charges are held in cells with no external windows, only a surveillance camera and a bench lining four bare walls.

Most young people who come into this sort of environment, especially for the first time, express some fear. Stereotypes about magistrates (more in the case of judges) that they are special, high-minded or intelligent, morally superior and wise lead young people to develop an attitude of awe towards them. In some jurisdictions, this sense is exacerbated by the austere black-robed, white-wigged and be-spectacled appearance of these judges. But the reverence soon dissipates as the young people discover that the judges are human, giving way completely to the fear that these judges would use their power to punish them heavily.

Several studies have found that many young offenders do not understand the proceedings in Children's Courts (ALRC 1981; O'Connor 1990; Australian Law Reform Commission and Human Rights & Equal Opportunity Commission 1997). In a Second Reading speech on Tasmania's *Youth Justice Act* 1997, the Minister categorically declared that the court 'is an alienating process' for young people (quoted in Szramka 2001). Thus, in Australia, most jurisdictions now have legislation promoting comprehensibility of proceedings. Typically, the legislation requires specific explanation of the elements of the offence charged, the allegations and their implications, and an explanation of the nature of court orders (Warner 1993).

In the 1980s, legislative changes in Australia introduced the right to be heard and the right to participate for young offenders.[1] Similarly, one of the main goals of the new youth justice approach which began in New Zealand in 1990 was to foster family involvement where young offenders and their families participate in making decisions for themselves and take control of their lives with a view to preventing further crime by these offenders. Three years into its implementation, research found that the system had failed to engage young people in the decision-making process. The reasons proffered in this research are interesting. At least one of these reasons relates to the point made at the beginning of this chapter about young people's willingness or ability to participate in agency-initiated partnership schemes such as family group conferencing in New Zealand:

> It may be that both families and professionals do not allow them to become involved; *or it may be that young persons themselves do not feel able to become involved.* It may be that young people have very little to say, at least in the presence of adults who are unknown to them, and that, therefore, they cannot be expected to participate more actively, whatever the forum. Many families do not encourage, or even actively discourage, the participation of young people in decisions about their own future. The problem may, thus, lie not in the system's response to young persons, but in the expectations of the wider society. (Maxwell 1993, p 120).

Young people's belief about the fairness of the system is a crucial factor. For instance, the Equal Treatment Benchbook, launched by the Judicial Studies Board in the UK in 1999, tells the results of a 1994 survey which found that only 11 per cent of young black people in that country believed that 'judges give fair and equal treatment to everyone in this country', compared to 25 per cent of young white people. Both 11 per cent and 25 per cent are depressingly low figures. Lord Irvine of Lairg, the Lord Chancellor who launched the book, stated in his speech that these figures 'represent damaging perceptions and we must work to change them' (London, 28 September 1999).

Youth attitudes toward detention

Even to the most daring young offender, the prospect of loss of freedom, isolation and loss of contact with family and friends generates some uneasiness about detention. Repeat offenders who have seen the inside of jails several times or the very disconnected young offenders may experience less fear about a custodial penalty. For most juvenile detention inmates, however, lack of privacy, restriction of creativity, a tensive atmosphere and punitive disciplinary regime are cause for resentment.

Research has shown that young detainees are adept at responding to and interpreting institutional regimes and programs in ways that allow them to maintain a sense of self and self-concept (Atkinson 1997, p 411). There is, however, no doubt that they still fight at least two enemies. First, boredom is a killer for young vibrant individuals who, before their imprisonment, felt imbued with unbounded energies. Secondly, many young people (including those who succeed in developing coping mechanisms) soon discover that they are in collision with staff who see their adjustment to the institution as a challenge to official meanings of detention experience as unpleasant and deterring.

The ensuing attitudes can be summarised by a poem that a young detainee wrote in South Australia:

Hate

I hate being told what to do
I hate being told what food to eat
I hate being told what time to go to bed
I hate being told what channel on TV to watch
I hate being told if I can read at night or not
I hate being told when I can play sport what sport
I hate being told what clothes to wear
I hate asking if I can go to the toilet
I hate being told what I can and can't say
I hate being told to do my work at school
I hate the fact that if you donat do what your told that you get into shit
I hate how the staff always have the last say in everything.

(quoted in Cunneen and White 1995, p 235)

The perception that young people are sent to detention to be punished means that young people generally doubt the claim about 'rehabilitation as the reason for their incarceration' (Youth Justice Coalition 1990, p 297) and make little effort to take advantage of most rehabilitative programs where they are available. It must be added that research which shows no significant rehabilitation in institutional settings supports young people's stance regarding the level of commitment to rehabilitation in most of the programs. Interviews with young detainees in some Australian jurisdictions revealed a high level of cynicism among them regarding the presence and uses of skills training. The Queensland Youth Advocacy Centre (1993, p 47) found that

> detention did little to assist young people to return to the community with income, housing or skills. Instead, it seemed to increase a young person's knowledge about crime and established a peer group from within the detention centre which extended to the outside on release – "you meet others you can do jobs with".

Segregation or solitary confinement, 'still a feature of detention centres throughout Australia' and a tool for managing disruptive inmates, generates uncomplimentary attitudes in young people:

> I was there for 12 hours. It's just a little cell, with carpet, a brick bench, with the floor coming up like that. No mattress or pillow or nothing. Just looking at the colour of the brick – makes you, starts to get you crazy after a while … at night time you think someone's going to come in and shoot you or something – its just the colour of the wall – it sends you crazy. Then you start to get um … schizophrenic … When I was little I got shut in a washing machine. This bloke put me in a washing machine when I was little … (Youth Justice Coalition 1990, p 324)

Confronted with loss of freedom, isolation and loss of contact with family and friends, young people would rebel, their weaker power position notwithstanding. A related issue is the problem of disturbances or riots. Riots have been a feature of the operation of juvenile institutions since the first reformatories were established in the 19th century, and they have occurred in both male and female sections of detention centres. We should acknowledge the point of desperation that is reached when prisoners (young or old) decide to rebel in a situation where they are largely without power. Cunneen and White (1995, p 237) rightly observe that 'riots are first and foremost rebellions against conditions of incarceration. They usually occur under regimes which manifest petty authoritarianism combined with a lack of programs'.

It's not all perception

It would be naïve in the extreme to suggest that the relationship between young people and criminal justice agencies is all perception game. Some reality lurks behind the perception. Page (1950, p 41) characterised it a foolish argument to say that young people 'have no faults which need to be corrected and, if necessary, punished, but complexes which need to be gravely studied and discussed'.

The analysis in this book so far shows clearly that neither the agencies nor young people are 'angels' being harassed by the unjust practices of the other. Although it goes without saying that 'power' lies on the side of the agencies, certain behaviours of young people tend to give credence to the images that these agencies hold about them. The following presentation on both victimisation and offending is evidence that young people can and do cause a considerable amount of harm and annoyance to their peers, society in general and the criminal justice agencies in particular.

Research reveals that some of the young would readily understand the reasons for criminal justice response to their behaviours. In relation to the police, for instance, a 13-year-old boy from Wester Hailes in Edinburgh said (in typically Scottish style):

> I've been chased by CID many a time, just like for minor things, like maybe smashing a windae or something. There used to be a big massive factory, was shut doon, right? When you walked past you usually just chucked a stane at the windae, all the windaes were smashed. The CID would see you right? They'd chase you for absolute miles. They take your name or take you doon the station. (Anderson et al, 1994, p 142)

Most police in the western world believe that sizeable portions of the youth population show little respect for them. In some countries, such as Australia and the US, police admit that they have been assaulted and harassed by young people in the course of their work: 'the nature of the harassment varied from verbal taunts, being shouted and sworn at, to outright assault, including kicks and punches' (Cunneen and White 1995, p 206). The case of Aboriginal youths referred to earlier who get involved with motor vehicle offences and 'seek out an interaction with police in the form of high-speed game of chase' suggests that such behaviours can escalate into fatal outcomes.

The story of three boys, aged between 15 and 16, in Racine County, Wisconsin, USA, who were charged with conspiracy to murder a dozen or more of their classmates and school officials in 1998, further illustrates the view that certain behaviours of young people create criminal images in the minds of law enforcers. The three were among five Burlington, Wisconsin high school students detained by police on 15 November 1998 (Davis 1998).

According to media sources, the five youth dressed in a distinctive style, called themselves 'Goths' (short for 'Gothics') and were devotees of music groups like Nine Inch Nails and Marilyn Manson. They apparently felt they were picked on by other students because of their looks and tastes in the small town of 9500, some 30 miles southwest of Milwaukee. They said other students taunted them and 'treated them like trash' (ibid).

One of the youth told reporters that the plotting was simply a means of getting revenge through fantasy. According to the account he gave *USA Today*, the scheme was fed by 'one boy's anger that he was being sent to a foster home in northern Wisconsin'. The others participated in the discussions mostly to 'make him feel good'.

Burlington police maintain that the group of boys had planned to cut telephone lines, take their assistant principal hostage and then look up the records of their intended victims and track them down. According to the town's police chief, some of the suspects said they planned to remain at the school after the killings and 'force a shootout with police or commit suicide'. Prosecutor Richard Barta also said the teenagers described their plot as a suicide mission. It is impossible to say how real this alleged conspiracy was, but then the consequences it generated regarding violent images of young people are quite real. However, given the record of police departments and prosecutors in the US, there is good reason to be sceptical of the police version.

Add to this story the following events in the US, and the evidence becomes somewhat overwhelming in support of the view that activities of some young people cannot but create images of 'crims on the loose':

- October 1997, a 17-year-old student shot and killed two classmates and wounded seven others in Pearl, Mississippi;

- December 1997, another high school student opened fire on a prayer circle in West Paducah, Kentucky, killing three girls;

- March 1998, four students and a teacher died in an ambush, allegedly carried out by two young boys in a suburb of Jonesboro, Arkansas;
- May 1998, two students were shot to death at a school in Springfield, Oregon;
- Two more attacks at schools in California in 1998;
- Columbine High School massacre, 20 April 1999.

In all, over 20 people died and dozens were wounded in attacks by youngsters on fellow students and teachers in the US during the 1997-99 period. This grim reality makes it difficult to sustain the image of youth as an embodiment of 'innocence'.

Reality behind the reality: the broader context of youth action

It would equally be naïve not to recognise the broader social processes that underpin some of what appear to be bizarre youth attitudes, actions and reactions. Bear in mind that some of the activities about which criminal justice agencies think negatively do lead to self-harm for these youth and the victimisation of fellow young people. Thus, it is not as if young people are necessarily at war solely with the agencies. Research has shown that most of those young ones whose attitudes and behaviours supply the canon fodder for negative image construction have themselves been victimised by crime, child abuse and other social problems which put them at risk of becoming anti-social. Put differently, many of the young people about whom the agencies have the greatest concern or distaste have multiple risk factors in multiple aspects in their lives.

Social transformation of inner cities, for instance, not only results in the concentration of the most disadvantaged segments of the youth population (Sampson and Lauritson 1997; Wilson 1987); many of them actually fall through the available safety-nets and lack basic economic supports. Some, of course, form the new mass of homeless and unemployed young people. While there are difficulties in asserting any simple relationship between homelessness or unemployment and youth crime, it is obvious that in the absence of other forms of legitimate income young people will be forced into a variety of 'underground' economic activities, including various forms of theft (Taylor 1999; Polk and White 1999).

Polk (1997) is right in his observation that the lifestyle of living in the streets for young people is often accompanied by a high level of alcohol use which further aggravates problematic contact with 'conventional' people. High levels of violence and assault, including homicide, can result especially when young males become involved, as Polk puts it, 'in masculine honour contests'. The sense of separation and alienation generates forms of anger that find expression in destructive activities such as vandalism, often against visible symbols of community order. In sum, there is a sociological backdrop to the 'cluster of problems of order posed by these alienated young people, ranging from vague concerns for public safety to highly concrete forms of crimes of burglary, assault and vandalism' (ibid, p 493).

In the 1980s and 1990s, the transition from Fordist economy to post-Fordist economy in most western societies left millions of young people struggling – ethnic minority youth alongside the 'poor white' population – for secure employment. The situation in the 2000s would not alter dramatically for the better, if at all. Those who can find no meaningful work will continue to form networks of street groups as one rational response. They will create an alternative economy in which they can find 'employment'. For some, having been excluded from the legitimate labour market, the alternative economy will become an avenue to 'reaffirm their muscular masculinity' (Taylor 1999). Earlier, James (1995) had argued that the struggles of young people in Britain in the mid-1990s represent the 'defensive/aggressive individualism which many young people exhibit in a "winner-loser" culture' arising from the turbo-charged capitalism which produces turmoil and constant change for society. In the ensuing post-Fordist market society, young people confront the challenge of transition into 'adulthood and independence' with many ending up with 'criminal' labels.

The experience of minority youth has a unique dimension. In indigenous communities for example, the historical processes which have produced mainstream social structure have failed to generate any accompanying institutional development. Thus, while the alien social structure has led to a decline in interdependency among people in these communities, it has not developed the support systems that are available in the mainstream society. The end result, as LaPrairie (1997) perceptively observes, is the emergence of socially stratified communities where limited resources and resource distribution create large groups of disadvantaged people, a growing youth subculture with few legitimate opportunities, decontextualised exposure to the mass media, and the lack of cultural and social resources to assist in identity formation which supports pro-social values.

Conclusion

For all intents and purposes, young people have never been, nor will ever be, passive recipients of social images. They actively engage with their immediate environment – in the mainstream or at the margin. In most cases, their sub-cultural expressions or lifestyles actually represent an intricate, at times abrasive, but nonetheless ingenuous way of coping with the strictures and stresses that social processes impose on their stage in life.

Cultural activities help them to define their identity and validate their presence, increasingly so in a highly abstracted civilisation that would rather construct them out of existence. Group orientation in public space ('hanging-out-together') is largely a mechanism for their own protection in the face of a highly conflict-prone society and a sense of their own vulnerability. The 'gentil', especially among the adult population, consider the visibility of both forms of lifestyle an affront. Criminal justice agencies smell delinquency and challenge to their own authority in these forms of lifestyle. Thus there exists a perfect pretext for an exclusionary response to young people who, instead of being a treasured asset, become a threatening liability.

While the forces of the wider society and the criminal justice agencies may seem overwhelming, some of the young people have little choice but to 'go down fighting', especially those intent upon countering a system-imposed inferiority. The destruction to property, assaults on public officers and self-harm that are inherent in such a countermanding response do little to project positive images for these young people. In fact, these collateral incidents feed back, in a rather vicious loop, into the basic antipathies that young people already attract by being 'youth'.

The political economy of the social context within which mainstream, affluent adults interact with less affluent and minority youth indicates how toxic interaction between these groups may arise. The uneven distribution of socio-political and economic powers, heavily tilted in favour of the mainstream adult population, means that the young, particularly those who are disadvantaged, will lose. There need not be war, but the images and responses that criminal justice agencies develop towards affected young people may be one critical factor that makes such a war redundant or inevitable.

Notes

1   For example, s 6(a) of the *Children's (Criminal Proceedings) Act* 1987 (NSW); s 18 of the *Children and Young Person's Act* 1989 (Vic).

3

Traditional criminal justice response to youth crime

Those with perception can see that the hardened criminal of tomorrow is the severely punished juvenile of today. Juveniles with socio-economic disadvantage, with lack of family and social support, without access to education and employment, will often resort to antisocial behaviour. Lack of normal life opportunities should not necessarily lead to further punishment via the criminal justice system. (Alder 1998)

In contrast to its rhetoric, the traditional western criminal justice response to youth crime has, in the main, arguably always been reactive and retributive. Despite the early optimistic notion that the juvenile justice system would be 'conspicuously a response to the modern spirit of social justice' and that, in it, the relations of the child to the society would be defined and adjusted according to the scientific findings about the 'best interests of the child' and his or her environment,[1] the system was doomed from birth to replicate the adult system's orientation towards determining guilt and inflicting punishment in an atmosphere of hostility.

This orientation embodies the traditional approach of the old-fashioned, taken-for-granted common wisdom that the best way to deal with adult crime is to catch criminals, take them to court of some sort, judge them and then, if they are found guilty, punish them.[2] This response consists of contacting, apprehending, referring to court and requesting secure detention of the offender (Wordes and Bynum 1995). In a somewhat phenomenological fashion, Tuck (1991, p23) defines this traditional criminal justice approach as follows:

> If one asked the ordinary man [sic] in the street or the average politician or journalist how society deals with crime, this would probably be the response: society deals with crime through the police, the courts, and the prisons, catching the guilty and punishing them when caught. Committing a crime is seen as the responsibility of the individual for which he can be punished as an individual.

The phrase 'catching the guilty' uncritically and wrongly presumes that only the 'guilty' get caught by the system. Nevertheless, it vividly shows that, in the traditional approach, 'reaction' is the best form of attack on crime. The fact that this approach may be based largely on the perception of the agencies rather than the actuality of crime is lost on its protagonists. The justificatory principle of retribution underpins this reactive mode of justice. With this principle the state absolves itself of any responsibility for the occurrence of crime and exerts 'backcasting' measures such as vengeance, denunciation and 'just deserts' on any persons convicted of crime, presumably on behalf of victims and the society at large (see Hudson 1996).

Vengeance, allegedly an instinctive demand active in every human being, is essentially punishment imposed once a wrong has occurred, even if it serves no useful purpose other than to negate a negation. Thus, the philosopher Immanuel Kant could urge capital punishment in his own days: 'even if we knew the world would end tomorrow, it would be our moral duty to hang a convicted murderer today' (quoted in Waller and Williams 1997, p 16). Although this idea of punishment is variously criticised today,[3] a close examination of the adult and juvenile penal policies and practices of the western world in the past 10 centuries at least will reveal the enduring attitude of vengeance. Predicting the future of the criminal justice 'traditional reactions' in Australia for instance, Grabosky (2001, p 227) states that 'the impulse to punish is deeply ingrained in many, if not all of us ... , the vengeful spirit is alive and well in Australia'.

Denunciatory punishment expresses an attitude of resentment and indignation on the part either of the punishing authority or of those in whose name the punishment is inflicted. Such punishment makes a statement that the offence is not to be tolerated by the society. Professor Hart once said, 'what distinguishes a criminal from a civil sanction... is the judgement of community condemnation which accompanies its imposition' (quoted in Feinberg 1965). The idea of 'just deserts', as another basis for punishment, has gained popularity since the 1970s. Its essence can be described thus:

> Under a general theory of political obligation all persons owe duties to others not to infringe their rights. Justice and fairness insist that all persons must bear the sacrifice of obeying the law equally. By committing a crime the offender has gained an unfair advantage over all others who have 'toed the line' and restrained themselves from committing crime. Social equilibrium in society must be restored. The offender deserves and must receive punishment in order to destroy his unfair advantage. (Clarkson and Keating 1990, p 7)

This idea is now embodied in the youth justice regimes of several western countries, especially those whose law enforcement pursues zero tolerance and whose courts apply sanctions 'commensurate with' or 'in proportionality to' the seriousness of the offence and deterrent in intent. Needless to say, all these forms of retributive punishment have left more questions than answers in the quest for an effective regimen for dealing with youth crime.

This chapter argues that youth justice in the western world, conducted essentially as 'a political enterprise' (Asquith 1983), carries on these reactive and retributive traditions. In this regard, far from being aberrant, the constant refrain in contemporary juvenile law and order rhetoric – 'get tough on youth crime!; more jails; lock'em up and throw away the keys' – faithfully reproduces the response of its adult pedigree to the prevailing images or representations of youth as a problem. By social inheritance, therefore, the resources of its agencies are fundamentally structured to deal with images of 'idle, anti-authoritarian, subversive youth', as opposed to the 'well schooled, clean, respectful, sporting and disciplined teenagers' (Brown 1998, p 3).

A history of official responses to offenders will establish the context in which we can better understand the traditional mechanisms through which young people are differentially selected, labelled and processed through the criminal justice system today. For obvious reasons, this history can only be presented here in an abbreviated form. This will be followed by an examination of the specific approach of each of the cornerstone agencies of the system to youth crime, with a view to highlighting the interface between social constructions of young people and their *modus operandi* in relation to crime prevention. Last, the chapter assesses the works of these agencies against international standards. Apart from the need to underline the many queries that the traditional approach has generated, the assessment will foreshadow the conditions that eventually tilted the agencies towards the 'partnership' model as a way forward in crime prevention.

A historical overview

The precise point in history at which the state in the western world decided to address the special needs of young people in the criminal justice systems may never be known with absolute certainty. However, fragments of history reveal some insights that are highly instructive for the purposes of this book. Between 700 and 1500 AD, children in western Europe were simply not seen as a distinct social group with unique needs and behaviours. However, while it is widely believed that adults and juveniles who violated the law were processed in the same manner and were subjected to the same types of punishments, there is evidence that, in the early Roman law, the severity of the punishment meted out to young people – though treated as adults – was to be tempered by their age. For example, an adult caught in manifest theft was subject to flogging and enslavement to his victim. However, a young offender convicted for the same crime would receive corporal punishment at the magistrate's discretion and was required to make restitution rather than to enter slavery (Wakefield and Hirschel 1996, p 91).

Up to the fifth century, whether an offender was too young to be punished was determined by his or her capacity to speak. The arbitrariness of this criterion was significantly reduced when, after the fifth century, the age was fixed at seven years. All those below this age were exempted from criminal responsibility. In other cases, it was when puberty set in (14 years for boys and 12 for girls) that young people were held totally responsible for their acts. But in some parts of the western world, punishment such as the death penalty was tempered for age. In the 10th century, Athelstane decreed that:

[M]en should slay none younger than a fifteen winters' man and provided that if his kindred will not take him, nor be surety for him, then swear he as the bishop shall teach him, that he will shun all evil and let him be in bondage for his price. (Barman 1934, p 23)

This shows that even as far back as a thousand years ago, society used to give some consideration to offenders' age, and thus gave them a chance for reformation.

Evidence suggests that, in the Middle Ages, there was a desire to discriminate between the adult criminal and the young delinquent. The Year Books of Edward I recorded that judgement for burglary was spared to some individuals of 12 years. Judgement or punishment at this time was generally severe. Thus, during the 10th and 11th centuries England, under Saxon and Norman kings, common criminals were mutilated in various ways, blinded, branded, amputated of feet and hands, and let crawl about the country as a warning to others, showing the fate of a criminal. These draconian penalties had not abated by the 16th century. For in Tudor times, boiling alive was the punishment for poisoners, and burning at stake the penalty paid by traitors, by a wife who killed her husband and by a servant who killed his master or mistress.

By the late 17th century, while punishment was somehow differentiated for young people, it did not lose its harshness towards this segment of the population. In 1686, for instance, a 10-year-old boy who stole 30 yards of satin ribbon was whipped. Four years later, in 1690, another 10-year-old boy convicted of stealing two gold rings and some money was 'burnt in the hand'. As Wakefield and Hirschel (1996, p 93) observe, 'these and other corporal punishment were the most frequent penalties for young offenders between the ages of 7 and 14 in England at that time'.

When transportation became the common penalty for adults in the 18th century, 'bind-out to a tradesman as an apprentice' was used in addition to the common penalty of corporal punishment for young offenders – especially with ordinary young people from poor families.[4] The death penalty also came into vogue for young offenders so that, in 1785, 18 of the 20 people executed in London were under the age of 18.

Early in the 18th century, a bankrupt was likely to be publicly scourged through the streets at the end of a cart, his tongue split, his nose cut off, his eyes put out, his property dispersed and himself finally hanged. Forgers, such as Rev William Dodd, one of the most fashionable preachers of London who had signed the name of his benefactor and friend Lord Chesterfield to a note, were usually hanged. The story of Andrew Branning, at the beginning of the 19th century, a luckless urchin aged only 13 who broke into a house and carried off a spoon shows that young people at this time were no longer spared the punishment meted to adult offenders. He was captured and brought to trial: 'his story ended in two words which were short and customary: Guilty – Death' (*Times* 18 January 1801, quoted in Barman 1934, p 20).

Clearly, the social outlook in the period up to the early part of the 19th century with regard to penal methods was pervaded by a spirit of retribution and revenge. The most dangerous aspect of the old retributive system was that it increasingly ignored the necessity of special treatment for juvenile offenders. The 17th and 18th centuries in particular witnessed the major erosion of the principle of awarding special treatment to young offenders. In the US, young offenders were treated as the same as adults at the time of the American Revolution. Young people in Canada continued to be similarly treated as in the US until 1908. During the period of undifferentiated systems, those convicted of offences in both countries could expect to receive fines, beatings and floggings; they could be put in stocks or driven through towns in carts for ridicule, and they could even be hanged, mutilated, burned or banished from the community (Bartollas 1996; Corrado and Markwart 1996).

In England, this period represents the height of punitiveness when the system sent young people 'to prison and condemned them to abandonment, misery and mendicity' (Barman 1934, p 22). Worse still, the prison at that time was a sewer throwing out into society 'a continuous flood of purulence, the germs of physiological and moral contagion'. It had a poisoning, brutalising, depressing and corrupting influence. It was a 'manufactory at once producing the phthisical, the insane and the criminal, and also exerting a severe, profitless taxation on the public purse' (ibid, p 21).

The early European settlements in Australia and New Zealand from 1780s onwards adopted the prevailing system in England that was applicable to young offenders, along with its lack of special procedures for dealing with children. In procedures and penalties, these countries inherited the draconian and punitive English regime. For instance the application of the death penalty to young offenders was demonstrated on 27 February 1788 when a 17-year-old boy who stole some butter, dried peas and salt pork in NSW was hanged, the first person to be penalised this way in the emerging European settlement (Mukherjee 2000). Another young person in his late teens was executed in May of the same year after being convicted of theft. And so on. Imprisonment was used widely for young people convicted of minor offences such as vagrancy.

Soon, it looked like a fundamental lesson was being learnt by the powers-that-be in these various countries, namely that severity is a double-edged weapon and if the offender leaves prison a worse person, a more embittered enemy of society than the prisoner was when he or she came in, society is injured equally with the offender. The changes that were introduced towards the mid-19th century, the dawn of modern civilisation, ostensibly emanated from this lesson. In the US, for instance, a report issued in 1822 by the Society for the Prevention of Pauperism (later renamed as the Society for the Reformation of Juvenile Delinquents) recommended the establishment of a separate and philosophically different penitentiary institution for juvenile offenders, saying:

> These prisons should be rather schools for instruction than places for punishment like our present State prisons ... The wretchedness and misery of the offender should not be the object of the punishment inflicted; the end

should be his reformation and future usefulness. (quoted in Bernard 1992, p 62)

The change of focus towards 'reformation' culminated in the opening of the first male juvenile institution, called House of Refuge in New York in 1825,[5] with the sole purpose of redeeming 'children in danger of growing up to be paupers and criminals'. The reformatory regimes in this institution were designed to address what the reformers believed to be the three main causes of pauperism and criminality among juveniles: (1) weak and criminal parents; (2) the manifold temptations of the streets; and (3) the peculiar weakness of children's moral nature. In 1838, the Pennsylvania Supreme Court took judicial notice of these causes in the case of Mary Ann Crouse who was sent to the Philadelphia House of Refuge. She had not committed any crime but was indicted on the ground that she was a poor child who appeared to be growing up to be a pauper. In rejecting the arguments of Mary's father who filed a writ of *habeas corpus*, the Court held:

> The object of the charity is reformation, by training its inmates to industry; by imbuing their minds with principles of morality and religion; by furnishing them with means to earn a living; and, above all, by separating them from the corrupting influence of improper associates. To this end, may not the natural parents, when unequal to the task of education, or unworthy of it, be superseded by the *parens patriae*, or common guardian of the community? ... The infant has been snatched from a course which must have ended in confirmed depravity; and not only is the restraint of her person lawful, but it would be an act of extreme cruelty to release her from it. (Bernard 1992, p 68)

Thus, although the justification for intervention in the lives of young people apparently changed from retribution to reformation, the explanation for deviance remained wedded to the classical view of crime-causation in which the state has no share. As the idea of the House of Refuge spread throughout the US (23 had been established in the 1830s and another 30 in 1840s), the underlying assumptions about the causes of crime and the reason for punishment went along.

In 1870, Massachusetts introduced a system of separate trial for young offenders and a 'State agent' was appointed to enquire about a child's family circumstances and to present the report in the court. However, it was the juvenile court established in Cook County (Chicago) of Illinois in 1899, based on the medieval English legal doctrine of *parens patriae*, that began a whole new judicial regime entirely devoted to young offenders. By 1920, more than 20 other States, including New York and Colorado, had established a separate system of hearings for 'delinquent' children or courts entirely devoted to juveniles. As with the reform institution, this new regime – with its emphasis on informality of proceedings and help, not punishment, as the goal, was endorsed by the Pennsylvania Supreme Court in the case of Frank Fisher.[6]

In England, the *Parkhurst Act* of 1838, deemed to be the first legislative recognition of separate treatment for the young offender,[7] was similarly founded upon a reformation doctrine where the aim of punishment was 'to work upon the heart of the evil-doer that he will be led voluntarily to forsake his wickedness' (Barman 1934, p 923). From this beginning and until the 1960s, English penal reformers were committed to a form of policy of intervention in the life of youth that would become known as the welfare model in the western world. Posterity had the works of Mary Carpenter, Sydney Turner, John Howard, and Matthew Davenport Hill in the UK and the 'childsaving movement' in the US to thank for this model.

From 1854 onward, several *Reformatory Schools Acts* were successively passed in England to give effect to the demands of society for reformation of the juvenile offenders. But it was not until 1908 that full effect was given to these new social demands under the provisions of the *Prevention of Crime Act* of that year. The Act provided for the establishment of institutions all over the country for the reformation of adolescent offenders of the age between 16 and 21. It was the first time that the problem of adolescence had received such careful consideration from the authorities; it was the first time that the doctrine of individualisation had also been adopted as the crux of the aetiological understanding of youth crime.

While setting up separate institutions for young people, England also simultaneously established the first separate juvenile justice system under the *Children Act 1908*.[8] The *Juvenile Delinquents Act 1908* introduced a similar system in Canada. In both countries, the legislation directed juvenile courts to sit in private and to apply a specific system of penalties for juveniles. Founded on the welfare-based juvenile justice model, the legislation stipulated that the courts must act 'in the best interest of the child'. The English *Children and Young Persons Act 1933* carried forward this approach and, in Canada, the approach remained intact until 1984.

The UK *Children and Young Persons Act 1969* significantly extended the reach of the welfare model. Of the several goals to which the Act was directed, three are noteworthy. One, it provided for the phasing out of existing punitive sanctions in the juvenile justice system such as detention, attendance centres and borstal training. Two, it elevated the need to dispose 'cases prior to court, where possible, through consultation between social services and the police'. Three, it directed courts to deal with cases informally so as to 'avoid the stigma of court appearances and the subjection of mainly working-class juvenile offenders to the scrutiny of unsympathetic middle-class magistrates'. With regard to this informal regime, the Act also determined that

> the court would be a place of investigation and enquiry, trying to find a course of action which would resolve the problem thought to have led to a child's offending. To this end social workers (the childcare experts) would replace probation officers in the courts and would prepare report for court. Sanctions would allow for full investigation into a child's background, would be non-punitive and quasi-indeterminate in nature and fitted to a child's needs rather than determined in advance by court order. (Pratt 1993, p 41)

More than anything else, it was the aspect of letting social workers into juvenile courts to replace more traditional probation officers that led the magistrates to criticise the English *Children and Young Persons Act 1969* regime. When England changed more towards the justice model in the early 1980s, with the enactment of the *Criminal Justice Act 1982*, some of these criticisms were taken into account and the determinate sentence of youth custody became fully entrenched against the backdrop of the emerging 'principle of least restrictive intervention'.[9] Canada took similar steps the same year with the enactment of the *Young Offenders Act 1982*.

Most jurisdictions in Australia enacted industrial and reformatory schools legislation between 1863 and 1874, modelled on the English laws, thus replicating the move elsewhere to establish separate juvenile institutional infrastructures for the neglected and the criminal or the pre-delinquent and the delinquent. Unlike in the US and the UK where the reformatory movement was led largely by philanthropists who were not directly involved with the judicial processing of the youth, Australia's experience was spearheaded by adult courts whose magistrates had become concerned about having to send convicted juveniles to adult prisons that had proved to be harmful. In fact, in Tasmania and Victoria where the first set of reformatory laws were enacted, magistrates not only led a series of petitions that preceded these laws but also actively partici-pated in drafting some of the laws (Seymour 1988, p 40).

More than two decades after Western Australia (the last jurisdiction to pass reformatory legislation) established its Reform School, South Australia became the first to establish a separate children's court in 1890. Within the next three decades, other States followed suit – Tasmania being the last State to do so in 1918. As to the motive for this change, all of the States emphasised that time had come for juveniles to be removed from the 'unhealthy surroundings, mixed up with drunkards and adult criminals' and from the 'farce and degradation' of trial by jury especially in minor charges (Seymour 1988, pp 69-70).

Clearly, the 19th century changes in justification for the social control of children, led to separate institutions and systems for needy and offending youth. The reformatory and court movements, increasingly separating young people from the adult justice and corrections systems and providing them with individualised treatment, were the outcomes. In place of the criminal justice's punitive policies were to be instituted the use of indeterminate procedures, preventative and/or rehabilitative approaches. The philosophical pillar upon which each of the movements was hung – childsaving for the reformatory and *parens patriae* doctrine for the courts, emphasised treatment, supervision and control rather than punishment (Feld 1998).

Thus, by the time the movements had fully crystallised several cultural and criminological fault lines, along with several binary conceptions for the respective juvenile and criminal justice systems, were institutionalised. You were either a child or an adult. As a child, explanation for your crimes shifted from free will to determinism. The way you were processed emphasised procedural informality as opposed to the formality of the adult system. Whereas judges felt bound by the rule of law in adult proceedings, they were encouraged to exercise a high degree of discretion in youth proceedings. If you were a confirmed case of neglect or delinquency, treatment and not punishment became the prescribed remedy (ibid).

Feld (1998) is right when he notes that serious youth crimes continually challenged these dichotomous constructs. Not surprisingly, several of the recent changes to juvenile laws that shifted the systems in the western countries towards the 'justice' model, have attempted to modify the 'bifurcations between these competing conceptions of children and crime control'. Although the next sub-section highlights some of these changes, the context for the changes will be addressed in detail in Chapter 5.

From welfare to justice model

Research shows that while the reformatory and judicial movements in relation to young people in several western countries appeared progressive or sound in intentions, they were rather disappointing in their actual performance. In the US, the efficacy of the House of Refuge approach began to be significantly questioned in the case of Daniel O'Connell in 1870. On the ground that he was in danger of becoming a pauper, Daniel was committed to the Chicago House of Refuge. He had not committed any crime. When his parents demanded that he be released, the case went to the Illinois Supreme Court for ruling.

In deciding to release Daniel, the Court held that reform school was only that in name – in reality. it punished rather than helped its inmates:

> Why should minors be imprisoned for misfortune? Destitution of proper parental care, ignorance, idleness and vice, are misfortunes, not crimes ... This boy is deprived of a father's care; bereft of home influences; has no freedom of action; is committed for an uncertain time; is branded as a prisoner; made subject to the will of others, and thus feels he is a slave (quoted in Bernard 1992, p 70).

By characterising committal to reform school as 'imprisonment' which could go for one year to 15 years depending on the age of the young person at the time, the Court called into question the so-called 'best interests' principle. The Court was also scathing of the state using the *parens patriae* doctrine to thwart the writ of *habeas corpus*, a writ for the securing of liberty for children; further, it underlined the need for the formal due process protection for children:

> the sovereign power of the State as parens patriae has determined the imprisonment beyond call. Such restraint upon natural liberty is tyranny and oppression. If, without crime, without the conviction of an offence, the children of the State are thus to be confined for the 'good of society' then the government [had better] acknowledge a failure ... Even criminals cannot be convicted and imprisoned without due process of law. (Ibid)

Edwin Lembert (1967, p 92) echoes this criticism of the underlying doctrine of *parens patriae*[10] when he says:

> Pious injunctions that 'care, custody and discipline of children under the control of the juvenile court shall approximate that which they would receive

from their parents' ... taken literally [is] meaningless either as ideal or reality. Neither the modern state nor an harassed juvenile court judge is a father; a halfway house is not a home; a reformatory cell is not a teenager's bedroom; a juvenile hall counsellor is not a dutch uncle; a cottage matron is not a mother ... [T]he people referred to ... are first and foremost members of organisations, enforcers of superimposed rules. Where conflicts arise between the interests of a youth and those of the organisation to which these functionaries are bureaucratically responsible there is no pattern of action which can predict that they will observe an order of value satisfaction favourable to the youth's interest.

Nearly a century after Daniel O'Connell's case, the US Supreme Court, in *In re Gault* 387 US 1 (1967), directed a full spotlight to the second movement of the reform era, namely the juvenile courts, in the history of responses to youth crime. In that case, the Court began to engraft 'some formal procedures at trial onto the juvenile court's individualised treatment sentencing regime and fostered a procedural and substantive convergence with adult criminal courts' (Feld 1998). Most of the works that attribute the origin of the shift towards a justice model to *Gault* gloss over the intricate issues that led the Supreme Court to instigate a major transformation in this area.[11] Bernard's work (1992) is an exception and his 'case analysis' will be summarised here in some detail.

Gerald Gault, a 15-year-old boy who lived in Gila County, Arizona, had been on probation for about three months for being in the company of another boy who had stolen a wallet from a lady's handbag. On 8 June 1964, he and his friend Ronald Lewis called their neighbour Mrs Cook and asked her: 'Do you give any?' 'Are your cherries ripe today?' and 'Do you have big bombers?'

Mrs Cook called the sheriff, who arrested the boys and placed them in detention without notifying their parents. When Gerald's mother came home at dinnertime she thought Gerald was over at the Lewis's and sent her older son to get him. But the Lewis's said that Gerald had been arrested.

The next day, Gerald's mother and brother went down to a hearing. No record was kept of this hearing and Mrs Cook did not appear. The judge later said Gerald admitted making the obscene remarks, whereas the Gaults said that Gerald only admitted dialling the phone. The judge said he would 'think about it'. Gerald was released from detention two or three days later.

A second hearing was held on 15 June, with Gerald's mother and father both attending. No record was kept of the hearing and Mrs Cook did not appear. Mrs Gault asked that Mrs Cook identify which boy made the remarks, but the judge said it was not necessary. The judge then committed Gerald to the State Industrial School for Boys until his 21st birthday. That meant he could be held for up to six years; but if he had been an adult, the maximum penalty for this offence would have been a fine of $5 to $50 and imprisonment for not more than two months.

The Gaults then retained a lawyer, who filed a writ of *habeas corpus*, demanding that the state justify holding Gerald. This writ ultimately made its way to the US Supreme Court. In the lower courts, the lawyer had argued that Gerald's treatment violated both Arizona statutes and the US

Constitution. But, in presenting the case to the Supreme Court, the lawyer narrowed the issue down to the denial of six specific constitutional rights in Gerald's adjudication hearing:

(1) the right to notice of the charges,

(2) the right to counsel,

(3) the right to confront and cross-examine witnesses,

(4) the privilege against self-incrimination,

(5) the right to a transcript of the proceedings, and

(6) the right to appellate review of the case.

The Supreme Court ruled that, in adjudication hearings that might result in being sent to an institution, juveniles had the right to adequate, written and timely notice, the right to counsel, the right to confront and cross-examine witnesses, and the privilege against self-incrimination. The court did not rule on the right to a transcript and appellate review, although it encouraged States to provide those rights to juveniles. The court also did not rule on due process rights in other stages of the juvenile justice system or in adjudication hearings that could not result in detention.

Because the decision, which presented a general line of reasoning for why due process protections should be introduced into the juvenile court, was based on the constitution, it applied to the entire nation, not just to Arizona. First, the Supreme Court concluded that Gerald was being *punished, not helped:*

> It is of no constitutional consequence – and of limited practical meaning –that the institution to which he is committed is called an Industrial School. The fact of the matter is that, however euphemistic the title, a 'receiving home' or an 'industrial school' for juveniles is an institution of confinement in which the child is incarcerated. ... Instead of mother and father and sisters and brothers and friends and classmates, his world is peopled by guards, custodians, state employees, and 'delinquents' confined with him for anything from waywardness to rape and homicide. (see Bernard 1992, p 116)

The conclusion that committing Gerald to an industrial home meant punishment was also based on an assessment of the *actual performance* of the juvenile justice system, not its *good intentions*: 'it is important, we think, that the claimed benefits of the juvenile process should be candidly appraised. Neither sentiment nor folklore should cause us to shut our eyes (to failures of the juvenile court)' (ibid). Next, in questioning and ultimately rejecting the *parens patriae* doctrine, the Court ruled that the meaning of this doctrine 'is murky and its historic credentials are of dubious relevance. ... There is no trace of the doctrine in the history of criminal jurisprudence' (ibid).

Finally, following a realistic appraisal of juvenile justice practices, the Court concluded that there was a need for *due process protections*:

> The essential difference between Gerald's case and a normal criminal case is that the safeguards available to adults were discarded in Gerald's case. The summary procedure as well as the long commitment was possible because Gerald was 15 years of age instead of over 18. (ibid, p 117)

In essence, *Gault* signalled a major shift of the focus of delinquency proceedings from a child's best interests to proof of legal guilt in adversarial fashion, and from procedural informality to 'due process' requirements. In the decades following *Gault*, several States revised their juvenile codes' statement of legislative purpose, de-emphasising rehabilitation and the child's best interest, and asserting the importance of public safety, punishment, and accountability in the juvenile justice system. A major change in philosophical direction from 'welfare' to 'justice' had taken place; and it reverberated throughout the western world.

The shift in emphasis in England from 'care' or 'welfare' in the 1960s to 'control' or 'justice' in the 1970s-80s owed a lot to the transformation in America. Notwithstanding the possibility that the *Children and Young Persons Act 1969* might have increased the punitive character of the juvenile justice system in the UK – despite the welfarist or rehabilitative rhetoric about it, the Conservative Party that took control of government after the 1979 election was determined to shift the system towards the 'justice' model. For the Party, this meant pursuing an agenda to 'toughen up' the laws and to make 'custodial care' system the centrepiece of the juvenile punitive machine. This agenda was implemented through various pieces of legislation: the *Criminal Justice Act* (1982 & 1988), the *Children Act 1989*, the *Criminal Justice Act 1991* and the *Criminal Justice and Public Order Act 1994*.

These laws had the effect of placing 'punishment' firmly at the centre of juvenile justice, popularising 'detention in a young offender institution' – with the Home Office Prison Department to determine the type of institution, transferring the civil care proceedings of the juvenile court to the Family Proceedings Court, providing new sentencing powers and providing for longer custodial sentences for juveniles (Wakefield and Hirschel 1996).

In Canada, the welfare model of the *Juvenile Delinquents Act 1908* came under a series of attacks from 1968 which advocated some changes towards the 'justice' model. An abortive attempt through a Bill introduced in the federal parliament in 1975 specifically sought to install the justice model principles. The change finally came with the unanimous passing of the *Young Offenders Act 1982*. That Act, while still acknowledging the special needs of young offenders as children, officially mandated 'formalised legal procedures' and stipulated that young persons were to be held responsible and accountable for their criminal acts. Critics of the law came to see it as a punitive 'kiddies' criminal code' – merely replicating the laws governing the adult justice system, a view vehemently rejected by the architects and proponents of the Act. Compared to the previous regime, there is little doubt that the reform trends were 'clearly toward crime control model principles of punitiveness, retribution, incapacitation, and deterrence' (Corrado and Markwart 1996).

The Australian experience in relation to this transition is rather different. In contradistinction to their American counterparts, the juvenile courts that were established in Australia since the last decade of the 19th century were modified adult (magistrates) criminal courts and never substantially departed from conventional principles and procedures of adult justice. Although much of the rhetoric about children's justice in the 20th century was drawn from the welfare model,[12] the adult courts dealing with juvenile offenders did little more than 'mitigate the harsh effects of [the] equality of treatment' between adults and children, with reduced penalties, separate custodial institutions and summary justice for the latter (Naffine 1993). Thus, although the ideology that the American *Gault* case embodied became influential in Australia, the actual decision 'has little direct relevance to Australia' (Seymour 1993, p 52).

Nevertheless, from the late 1970s the dissatisfaction with the welfare aspects of some systems in Australia led to legislative changes aimed at unambiguously committing Australia to the 'justice' model. South Australia was first with its *Children's Protection and Young Offenders Act 1979*. Eight years later, New South Wales followed with its *Children's Court Act 1987* and *Children (Criminal Proceedings) Act 1987*. Victoria enacted its own law two years later: the *Children and Young Persons Act 1989*. In other Australian jurisdictions, a clear shift from the welfare approach occurred in the 1990s, Queensland and Western Australia passing their own laws in 1992 and 1994 respectively.

What is significant about this shift for our present purpose is that, despite the rhetoric of rehabilitation being the major principle in juvenile sentencing, it brought *retribution* to the forefront of crime policies in general and juvenile justice (re)actions in particular. This was evident, for example, in the Western Australia's *Crime (Serious and Repeat Offenders) Sentencing Act 1992*, Queensland's *Juvenile Justice Act 1992*, South Australia's *Young Offenders Act 1993*, and Western Australia's *Young Offenders Act 1994*. In the last five years of the 20th century, this trend intensified as evidenced by Western Australia's *Criminal Code (Amendment) Act 1996* which introduced mandatory detention for young offenders convicted for a third offence of home burglary. The Northern Territory's *Juvenile Justice Amendment Act (No 2) 1996* also introduced mandatory imprisonment for offenders who commit a range of property offences twice or more. And, by the now repealed *Sentencing Amendment Act (No 2) 1999*, the NT government extended mandatory sentencing to violent and sexual offences.

All these retributive laws permit courts to sentence juveniles 16 years of age and over to adult prison for periods ranging from a maximum of three months in Western Australia to two years in Queensland.[13] More significantly, they illustrate the unwritten state policy towards young people: *treat them as adults in crime but as youth in citizenship*. The trend in this retributive governance is also manifested in the use of curfews, operation sweep and zero tolerance.

Contemporary modes of processing young offenders

In the post-19th century period, the processing of young people through the western justice system has generally continued to follow an identifiable sequence: from law violation to police apprehension, from trial to judicial dispositions, and from sentencing to probation/conditional release or correctional confinement. Although the organisation of the systems varies from country to country or, in some cases, between jurisdictions in one country, two options are generally provided for processing young offending cases especially in the first phase: informal and formal. An authorised official of the system (eg police officer, juvenile prosecutor or juvenile probation officer) decides whether to process the case informally by diverting the case from the juvenile court or formally through the court system. In all the countries, this discretionary decision is made within legislative, judicial and political frameworks.

Juvenile codes, the judge-made laws and politics affect police discretion in the investigation of youth offenders in the same way as in adult crime. When young persons are apprehended, police must decide whether to release them (with or without counsel or warning), divert them to community resources or bring them to the attention of juvenile courts. Where they decide to process them through the courts, they must draft and lodge a charge or complaint, file a petition (as in the US) to provide notice of the offences that will be pursued and to request the court to adjudicate (judicially determine) whether or not the youth is guilty of the offences as charged.

Recent politico-legal developments have resulted in the police or juvenile prosecutors having the power to send a juvenile to adult (criminal) court. In the US, this is done by one of the following three methods:

- judicial waiver, which allows juvenile court judges to transfer juveniles to criminal court. Generally, prosecutors initiate judicial waiver by filing a waiver petition asking the judge to consider the case for waiver;

- prosecutor direct filing, which allows prosecutors to decide whether to file certain cases in juvenile or criminal court;

- application of statutory exclusion laws, which specify crimes or juveniles with certain prior records that are excluded from juvenile court jurisdiction, and who must therefore go to the criminal court.

A Report to Congressional Requesters, titled *Juvenile Justice – Juveniles Processed In Criminal Court And Case Dispositions* in August 1995, identified (1) judicial waiver laws in 47 States and the District of Columbia; (2) prosecutor direct filing laws in 10 States and the District of Columbia; and (3) one or more statutory exclusion laws in 37 States and the District of Columbia.[14]

The number of delinquency cases judicially waived to criminal court reached a peak in 1994 with 11,700 cases. This represented a 73 per cent increase over the number of cases waived in 1988 (6700). Since 1994, however, the number of cases waived to criminal court has declined by 28 per cent to 8400 cases. Throughout 1992, property offences outnumbered person offences among waived cases. This trend reversed in 1993, as person offence cases accounted for a greater proportion of the waived caseload than property offence cases (43 per cent versus 38 per cent).

Between 1994 and 1997, the decline in waived person offence cases (35 per cent) outpaced the decline in waived property offence cases (26 per cent). By 1997, the proportion of formally processed person offence cases (40 per cent or 3300 cases) that were waived was about the same as for formally processed property offence cases (38 per cent or 3200 cases).

From 1988 to 1997, the number of judicially waived cases involving black youth increased 35 per cent, compared with a 14 per cent increase for white youth. Property offence cases made up the largest share of the waived caseload for black youth in 1988 and 1989. From 1990 to 1997, however, person offence cases made up the largest share of the waived caseload for black youth. Comparatively, property offence cases constituted the largest share of judicially waived cases for white youth each year from 1988 through 1997 (Puzzanchera 2000).

In Australia, several jurisdictions have introduced waiver mechanisms for serious and violent young offenders since 1979. Before 1993, the decision to transfer young offenders to adult courts in South Australia rested with a judge of the Supreme Court on application from the Attorney-General. The *Young Offenders Act 1993* of that State changed that process to allow the police prosecutor to apply directly to the Youth Court.[15]

Observers have noted that the prosecution of children as adults (eg the 12-year-old Nathaniel Abraham in the US, and the two 11-year-olds, Jon Venables and Robert Thompson, in Britain[16]) is part of a wider cross-national development which is bound up with the dismantling of welfare programs and social reforms associated with the post-World War Two period (Mason 1998). While most jurisdictions are now careful to distinguish between the way serious indictable offences and other offences are handled under the waiver mechanisms, all jurisdictions have largely shifted from the welfare orientation in the treatment of most young offenders.

Policing youth crime

In the western world, the police as a sub-system of the juvenile justice system are the gatekeepers who determine not only which young persons enter the system, but also how they enter and with what frequency. All of this has significant implications for the experience that such young persons would have from the system. Without overdramatising the role of the police, it is correct to say, as Edwards (1999, p 49) did, that 'without police providing the corn, there is nothing for the mill of justice to grind … The criminal justice system cannot operate unless police supply both a suspect and credible evidence collected against that suspect'.

The traditional police approach to garnering 'young corn' for the 'justice mill', usually articulated in crime prevention or reduction terms, has been fraught with problems. In the US, police have been noted to demand mandatory and enhanced policing and sentencing practices for targeted young offenders. For example, although a research by Wolfgang, Thornberry and Figlio (1987) pointed to the need to further explore the nature of the progression of a criminal career and the process through which adolescent offenders become career adult offenders, the police went to the legislatures to seek extra powers to be tough on such offenders without having the benefit of the much needed research. The belief was that such selective enforcement and penalty would net the offenders and keep them behind bars in order to achieve a significant reduction in crime. The police have been shown to get involved in 'frontier justice' or 'vigilantism' in spite of its failure to protect Americans as their proponents had claimed (*Wall Street Journal*, 26 June 1988).

The UK police response in the James Bulger case in 1993 showed several hallmarks of this approach. In February 1993 Jamie went missing while shopping with his mother in a mall in Bootle, near Liverpool. His body was found two days later on a railway track about two-and-a-half miles from the mall. Footage from video security cameras along the route showed Jamie in the company of two older boys.

Accompanied by sensationalist reports in the media, the police launched an investigation in which 160 juveniles were taken into custody in just five days. In some of the cases, the police response appeared to be an overkill. For instance, 12-year-old Jonathon Green was arrested at home in the glare of publicity by a force of 15 detectives and six police vans, even though it was Jonathon's father who had contacted the police after seeing the video images of the two boys on the television. The boy was released after 23 hours and eliminated from the inquiry. Needless to say, he suffered mental distress for which he had to receive counselling and treatment (Mason 1998).

Thompson and Venables were later arrested and given no counselling during their detention, on the grounds that this would prejudice their trial. They were tried as adults in an adult court, convicted and sentenced to be detained indefinitely at Her Majesty's pleasure, first in secure accommodation and, then, at the age of 18, they were to be transferred to an adult prison (ibid).

In Australia, contemporary policing of youth in 'public space' is one site in which elements of the traditional approach are evident. On occasions, police would 'mould and shape a situation until it will come within the ambit of the legal system and allow them to 'take the kid off the streets' (Blagg and Wilkie 1995, p 5). Simply implementing the letter of the law 'will not allow them the flexibility they need to maintain social order and keep the peace as they see fit'. In those circumstances, police feel obliged to use a salutary 'short, sharp, shock' method, administering 'kerb-side justice', or using discretion to deal informally with some offences (ibid). It's all about police being 'quick to exact their own justice', especially in relation to minorities (see Omaji 2001b, p 240).

Similarly, as the research by Anderson and his colleagues (1994) shows, police in Edinburgh regularly spend half their time chasing young people about and do not care to establish whether these young people who never seem to fight with the police treat this as a game. A police officer was quoted as saying:

> You're just moving them on from one place to another. Well, they were hanging about Broughton Street and down that area and my inspector, he was quite good, he says 'Right, tonight we'll just lock em all up – do them for breach of the peace.' It solved the problem for the Broughton Street area because they just went somewhere else because they realised they'd just get locked up if they stayed there. If that was happening to them in every division where they congregate, they'd soon get the message. (1994, p 140)

In Australia, research conducted for the National Youth Affairs Research Scheme in the early 1990s found a similar emphasis on street policing. Not only was a high proportion (an average of 83 per cent) of the young people interviewed stopped and spoken to by the police (Table 3.1 on following page); all except 17 per cent of those stopped said that they were stopped in the street (Alder, O'Connor, Warner, and White 1992, pp 20-22). While the contacts involved taking the young interviewees to police station and holding them in police cells in large proportions, the youth experience (see Table 3.2 on following page) tends to support other research findings that police procedures turn out to be essentially 'degradation ceremonies' in their own right (Blagg and Wilkie 1995, p 5).

Stereotypical images that police use as cues to assess demeanour also reveal a down side to traditional policing. Patrol officers view juveniles who appear contrite about their infractions, respectful to officers and fearful of the sanctions that might be employed against them as basically law-abiding or at least 'salvageable'. For these young people, police usually assume that reprimand would suffice to guarantee their future conformity. By contrast, youthful offenders who are fractious, obdurate, or who appear nonchalant in their encounters with patrol officers are likely to be viewed as 'would-be tough guys' or 'punks' who fully deserve the most severe processing technique – arrest.

The following observation notes from Piliavin and Briar (1991) illustrate not only the importance attached to demeanour by police in making disposition decisions but also the influence of the media in the direction of such decisions. An 18-year-old upper-class white male was accused of statutory rape. The police sergeant assigned to interrogate him, highly experienced in the service, expressed his uncertainty as to what he should do with this young man. On the one hand, he could not ignore the fact that an offence had been committed; he had been informed, in fact, that the youth was prepared to confess to the offence. Nor could he overlook the continued pressure from the girl's father (an important political figure) for the police to take severe action against the youth. On the other hand, the sergeant had formed a low opinion of the girl's moral character and he considered it unfair to charge the young man with statutory rape when the girl was a willing partner to the offence and might even have been the instigator of it. However, his sense of injustice concerning the accused was tempered by his image of the youth as a 'punk', based, he explained, on information he had received that the youth belonged to a certain gang, the members of which were well known to, and disliked by, the police. Nevertheless, up until the time to leave his office for the interrogation, the sergeant was still in doubt as to what he should do with the accused.

Table 3.1: Per cent of specific groups of young people who reported specific types of police contact in Australia

Type of contact	Aust/English (%) n=228	Aboriginal/Torres Strait Islander (%) n=50	Born overseas or NESB (%) n=105
Asked for help	39	22	38
Stopped/spoken to	82	98	69
Police officially cautioned	25	34	15
Taken to police station	52	80	31
Held in police cells	55	65	30
Strip searched/asked to undress	24	37	11
Roughed up	33	56	21

Source: Adapted from Alder, O'Connor, Warner, and White (1992, p 20)

Table 3.2: Experience of young people in the hands of police

Experience in the hands of police	Percentage of young interviewees n=102
Spoken to nicely	28
Try to make comfortable	22
Overall treated fairly	37
Told about rights	28
Explained what happened	57
Police tried to get support person	29
Told could make phone call	21
Other person present during questioning	35
Fingerprinted	53
Fingerprinted and not arrested	22
Held in police cells	53
Police yelled/swore	70
Police hit	40
Police pushed around	55
Asked to remove pieces of clothing	42

Source: Adapted from Alder, O'Connor, Warner, and White (op cit, p 24)

On the way to the interrogation room, the sergeant was stopped by a reporter from the local newspaper. In an excited tone of voice, the reporter explained that his editor was pressing him to get further information about this case. The newspaper had printed some of the facts about the girl's disappearance and as a consequence the girl's father was threatening suit against the paper for defamation of the girl's character. It would strengthen the newspaper's position, the reporter explained, if the police had information indicating that the girl's associates, particularly the youth the sergeant was about to interrogate, were persons of disreputable character. This stimulus seemed to resolve the sergeant's uncertainty. He told the reporter, 'unofficially', that the youth was known to be an undesirable person, citing as evidence his membership in the delinquent gang.

Furthermore, the sergeant added that he had evidence that this youth had been intimate with the girl over a period of many months. When the reporter asked if the police were planning to do anything to the youth, the sergeant answered that he intended to charge the youth with statutory rape. In the interrogation, however, three points quickly emerged which profoundly affected the sergeant's judgment of the youth. First, the youth was polite and cooperative, he consistently addressed the officer as 'sir', answered all questions quietly and signed a statement implicating himself in numerous counts of statutory rape. Second, the youth's intentions toward the girl appeared to have been honourable; for example, he said that he wanted to marry her eventually. Third, the youth was not in fact a member of the gang in question. The sergeant's attitude became increasingly sympathetic and, afterwards, he announced his intention to let the young man 'off the hook', by reducing or possibly dropping the charges.

In another incident, two officers brought into the police station a 17-year-old white boy who, along with two older companions, had been found in a home having sex with a 15-year-old girl. The boy responded to police officers' queries slowly and with obvious disregard. It was apparent that his lack of deference toward the officers and his failure to express concern about his situation were irritating his questioners. Finally, one of the officers, obviously angry, commented that in his view the boy was simply a 'stud' interested only in sex, eating and sleeping. The policemen conjectured that the boy 'probably already had knocked up half a dozen girls'. The boy ignored these remarks, except for an occasional impassive stare at the police officers. Turning to the boy, the officer remarked, 'What the hell am I going to do with you?' And again the boy simply returned the officer's gaze. The latter then said, 'Well, I guess we'll just have to put you away for a while'. An arrest report was then made out and the boy was taken to Juvenile Hall.

Although anger and disgust frequently characterised officers' attitudes toward recalcitrant and impassive juvenile offenders, their manner while processing these youths was typically routine, restrained and without rancour. While the officers' restraint may have been due in part to their desire to avoid accusation and censure, it also seemed to reflect their being accustomed to these frequent experiences. By and large, only their occasional 'needling' or insulting of a boy gave any hint of the underlying resentment and dislike they felt toward many of these youths.

Police officers' animosity toward recalcitrant or aloof offenders appears to stem from two sources: moral indignation that these juveniles were apparently assured and indifferent about their transgressions, and resentment that these youths failed to accord police the respect they believed they deserve. Since the officers perceive themselves as honestly and impartially performing a vital community function warranting respect and deference from the community at large, they attribute the lack of respect shown them by young people to the youth's immorality.

Traditional policing in contemporary times is also characterised by models that carry high risk for young people: (1) preventive patrol or monitoring model and (2) the 'professionalisation' model to apprehend criminals and deter crime. With regard to preventive patrol, the assumption is that by increasing the number of officers and ensuring 'rapid response police cars ..., the certainty of apprehension and conviction would result in an arrest rate that would be high enough to deter the general population from committing a crime' (Wiatrowski 1996, p 124). Preventive monitoring (eg in Australia) derives from police statutory power to remove children from public spaces in circumstances where the children are not suspected of illegal activity but are considered 'in physical or moral danger' or 'at risk' of offending.[17]

In reality, images of youth – generalised on the basis of race/colour, class, gender, and subculture (demeanour and appearance are usual handles) together with the prevailing law and order ideology affect the character of these response-types. Officers operating within this framework initiate contacts with young people not so much because of the seriousness of the offence or the nature of the call, but when the young people look 'suspicious',[18] funny, out of place or are hanging out on street corners. Despite the high chance of the statutory powers being misused, such as the police acting on stereotypes about young people, there is little or no accountability for, or judicial supervision of, police actions (Australian Law Reform Commission and Human Rights & Equal Opportunity Commission 1997, p 86).

Paradoxically, the professionalisation model also produces a tendency towards punitiveness based on stereotypical images. Wilson's (1968) study of two cities in the US provides an illustrative finding that remains pertinent. A 'fraternal' police department is moralistic in outlook and holds that faulty personal or family morality produces delinquents and, although verbalising restrictive and punitive attitudes toward offenders, it formerly processes few young offenders. Conversely, a 'professional' police department is bureaucratic in outlook and, although holding therapeutic attitudes toward offenders, it formally processes a large number of offenders, pursues a stricter enforcement of the law and draws more young offenders into the system.

The Los Angeles Police Department has an organisational culture that emphasises crime control over crime prevention and that isolates the police from the communities and the people whom they serve. With the full support of many, the LAPD insists on aggressive detection of major crimes and a rapid seven-minute response time (professionalist model). This style of policing produces results, but does so at the risk of creating a siege mentality that alienates the officers from their community and a propensity for aggressive policing especially towards the youth (Warren's 1992 Report, quoted in Kucera 1993, p 235).

After deciding to process cases officially, police are more likely to refer to court 'surly or defiant youth than polite, contrite youngsters' (Goldman 1963). Those who seemed to be members of gangs, who were blacks, who dressed like 'cats' or who were flippant ended up in juvenile courts disproportionately to their number in the general population (Piliavin and Briar 1964). An Australian research shows that the 'degree of cooperation' and 'attitude' of young people rank equally strongly with the 'seriousness of the offence' among the factors that influence police decisions on how to process suspected young offenders (see Alder et al 1992, p 33).

It is in the policing of minority youth that the worst of the practices described above do tend to be manifested. Police-Aboriginal relations, for instance, exhibit what appears to be a lot of game playing. However, as Beresford and Omaji (1996) demonstrate, several aspects of old police practices in relation to Aboriginal youth end up marginalising and criminalising this minority youth:

> Often kids just have to walk out onto the streets and they are accosted by the police who ask them for their name and address. They will walk around the corner and another police officer will do exactly the same. Therefore, these young people think they may as well sniff glue with their mates. (ibid, p 71)

Police would then charge them with offences concerning substance abuse or other perhaps spurious, minor public order offences, then put these youths under continuous surveillance. These stereotyped youths become the subjects of aggressive policing and subsequently end up in the criminal justice system as offenders.

Police use less cautioning or other informal systems and summonsing, and more of arrest for minority suspects (Omaji 1997 and 1999). Their approach to questioning minority youth takes little or no account of language and cultural differences. Police used violence in the process of all this, as the experiences of Aboriginal youth show:

- constantly calling around to their private houses if any offences were committed in the area (targeting and harassment);
- bashing them when arrested and over-tightening handcuffs at wrists and ankles;
- stripping them to undies and belting them on bare bodies with batons; and
- dropping a brick on their toes, jamming their fingers in drawers, belting with batons on the chest over a phone book so that no bruises will show (Beresford and Omaji 1996, p 81).

In addition to the above-mentioned physical violence, police constantly question these young people: 'What are you doing? Where are you going? Where were you at 8pm last night when a crime was committed? Can you prove it?' all of which further contributes to the view that 'police and young Aborigines are involved in a private war' (see Cunneen 2001 for a detailed analysis of police interaction with indigenous communities).

A close examination shows that these young people experience all elements of a three-part typology of police violence:

- physical abuse/excessive force;
- verbal/psychological abuse; and
- legal abuse/violation of human rights.

To these young people, police have become more than an enforcement agency; they are the punishers as well. Police violence is not gratuitous: it serves an instrumental purpose – to gain admission; to dispense summary justice under the perception that the courts are too lenient on the criminals that they labour to catch or to reassert their authority. Either of these objects reinforces and legitimises the negative perceptions that tend to dominate the relationships between police and young people.

As in Australia, research has shown that popular anxieties around minority youth in other countries have generated and/or legitimised intensive police intervention in the lives of these youth, at times resulting in widespread civil disorders as with the policing operations which led to urban riots in Brixton in the 1980s and the Rodney King riot in Los Angeles in the 1990s.

In all aspects of traditional methods of policing – preventive or professionalist – most western countries have experienced massive failures in relation to preventing youth crime. This is particularly so where there is overuse of one of five role-identity orientations adopted by police officers, namely the 'authority figure'. In this orientation, police use intimidation to move teenagers on from the public space. Other orientations that are less likely to antagonise young people but not used routinely are:

- peacemaker and problem solver – trying to get everybody to get along and understand the other person's viewpoint;
- competent law enforcer – staying within the law and obtaining proper evidence to make a case;
- friend or peer – jogging with kids, talking to them (not down to them), letting them know police officers are human with their own needs and explaining the situation to them; and
- knight in shining armour – presenting the 'we are here to save the day, everything will be fine, and call again if the problem arises' attitude (Hess and Wrobleski 1993).

Why are they less used? While this may sound rhetorical, the ideological, sociological and media factors that we examined in Chapter 1 clearly underline the political significance of the choices that law enforcement officers make when they come in contact with young people.

Judicial response to youth crime

Barely 70 years after juvenile courts came into existence in the western world, they had to move in the direction of greater formality and coercion. This meant departing, radically in some countries or notching up in others, from what the founding thinkers of children's courts in these countries wanted. It may be recalled, as several parliaments in Australia expressed, that these thinkers wanted a system that would:

- correct offending children in a 'fatherly manner';
- save the children 'from becoming criminals';
- endeavour to lead children 'on to a new career, in which [they] may rise to higher things, and prove in the future a good citizen; and
- avoid the 'terrorism of the ordinary courts of the land' (Seymour 1997, p 294).

No doubt, the history of dealing with young people in these countries would have convinced even the most optimistic person that the required changes were a tall order. In fact, in Australia, this was requiring an essentially police court of summary jurisdiction to adopt a paternal, non-punitive approach. If we go back in the history of all the countries, we would clearly find a large proportion of children who came before their courts being whipped, fined, bound over and imprisoned. Nonetheless, few, except those aided by the analytical power of the critical political economy of justice, could have predicted that, under the 'justice' model, the courts would adopt such a severe and punitive response to young offenders as they did in the 1980s and 1990s.

Evaluations of juvenile court sentencing practices, treatment effectiveness and conditions of confinement reveal an increasingly punitive system. Despite juvenile courts' persistent rehabilitative rhetoric, the reality of *treating* juveniles closely resembles *punishing* adult criminals. There is jurisprudential and administrative convergence eroding the justifications for a separate criminal system for young offenders. For instance, the Western Australian Ministry of Justice has been merging the management of its juvenile justice division with the adult offender management division since 1996 (Omaji 1997b). In the US, four procedural and substantive developments – removal of jurisdiction over status offenders, waiver of serious offenders into the adult system, increased punitiveness and procedural formality – have led virtually to 'the criminalising of the juvenile court' (Feld 1992, p 60).

The tendency of the courts with this ideological bent to fight the 'misguided sympathy' image by wanting to be seen to be tough on young offenders is compounded by the fact that most of its judicial officers would be strongly beholden to the 'classicist' thinking of individual responsibility for youth crime. Further, the inclination of these officers is, by and large, to 'get troublesome kids out of the community' (Beresford and Omaji 1996, p 97). Much of this can be accounted for by the fact that these courts do subscribe to prevailing negative perceptions of young people. As Feld (1992, p 60) observes, juvenile courts, like other child-centred laws and institutions, reflect and advance the changing conception of childhood. They are thus bound to be caught up in society's ambivalence about its responses to youth in general which was highlighted in Chapter 1.

One significant casualty of this situation is the 'ideological legitimacy of a separate juvenile court system' (Seymour 1997, p 298). The Nevada Supreme Court did not seem to care when it endorsed punishment as an appropriate function of juvenile courts in its *In re Seven Minors* decision:

> By formally recognising the legitimacy of punitive and deterrent sanctions for criminal offences juvenile courts will be properly and somewhat belatedly expressing society's firm disapproval of juvenile crime and will be clearly issuing a threat of punishment for criminal acts to the juvenile population.[19]

As stated in Chapter 2, moral assessment of physical appearance – differentiated by several artefacts of identity – plays a significant role in the perceptions that influence the courts' treatment of young people. It is more than an important influence on sentencing; it is actually a key element, especially for juveniles (Parker, Sumner and Jarvis 1989). The caution that an ex-juvenile court judge in South Australia issued some years ago appears as valid today as it was then.

> A necessary aspect of the approach in juvenile courts is the need to be 'philosophical', tolerant and non-judgemental with reference to matters of dress, physical appearance, and demeanour. One firm conviction I have after serving in a juvenile court is that it is unsafe to allow such matters to influence on the final decision-making process. (Wilson 1974, quoted in Omaji 1995)

The literature on indigenous or ethnic minority youth being portrayed stereotypically in language that is value-laden and which sustains pre-judicial decision-making processes based on physical appearance is substantial (Leonard et al 1995; Walker et al 1996). Contrary to the view that a 'colour-blind' approach ensures equality of treatment, the absence of a consideration of 'race' or other markers of disadvantage within the ideo-logical stances that frame and inform the operation of the justice system is contrived to perpetuate discrimination against the minorities. Invariably, racial minority youth are consistently disadvantaged by institutions such as the mainstream courts operating mono-cultural policies under the guise of 'colour-blind' or culture-neutral justice (Kirk 1996, Hogg 2001).

A major point in all this discussion is that the way the courts treat young people is not a purely mechanical judicial response to the belief in the 'crime problem' – real or imagined. Box (1987, pp 133-134) could not be more right when he says:

> [T]he judiciary responds actively, changing its practices to fit what it perceives to be a changed situation. Not only is it more receptive to the idea that [its host country] has been experiencing a massive crime wave ..., but it is

also more in touch with those social groups who clamour for more prisons, police, and punishment. It therefore responds actively by increasing the use of prison sentences and reducing the use of non-supervisory sentences ... The outcome is the imposition of more sentences at the higher end of punishment tariff over and above the changes in the volume and pattern of crime. This effect is ... mediated by judicial attitudes and ideological positions which prepare a sufficiently large proportion of judges and magistrates to respond to deteriorating economic conditions by resorting more frequently to severe penal sanctions.

Detention: 'banging up the youth'

The ambivalence that afflicted the police and courts in their traditional response to youth crime did not spare custodial staff. During a turbulent history of change from reformation through rehabilitation to warehousing, these staff have had to perform 'a multi-functional, at times conflicting, role': they run programs, provide informal counselling, provide links with professionals engaged to work in particular program areas, and maintain security and safety (Atkinson 1997, p 412).

With the advent of the 'justice' model, custodial officers have generally given up rehabilitation in favour of punitive custody. The fact that this approach has hardly dented the 'recidivism problem' in any of the western countries serves as no check on the orientation. Infatuation with warehousing is so strong now that science fiction writers are now promoting 'the use of the moons of Jupiter as penal colonies', no different from those established by 18th century and 19th century colonial powers like Britain and France in the US, Caribbean, the Indian Ocean and Australia (Wiatrowski 1996, p 119).

As with the other agencies that operate the juvenile justice system with the 'classicist' thinking, youth detention centres use crude behaviour modification techniques designed to redress individual pathology that is thought to be responsible for young people's criminal actions. Yet, the reality is that prison or detention musters 'are drawn predominantly from the nation's burgeoning underclass: the under-educated, poorly socialised, family deprived, substance-dependent, previously unemployed, physically unhealthy, high-risk lifestyle and psychologically damaged segments of the population' (Harding 1999, p 119). The outcome of the prevailing classicist response is a 'tyranny of treatment' within these centres (Beresford and Omaji 1996, p 93). Until recently, detention programs in Western Australia, for instance, were generally not suitably structured to take account of the cultural needs of the inmates. For example, school programs were substantially based on the classroom model from which most Aboriginal detainees felt alienated (Beresford and Omaji 1996, p 118).

The sterile nature of the environment in most detention centres is enough to build up aggression and to leave young inmates at their most dangerous at the time of release. Ex-prisoners describing how they were brutalised in New Zealand correctional systems said: 'your senses are under attack – by noise, by yelling from guards and inmates ... You adapt and cope but are desensitised in so doing' (Consedine 1996, p 32). Research shows that staff aggravate this problem by their *'rattle the keys'* mode of operation. Some officers use this approach to 'punish' or make life unbearable for inmates (Beresford and Omaji 1996, p 169).

One 16-year-old inmate of a youth custody centre in Plymouth, UK, described the formal routine of the centre in which key rattling would no doubt be a prominent feature:

> Normal you get up. They come around about seven in the morning and bang on the door and tell you to get out of bed ... Bang you up till half-ten and then they get you to scrub your cell out. And then they bang you up again and then about half-eleven you get dinner. And then they bang you up straight after dinner ... Half one-two o'clock and you might have association in the afternoon. Then they'll bang you up again before tea. They let you out for tea and then banged up again. (Little 1990, p 105)

Abuse of power, resulting in staff committing physical violence on young inmates, is not a rare phenomenon in the detention centres of most of the western countries. A 1998 investigation by the US Department of Justice of the juvenile section of Davies County Detention Centre in Kentucky found that staff regularly used stun guns and pepper spray to control uncooperative youth. Young people also report being hit by staff.

Not all the incidents come to public attention, but from time to time some of these violent acts are so vicious and revolting to ordinary conscience that they end up in courts. Vikram Dodd report one such act in which three prison officers who committed a vicious premeditated attack on an inmate were jailed in September 2000. The officers kicked and punched Timothy Donovan, a convicted murderer, in his cell at Wormwood Scrubs prison, west London, two years ago (Dodd 2000).

According to Vikram, one stood on the victim's face to prevent him escaping. Donovan was then handcuffed and spent 14 days in solitary confinement after one of the officers claimed Donovan had attacked him. The men were charged after fellow officers reported the attack. A jury found them guilty and Judge Charles Byers sentenced the three to 12, 15 and 18 months imprisonment respectively. Judge Byers said: 'you abuse the trust and authority placed in you ... During the course of that incident, not only did you let yourselves down but also the public and the prison service' (ibid). Needless to add, punitive attitudes further serve to crush the criminal, isolate him from the rest of the society and, as a result, paralyse society's good intentions of reform.

Traditional response to youth crime and international standards

The past four decades have seen the emergence of international standards against which the various developments in criminal justice response to youth crime can be measured. Developed mostly by the United Nations, these international standards address general civil and political rights in which the position of young people is acknowledged,[20] including specific rights for children,[21] the treatment of children in the justice system,[22] the protection of children deprived of their liberty[23] and the prevention of juvenile or youth crime.[24]

Juvenile justice decalogue

A comparative analysis of all the relevant international instruments reveals several justice-oriented provisions that can be synthesised into the following 10 standards (I call them Juvenile Justice Decalogue):[25]

(1) Every dealing with young people should aim to promote the principles of the 'best interests of the child' and the well-being of the juveniles (Beijing Rules 5.1 & 14.2; CROC Article 3(1); Riyadh Guideline 52; and Havana Rule 1).

(2) Young people's freedom to associate or assemble peacefully with their peers should not be restricted unless it is legally necessary to do so (CROC Article 15).

(3) Separate and different laws, procedures, authorities and institutions should be established to deal with children in trouble with the law (Beijing Rule 2.2(a); CROC Article 40(3); and Havana Rule 29).

(4) Personnel in juvenile justice services should be competent in their methods, approaches and attitudes and reflect the diversity of the juveniles that come into their services (Beijing Rule 1.6 & 22.2).

(5) Young people charged with offences should be given all the minimum guarantees including the presumption of innocence (Universal Declaration of Human Rights Article11; ICCPR Article 14(2); Beijing Rule 7; and Havana Rule 17)] and the right not to be compelled to testify against themselves or to confess guilt (ICCPR Article 14(3)(g); and CROC Article 40 (2)(b)).

(6) In all cases, reaction to young people should respect the principle of proportionality in a manner that takes account of age and seriousness of the precipitating behaviour (Beijing Rule 5).

(7) Official response to youth crime at all stages should not involve the use of torture or any form of violence and harm; and, in consequence, no instruments of restraint or force should be allowed (Beijing Rule 10.3; CROC Articles 19 & 37; and Havana Rule 63-64).

(8) Young people should not be subjected to harsh and degrading corrections and the use of detention or institutionalisation for young people should be the last resort; it should also segregate according to age, be rehabilitative or socially transformative, and treat inmates with humanity, dignity and appropriate recreation (ICCPR Article 10; Beijing Rule 19; CROC Article 37; Riyadh Guidelines 46; and Havana Rule 32 & 47).

(9)   The death penalty should not be applied to young people convicted of any offence (ICCPR Article 6(5); Beijing Rule 17.2; and CROC 37(a)).

(10)   Young people should be allowed to have an active role or participation and partnership in all fora including the juvenile justice system, with the right to express their views; they should not be considered as mere objects of socialisation and control (CROC Articles 12-13; and Riyadh Guideline 3).

Western juvenile justice systems breach the standards

Most responses to youth crime in the western world have increasingly diminished the rights that international instruments confer on young people in relation to how they are served by the justice system (Boss, Edwards, and Pitman 1995).

The studies between 1994 and 1998 in which the Human Rights Watch (1999) documented fundamental challenges for juvenile justice systems worldwide reveal that far too often children were locked up with adults, sometimes for very minor offences or no offence at all. Many countries failed to use more effective and less costly alternatives to incarceration, such as day treatment, release to parents with restrictions on activities, or shelter care in small group homes. Further, in the 1990s at least six countries were known to have executed persons who were juveniles at the time of their offences, in violation of international standards.

According to Amnesty International USA (1999), many children in the US are subjected to a juvenile justice system of brutal physical force, cruel punishments and extreme overcrowding. The notion of the 'super predator' or the 'teenage time bomb' has fuelled irrational and short-sighted policies which ultimately strip young people of their human dignity and rob our society of untapped human potential. In the US, as well as in some other western countries, there has been an increasing tendency to try children as adults and to commingle children with adults in detention. Between 1992 and 1998, at least 40 US States adopted legislation making it easier for children to be tried as adults. While African American youths are only 15 per cent of the population 10-17 years old, they comprise 50 per cent of all cases transferred to adult criminal courts.

All too often, the trial of juveniles as adults in the US failed to provide children with the special safeguards and care to which they were entitled under international law. The adult criminal system deprived children of the variety of rehabilitative dispositions that were available in juvenile adjudications; in particular, children charged as adults could expect to spend a minimum of six months in jail even before their cases came to trial, with no real alternatives to institutional care available to them.

Adjudication in the adult courts also denies children the right to have their privacy respected in all stages of the proceedings against them. Despite the declining percentage of violent juvenile offenders, and in spite of the fact that incarceration is shown to be more expensive than the use of community placements and less effective in reducing future delinquency (see Chapter 4), most US States continue to incarcerate high numbers of children for non-violent offences. A 1994 study by the National Council on Crime and Delinquency concluded that less than 14 per cent of young inmates in 28 State juvenile corrections systems were in detention for serious violent crimes. Indeed, the US Department of Justice's Office of Juvenile Justice and Delinquency Prevention reported that in 1995, over 8 per cent of detained juveniles nationwide were held for status offences, acts which would not be crimes if committed by adults. As Mark Soler, president of the California-based Youth Law Center, commented, America has seen 'juveniles locked up for repeated truancy, running away from home, violating curfew, possession of alcohol, possession of marijuana, shoplifting, and missing even a single meeting with a probation officer' (Soler 1996).

Despite the directive of Article 37(c) of the Convention on the Rights of the Child that 'every child deprived of liberty shall be separated from adults unless it is considered in the child's best interest not to do so', children continue to be held with adults in many parts of the western world. In at least 12 US States, children charged as adults are held in adult jails pending trial, in violation of international standards. The juveniles held in many of these facilities have daily contact with inmates 29 and 30 years older, many of whom are repeat offenders. Most adult jails offer incarcerated youth little or no education or other programming, virtually abandoning any effort to rehabilitate these youth or to assist them 'to assume socially constructive and productive roles in society' as required under Article 26 of the Beijing Rules.

On 7 September 1999, Amnesty International wrote an *Open Letter to the United States Congress* to express urgent concern about two pieces of pending Juvenile Justice Legislation (Bills S 254 and HR 1501) that have the potential to open up the possibility of children as young as 13 being held in the same cell with adults before their trial.

All but a handful of US States incarcerate children in adult correctional facilities after sentencing. The US Bureau of Justice Statistics reported that from mid-year 1990 to mid-year 1995, the number of inmates under the age of eighteen in State and federal correctional facilities rose from 3600 to 5309, an increase of nearly 50 per cent. According to these data, Florida, Connecticut, New York, North Carolina and Texas had the highest number of children incarcerated in adult correctional facilities at midyear 1995. Amnesty International's November 1998 report, *Betraying the Young: Human Rights Violations against Children in the US Justice System*, found that at least 3700 under-18-year-olds, prosecuted and convicted as adults under State laws, were being held with adults.

The US Department of Justice (DOJ) concluded a year-long investigation of the States' juvenile detention facilities in February 1998. It identified a 'pattern of egregious conditions' that violated children's rights, including overcrowded and unsafe conditions, physical abuse by staff and excessive use of disciplinary measures, and inadequate educational, medical, and mental health services. Its investigators also found that three-quarters of the children in detention were non-violent offenders, sometimes held for offences such as painting graffiti, making harassing telephone calls or disobeying a parent's rules. These children were incarcerated in jail-like facilities, where they were shackled to cell furniture for being too noisy, were physically or sexually abused by other detainees or staff, and stripped naked and shackled to a toilet for showing signs of suicidal behaviour.

The DOJ conducted at least two other investigations of juvenile facilities in 1998 and found violations of international standards in the county detention centres in Owensboro, Kentucky, and Greenville, South Carolina. In each of these facilities, the DOJ found evidence that staff employed excessive force against juvenile inmates. Each facility failed to provide adequate medical and mental health care to children in detention. Juveniles in both facilities received little or no education even though many were housed in the detention centres for extended periods of time.

In the US, several young people have been executed for acts committed before the age of 18, in violation of international standards. The imposition of the death penalty on persons who were under 18 years of age at the time of their offence violates the provisions of several international and regional human rights instruments, including the International Covenant on Civil and Political Rights (ICCPR), the Convention on the Rights of the Child, the Beijing Rules and the American Convention on Human Rights. In contrast to this international consensus, some US politicians call for children as young as 11 to be made eligible for the death penalty. For its part, the US Supreme Court, while recognising that the law should treat children and adults differently, has determined that 16 should be the minimum age for execution, not 18.

More than 70 juvenile offenders were on death row in the United States as of 1 July 1998. As Americans faced the prospect of three prisoners in their 20s being executed in January 2000 for murders committed when they were 17 years old, US Senator Russ Feingold observed, 'I don't think we should be proud of the fact that the United States is the world leader in the execution of child offenders' (Amnesty International 1999b).

In January 1995, the UN Committee found fundamental violations of children's rights in the UK following its examination of that government's report to Geneva with respect to its implementation of the UN Convention on the Rights of the Child:

> Policy after policy 'has broken the terms of the UN Convention' ... a report of the UN monitoring committee adds up to a devastating indictment of minister's failure to meet the human rights of Britain's children ... the Report is not all bad ... however, the 'positive aspects' cover only four paragraphs, and the remaining 39 are either critical or are recommendations for action. (*The Guardian*, 28 January 1995; see Goldson 1999, p 4)

Of particular concern to the UN Committee was the government's harsh policies in relation to juvenile crime, which were underpinned by retributive and punitive imperatives. The intensification and diversification of custodial institutions for children, and their pre-eminence within contemporary state responses to juvenile crime, places the UK in conflict with the overall spirit of the UN Convention on the Rights of the Child and, more specifically, some of its principal articles, most notably Article 37 which states that the 'arrest, detention or imprisonment of the child ... shall be used only as a measure of last resort and for the shortest appropriate time'. This failure means that other related international instruments to which the UK is also formally committed have also been breached: the Beijing Rules 1985, the Riyadh Guidelines 1990, and the Havana Rules 1990 (Goldson 1999, p 11.)

Several UK juvenile detention facilities have also been found to be appalling. For instance, reporting in 1998 on the conditions under which young offenders were being held in Warrington Young Offenders Institution, the Chief Inspector of Prisons says:

> I ... find it quite incredible that the Prison Service should have thought it appropriate to remove tolerable although not ideal arrangements for the treatment of children in custody in favour of utterly unsuitable conditions ... [S]enior management failed to provide sufficient, or appropriate, resources to go with the increased numbers. To find children no longer eating together, but forced to take their food back to their cells, which are little more than lavatories ... would be bad enough. To find that adult prison conditions have been deliberately introduced ... is nothing short of disgraceful. (quoted in Pitts 1999, p 153)

Together with poor social services such as education and health, the bullying and abuse of inmates make these unsatisfactory physical conditions all the more intolerable and the institutions highly inconsistent with international standards.

Blagg and Wilkie (1995) have argued that few States in Australia appear to have heeded the UN International Covenant on Civil and Political Rights (1966) charges for governments to ensure that children have the right to such powers and measures as required by their status as minors. Fewer still now emphasise the UN Beijing rules (Standard Minimum Rules for the Administration of Juvenile Justice 1985) which provide guidance to States for the protection of children's rights and respect for their needs in the development of separate and specialised systems of juvenile justice.

At the close of the 20th century, Australian States and Territories seemed to have paid less and less attention to the United Nations Guidelines for the Prevention of Juvenile Delinquency (the Riyadh Guidelines) which outline social policies to be applied to prevent and protect young people from offending. Similarly ignored is the United Nations Rules for the Protection of Juveniles Deprived of their Liberty (the JDL Rules) which established measures for social re-integration of young people once deprived of their liberty, whether in prison or other institutions. Australia also falls short of the standards that the UN Convention on the Rights of the Child embodies (ibid, p 7).

In recent times, the work of the Australasian Juvenile Justice Centre Managers (from across Australia and New Zealand) to strengthen links between the community and young people in custodial facilities to increase their chances of reintegration on release represents a bright spot in an otherwise bleak record. Of particular significance is their work on the Australasian Standards for Juvenile Custodial Facilities which became a focal point for discussion during their second annual conference in 2000 (Department of Human Services 2000). Be that as it may, of the countries selected for this research, none can wholly present an enviable record of compliance with most of the juvenile justice decalogue that I formulated at the beginning of this section.

As Amnesty International (2000) observes recently, the Western Australia and the Northern Territory mandatory sentencing laws for juveniles were clearly inconsistent with Australia's international human rights obligations. The Northern Territory legislation was repealed in 2001 by a new government formed by the Australian Labor Party, but there is no gainsaying the fact that wherever these laws exist they take away the ability of the courts in those jurisdictions to sentence juvenile offenders according to international human rights standards.

Conclusion

To be a young, poor, unemployed and ethnic-minority male is to be in no position to protect oneself against or present much trouble to the legal process. When this coincides with the image of a 'villain', an image mostly constructed by the media and widely accepted by the public and the criminal justice agencies, one becomes most vulnerable to apprehension, arrest, prosecution, and detention, whether or not one commits crimes or does so disproportionately to others.

The seemingly intractable nature of the perceived rising rate of youth crime and the strong verdict that the punitive system is out of step with the international standards for wholesome development of children suggest that the traditional criminal justice approach to youth crime is anachronistic. In all the countries studied in this book, there is the appearance of acute awareness of this fact, yet these countries nevertheless appear firmly wedded to this anachronism.

Notes

1   Herbert Lou of juvenile courts in the United States in 1927. 'Best interest' approaches are still common today in several western systems of juvenile justice.

2   As I will show later in this chapter, even the post-19th century American system which seemed to have a distinctive origin and focus on treatment rather than punishment parallels the adult orientation at least in process, if not in outcome.

3   See, for examples, Consedine 1996; Rutherford 1998; and Wundersitz 2000.

4   In fact, the practice of apprenticing out the poor youths had commenced in the US by the early 17th century. This was based on a similar practice in England since the Poor Law of 1601 where 'young paupers were taken into poorhouses and then apprenticed out to rural areas' (see Bernard 1992, p 67).

5   It would appear that a House of Refuge for female juveniles had already been opened in 1823 (See Bartollas 1996, p 302).

6   A 14-year-old boy indicted for larceny, tried and sent to the House of Refuge by the newly established juvenile court in Philadelphia. The Supreme Court held that 'due process' was not necessary for the State, when compelled as parens patriae, to lead a child into one of its courts for the purpose of saving and shielding the child 'from the consequences of persistence in a career of waywardness'.

7   Under this legislation, the first separate juvenile institution, the Parkhurst Prison for boys, was opened in 1838.

8   It should be recalled that in the US the so-called welfare-based juvenile court system was introduced about 50 years after the first separate holding institution for juveniles was established.

9   The change in policy and law towards the justice model will be discussed in detail in Chapter 5.

10   In criticising this doctrine, Gibbons (1977, p 97) was rather unrestrained, arguing that it made juvenile courts little more than 'a crude piece of social apparatus'.

11   In an earlier case of Morris Kent, the first ever juvenile case to be heard by the American Supreme Court, the Court had shown inclinations to replace parens patriae with 'due process' as the main protection for children processed through juvenile courts.

12   The fact that most of the States' legislative frameworks were titled 'Child Welfare Act' suggests this inference.

13   As at the time of writing, NSW was one exception to this trend.

14   Interestingly, the Report also identified 21 States with provisions for 'reverse waiver', allowing criminal court judges to transfer cases from criminal court to juvenile court under circumstances specified in the law. For example, in Arkansas, when a prosecutor directly files a case in criminal court, the criminal court judge may remand the case to the juvenile court.

15   Unlike the US and the UK, Australia's jurisdictions named their juvenile courts as Children's Courts. In 1993, South Australia changed the name to Youth Court 'ostensibly to reflect the perception that the court is not dealing with vulnerable children but with young adults who need to be held responsible and punished for their actions' (Wundersitz 2000, p 105).

16   Details about the British case are presented later. In the US case, the youth was shooting a 30-year-old rifle with the stock missing on 29 October 1997 when, according to ballistic evidence, a bullet that had probably ricocheted off a tree accidentally killed a young man leaving a convenience store nearly 100 yards away. Under a law promulgated by the Michigan State Legislature, the prosecutor may request permission to try any youth as an adult, with no lower age limit. Arrested at age 11, Nathaniel was held in custody for two years until trial and brought into court shackled.

17   For example, s 138B(1) of the Western Australian *Child Welfare Act* 1947 gives power to the police to apprehend a child who is away from his or her place of residence, not under the immediate supervision of a responsible person and who is 'in physical or moral danger, misbehaving or truanting from school'. Part 3 of the New South Wales *Children (Parental Responsibility) Act* 1994, now repealed and replaced by *Children (Protection &Parental Responsibility) Act* 1997, gave police in certain regions powers to 'prevent' juvenile offending.

18   In several countries, this actually means a black kid in a white neighbourhood.

19   99 Nevada at 432, 664 at 950 (1983).

20   See the International Covenant on Civil and Political Rights (ICCPR).

21   See the Convention on the Rights of the Child (CROC).

22   See the Standard Minimum Rules for the Administration of Juvenile Justice (the Beijing Rules).

23   See the UN Rules for the Protection of Juveniles Deprived of Their Liberty (Havana Rule).

24   See the UN Guidelines for the Prevention of Juvenile Delinquency (the Riyadh Guidelines).

25   My formulation of these standards does not faithfully reproduce the wordings of the provisions of the various instruments that I reviewed. Readers should consult these instruments for the actual wordings of the standards.

4

Trends and costs of traditional criminal justice response to youth crime

Until our society grapples adequately with the shortcomings of a retributive criminal justice philosophy, we will continue to have increasing crime rates, higher imprisonment numbers, less safety in the community, and an extremely expensive ever-expanding prison system. (Consedine 1995, p 40)

Traditional criminal justice practices in the Western world, reinforced by mutual stereotyping between criminal justice agencies and young people, have produced disturbing trends and fiscal costs in relation to youth crime since the 1980s. Unlike most conventional works in criminology, this book takes the view that the trends and costs of youth crime are as much a function of stereotypy and how all parties react to it as they are of socio-structural factors usually presented as 'criminological facts'.

For instance, none of the widely accepted 13 'facts', identified by Braithwaite (1989, pp 44-49),[1] highlights the role that operational practices of the justice agencies play in criminal statistics. Nor do the facts show that many of these practices represent on the one hand the agencies' reaction to their own socially constructed images of youth and, on the other, young people's active contribution to this imaging as shown in Chapters 1 and 2 of this book. Six of the 'facts' directly attribute a greater proportion of crime to young males between 15 and 25 years old who are less attached to their schools, have low educational and occupational aspirations, do poorly at school, are weakly attached to their parents and have friendships with criminals. Three other 'facts' identify marital status, high residential mobility and weak belief in complying with the law as pre-disposing conditions in youth crime. The remaining four 'facts' are only remotely concerned with youth. On the whole, none makes reference to reactive policing, punitive judging, destructive detention and negative stereotyping as factors that contribute to the rates and costs of youth crime.

Conventional criminology also presents juvenile crime statistics in terms of a simple direct link between trends in youth crime and the pro-portion of young people in the total population of an area. I argue that the relationship is both complex and highly contingent. The emphasis of the chapter, though, is on two main issues: first, to show the disjuncture between the types and trends in youth crime on the one hand and, on the other, the punitive responses of the criminal justice agencies. While the level of youth crime as measured by police arrests goes down, court processing and detention go up (for example, see LaPrairie 1999 on Canada and Zimring 2001b on the US). Next, the chapter illustrates the fiscal costs of these responses in terms of how much the state, on average, expends on policing, prosecuting and correcting young offenders and the 'value' accruing from the costs. All this will shed further light on the context within which the new preventive 'partnership' paradigm began to attract the attention of the criminal justice agencies as sections of the state apparatus in search of creative solutions to the crime problem.

Trends in youth crime:
demography is not destiny

Traditionally, trends of youth crime have been attributed to the proportion of youth in the total population.[2] While this attribution cannot be dismissed outright, any claim that there is a direct relationship between the two variables is, at best, simplistic and, at worst, misleading. As with other 'criminological facts', this claim does not acknowledge other compounding factors in the movement of crime trends.

Proponents of the direct relationship frequently call time series studies to their defence. For instance, one such study found that during the two World Wars countries that sent a large number of young soldiers to fight overseas, thus decreasing their youth populations, also recorded a significant drop in the level of crimes during the war years (Mukherjee 1997). Commenting on the Australian crime trends in the 1850s to 1970s period, Mukherjee (2000, p 50) says:

> [D]uring the two wars, offences against the person and good order offences declined substantially. These are offences committed predominantly by young males. A significant proportion of such young males were in the defence forces at this time.

Recently, a predicted rise in the sheer number of juveniles in the US, with demographers estimating a 31 per cent increase in juvenile population by 2010, has been used to project an increase in youth crime in the US. This is dubbed 'a potential time bomb' for the 21st century (American Psychological Association 1996; Gest and Pope 1996; Governor's Crime Commission, North Carolina 1996).

However, other research works have shown an inverse relationship between youth crime and youth population. For instance, while America's youth population decreased from 14 per cent of the total US population in 1983 to 11 per cent in 1993, the arrest rate (still one of the best official indicators of criminal justice response to crime) for juveniles who committed index violent crimes increased from 16.4 per cent to 18.4 per cent. When the juvenile population grew between 1993 and 1997, the arrest rates for juveniles for homicides declined by about 39 per cent following a similar pattern to youth crime in general (Bilchick 1999).

In England and Wales, recorded crime committed by juveniles (10-17 year olds) rose by 54 per cent in the 1980s when the youth population fell by 25 per cent (Pitts and Hope 1998, p 38). Australian experience equally challenges the direct relationship proposition. In two decades, 1973-74 to 1994-95, the total number of reported major violent and property crimes and arrest rates for young people (males in particular) increased, while the proportion of young people under 18 years old declined from 35 per cent to 25.4 per cent of the Australian population.

Walker and Henderson (1991) had argued that the strong increases in property crime in Australia during the early 1970s were demography-related: the 10-17 year age group was expanding. So also was the increase in the violent crimes as this cohort moved into the 18-24 year group. Yet, these crimes kept up their momentum for most of the 1980s and early 1990s when the population of the 10-24 year olds was in fact in decline. In those States where the actual number of young people arrested for serious offences declined especially in the 1990s, the increase in the overall rates suggests that the youth population was declining during the same period.

The tyranny of 'small numbers'

In addition to the unsettled relationship between demography and youth crime trends, crime statistics distort the picture of juvenile crime in comparison with adult crime. At least four 'direct' reasons account for this. First, young people are more likely than adults to be caught. Secondly, they tend to commit offences in groups, so that for one offence there are a number of offenders. Thirdly, they tend to commit offences which have high reporting rates, such as car theft and break and enters. Last, figures do not differentiate well between the different offending patterns of young people of different age groups.

As an indirect reason, crime statistics usually cannot distinguish whether increases or decreases are related to:

- levels of reporting of crime (eg car theft is usually reported because of insurance);

- population changes (especially the growing numbers of young people in absolute and relative terms); and

- changes in juvenile justice laws and practices (especially in police numbers, location and priorities; the number of behaviours criminalised; the age bracket prescribed as juvenile; and the age of criminal culpability).

On their own or in combination, these reasons create a distorted view of juvenile offending. It has led the media and others to exaggerate the contribution of juveniles both to the total volume of violent crime and to the increase over a period, giving rise to what is known as the 'tyranny of small numbers' syndrome (Howell 1997, p 50). In the analysis of increases in arrests for violent crimes between 1985 and 1994 in the US, for instance,

Snyder and his colleagues illustrate the 'tyranny of small numbers' principle, as shown below (Snyder, Sickmund and Poe-Yamagata 1996).

The number of violent crimes reported to law enforcement agencies in the US increased 40 per cent between 1985 and 1994. Knowing that over the same period juvenile arrests for violent crimes grew 75 per cent, while adult arrests increased 48 per cent, some may conclude that juveniles were responsible for most of the increase in violent crime. However, even though the percentage increase in juvenile arrests was more than the adult increase, the majority of the growth came from the adults. The following example shows how this apparent contradiction can occur.

Assume that of the 100 violent crimes committed in 1985 in a small town, juveniles were responsible for 10 and adults for 90. If the number of juvenile violent crimes increased 70 per cent in 1994, juveniles would be committing 17 in total or 7 more violent crimes. A 50 per cent increase in adult violent crimes would mean that adults were committing 135 or 45 more. This brings the total of violent crime in 1994 to 152, 52 per cent higher than the 1985 number. If each crime resulted in arrest, the percentage increase in juvenile arrests would be more than the adult increase (70 per cent versus 50 per cent). However, 87 per cent of the total increase (45 of the additional 52 violent crimes) would have been committed by adults. A large percentage increase in juvenile arrests does not necessarily translate into a large contribution to overall crime growth. Thus, growth cannot be attributed to juveniles without establishing what the base figures were in the first place.

This syndrome is used to further illustrate the tenuous nature of the argument that, because there is overall growth in youth population, the rate of youth crime will necessarily increase. The underlying relationships are far more complex and will not be adequately understood if the broader factors such as political ideologies, legislative changes, perceptual frameworks and criminal justice activities are not examined.

The next three sections should be read with this caveat in mind. Further, readers should be careful not to draw comparative conclusions about the various countries from the face value of the crime figures mainly because of differences in 'crime' and 'youth' definitions or classifications and criminal justice cultures. Although 'juvenile' and 'youth' are used interchangeably for convenience, the two concepts refer to different age categories in some of the countries.

Trends in police arrest

In the US, juveniles accounted for about 49 per cent of the total arrests in 1965. This figure decreased to 31.3 per cent in 1974, 31 per cent in 1984 and 21.7 per cent in 1994 (Siegel and Senna 1988; Shepherd 1997). Figures from the Federal Bureau of Investigation's *Uniform Crime Reporting Program* indicate that in 1997 juveniles accounted for only 19 per cent of all arrests (Snyder 1998; Bilchik 1999). Thus, between 1965 and 1997, the juvenile proportion of total arrests declined by 30 per cent. The decline may be puzzling, but it nonetheless provides no obvious support for the screaming media about juvenile crime wave.[3]

The juvenile violent crime rate increased more than 60 per cent between 1988 and 1994, but then decreased 23 per cent from 1994 to 1997 (Snyder 1998) and was still going down at the close of the 20th century. Similarly, arrest rates of juveniles for homicide increased substantially between 1988 and 1994 but declined 39 per cent from 1994 to 1997. These decreases occurred at the same time that there had been continuing growth in the juvenile population. It is also important to note that, in 1997, only a fraction – less than half of 1 per cent – of juveniles age 10 to 17 were arrested for a violent crime (ibid). Further, less than 20 per cent of juvenile offenders were being arrested for the great majority of violent juvenile crime in American communities (Sickmund, Snyder, and Poe-Yamagata 1997).

Across Canada, the UK and Australasia, the arrest rates for young offenders generally declined in the last five years of the 1990s. In Canada, the rate of young people arrested for violent crimes fell 1 per cent in 1998, the third straight annual decline. The general arrest trends in Australia for serious assault, break, enter and steal, motor vehicle theft and fraud, increased gradually, peaking in 1992-93 (Mukherjee and Graycar 1997, p 47). Since then, the arrest trends have been declining. In Western Australia for instance, the total arrests of juveniles declined consistently from 3414 in 1994 to 3132 in 1998 (Ferrante, Fernandez and Loh 1999).

The New Zealand total juvenile arrest trends in the 1990s involving 14 to 16 year olds increased by 19 per cent over the decade (Table 4.1). However, in rate terms, the trends only increased from 129 per 1000 in 1990 to 196 in 1995 before declining to 186 in 1998 (*Justice Matters* 1999).

The reasons for all these declining trends in all the countries are yet to be fully determined, but it can be said with some certainty that they coincided with the height of public dissatisfaction with the old ways and the criminal justice agencies embracing a more enlightened approach to crime control.

The gender of those apprehended in all the countries cited presents an interesting picture. Juvenile female arrests and involvement in at-risk and delinquent behaviour continue to rise at a rate which is quickly drawing attention to the needs of girls. In 1997, females accounted for 26 per cent of all juvenile arrests in the US (Snyder 1998). Females are increasingly becoming involved in violent offending as well. The growth in juvenile violent crime arrest rates between 1987 and 1994 was far greater for females than for males and the decline after 1994 was less for females than males (ibid).

In recent years, concern has grown in Canada about increasing violence by young women. The rate for female young people charged with violent crime is still only one-third the rate for their male counterparts. However, since 1988 the rate of violent crime among female young people has more than doubled (+127 per cent), compared with an increase of 65 per cent among male young people. Females charged with violent crime tend to be

Table 4.1: Number of offenders aged 14 to 16 apprehended by the police in New Zealand for non-traffic offences, by type of offence, 1987 to 1996

Offence Type	1987	1988	1989	1990	1991	1992	1993	1994	1995	1996	Overall % change
Violence	1841	1786	1641	1484	1681	1813	2447	2881	3139	3195	+74%
Sexual	170	166	150	163	148	113	158	157	121	163	-4%
Drugs/Anti-social[1]	4275	3920	3542	2841	2487	2244	2995	3357	3616	3964	-7%
Dishonest[2]	17164	14439	15649	14200	14440	15529	17323	17271	18089	18094	+5%
Property damage	1306	1449	1271	1360	1670	1676	2109	2642	2694	2977	+128%
Property abuse	1440	1643	1428	1355	1687	1708	2023	1884	2153	2193	+52%
Administrative	182	224	282	221	244	263	324	487	577	684	+276%
Total	26378	23627	23963	21624	2357	23346	27379	28679	30389	31270	+19%

Notes:
1. Includes all drug offences, obstructing or resisting police officers, disorderly behaviour, language offences, 'family' offences, and Sale of Liquor Act offences.
2. Burglary, vehicle conversion, theft, receiving stolen property, and fraud.

Source: Adapted from New Zealand Ministry of Justice (1998)

younger than their male counterparts. Among males, the violent crime rate increased gradually with age, the highest rate being among 17 year olds. Among females, the rate peaked at the ages of 14 and 15.[4] For girls in Australia, the arrest proportion increased fourfold, from 4 per cent to 18 per cent between 1974 and 1994.

Ethnic background is another operative factor in arrest trends. In North America, the UK and Australasia, ethnic minority youth comprise a disproportionately higher percentage of youth arrests than the majority youth. For instance, although blacks and whites in the US have approximately the same rate of drug use, blacks who are no more than 15 per cent of the juvenile population constitute more than 34 per cent of those arrested for drug offences. From 1986 to 1991, arrests of white juveniles for drug offences decreased 34 per cent, while arrests of minority juveniles increased 78 per cent (Leadership Conference on Civil Rights 2000, p 37). Similar disparities appear in relation to non-drug-related crimes. African-American juveniles accounted for 49 per cent of arrests for violent crimes in 1992. US law enforcement agencies made an estimated 2.6 million arrests of persons under age 18 in 1998. More than 26 per cent involved black youth, clearly establishing a case of over-representation (Building Blocks for Youth 2000).

Similarly, West Indians in the UK are more likely to be arrested. Analysis of the 1994 and 1996 British Crime Surveys shows they were more likely than white or Asian people to be stopped while in a vehicle or on foot and 12 per cent of those stopped were more likely to be arrested compared to 6 per cent of Asians and 3 per cent of whites. The story is similar, in some cases worse, for indigenous youth in Australia, Canada and New Zealand. For instance, National Police Custody Surveys in Australia show 'a continuing heavy involvement of indigenous children (compared to non-indigenous children) in the criminal justice system, in particular the elevated portion of Aboriginal children being [arrested and] held in cells by police' (Commonwealth of Australia 1997, p 491).

Trends in court processing

Juvenile courts in the United States processed an estimated 1.5 million delinquency cases in 1992 and the number rose to 1.8 million in 1996 before dropping slightly to 1.76 in 1997 (Table 4.2). In the UK, the total number of persons prosecuted in the courts rose from 1.92 million in 1987 to 2.05 million in 1992, and fell to 1.86 million in 1997. The proportion of these numbers that were 10-21 years old remained fairly constant at 19 per cent (Home Office 1999). Similarly, the proportion of youth prosecuted for criminal offences in Canada remained constant at 22 per cent during 1995-99 (Table 4.3).

Australia and New Zealand present a unique feature in that the trends of the cases prosecuted in court involving young persons for all offences declined substantially over a similar period. In Australia, the Western Australia experience is noteworthy in this regard. The number of juveniles dealt with by the Children's Court in this jurisdiction fell 40 per cent from 10,513 in 1990 to 4155 in 1998 (Ferrante, Fernandez and Loh 1999, p 111). The most dramatic fall occurred in 1995 when the diversionary scheme of referring juveniles away from the Court to Juvenile Justice Teams that was formalised in 1994 came into full operation.

Table 4.2: Delinquency cases processed by juvenile courts in the US, 1992-97

Year	Estimated number	Percentage change
1992	1,471,200	–
1993	1,506,788	2.4
1994	1,555,200	3.2
1995	1,700,000	9.3
1996	1,800,000	5.9
1997	1,755,100	-2.5

Sources: Constructed from Butts (1992) and Stahl (1997)

Table 4.3 Youth and adults charged in all criminal incidents in Canada, 1995-99

Year	Youth	Adults	Total	Youth %
1995	128,809	454,465	583,274	22
1996	128,542	454,971	583,513	22
1997	120,208	429,898	550,106	22
1998	117,542	427,608	545,150	22
1999	111,474	426,838	538,312	21

Source: Constructed from Statistics Canada, Catalogue no 85-205-XIB

In New Zealand, the decline was by 64 per cent from 10,910 in 1987 to 3908 in 1996 (Table 4.4) and, like Western Australia, this coincided with the introduction of the *Children, Young Persons, and Their Families Act* 1989 (CYP&F) with its emphasis on diverting young people from formal pro-secution processes in court. It resulted in a large drop in the total number of cases involving young people that came before the courts in 1990. Although the number was decreasing steadily anyway, the introduction of the CYP&F Act saw the total number of cases drop sharply from 8193 in 1989 to 2352 in 1990. There has generally been a slowly increasing trend in the number of cases since then. In 1996, there were 3908 cases involving young people which came before the courts, but as indicated earlier this was still 64 per cent less than in 1987.

Table 4.4 Outcomes of prosecutions involving young people for all offences except non-imprisonable traffic offences, 1987 to 1996 in New Zealand*

Outcome	1987	1988	1989	1990	1991	1992	1993	1994	1995	1996	Overall % Change
Convicted	1344	1368	1213	286	255	228	440	488	290	341	-75%
s.19 Discharge	27	8	6	3	9	1	4	6	3	3	–
Youth Court Proved	7944	6856	5410	855	991	846	859	871	1141	1220	-85%
Not Proved	1526	1231	1551	1202	1619	1624	1874	2104	2442	2326	+52%
Other	69	56	13	6	2	0	0	4	10	18	–
Total	10910	9519	8193	2352	2876	2699	3177	3473	3886	3908	-64%

* Includes cases where there was a stay of proceedings. Also includes cases where the person was found to be under disability or was acquitted on account of insanity, and was committed to a hospital under s 115 of the *Criminal Justice Act 1985*.

Source: Adapted from New Zealand Ministry of Justice (1998)

A gender analysis shows that in 1992, four out of five delinquency cases in the US involved a male juvenile (81 per cent). This proportion declined to 79 per cent in 1994 and further by 1 per cent from 1995 to 1997. The implication of this is that the proportion of female juvenile involvement rose from 19 per cent in 1992 to 22 per cent in 1997. In fact over a more extended period (between 1988 and 1997), the number of delinquency cases involving females increased 83 per cent (from 225,100 to 412,200), compared with a 39 per cent increase for males (960,800 to 1,342,900). The growth in female cases outpaced the growth for males for all offence categories except drug violations.

All things considered, youth crime in the other countries studied remains essentially a male phenomenon. In Australia, as in Canada, the UK and New Zealand, although the gap between rates of involvement by males and females in crime has been narrowing since the late 1980s, the young perpetrator of serious offences is five times more likely to be male than females. Inter-jurisdictional data in Australia show that gender differences in relation to robbery during late 1970s and most of 1980s did not change much (Mukherjee and Dagger 1990, p 75).

The number of females charged with an offence in Australia during the 1981-98 period increased, but this did not translate into an increase in incarceration as it did for young males. The type of offences committed by young females seems to be of a less serious nature than the type committed by their male counterparts; and females had reduced recidivism rates or took a longer period to reoffend. In fact, the rate of female detainees generally declined from 17.2 per cent in 1981 to 6.3 per cent in 1998. This decline was driven mainly by the trends in NSW, Victoria and Queensland. Western Australian and South Australian figures 'remained relatively stable' over the period.

With regard to racial characteristics, court-processed cases show a remarkable disparity. Following the arrest trends we saw earlier, this is hardly surprising, except that the ratio at this level increased rather significantly. During most of the 1990s (1992-97), the juvenile population of the US was about 80 per cent white and 15 per cent black. White juveniles, however, were involved in an average of 65 per cent of the delinquency cases handled by juvenile courts. For the black juveniles, the average was 32 per cent of these delinquency cases, again clearly showing an overrepresentation. The 5 per cent 'other' youth had only 3 per cent involvement with the court system.

In 1997, for instance, although the majority of cases referred to juvenile court involved white youth the proportion involving African-American youth was twice their proportion in the population. Thus, of the estimated 1,755,100 delinquency cases referred to the nation's juvenile courts in that year, 66 per cent involved white youth whose proportion of the entire youth population was 79 per cent, 31 per cent involved African-American youth with 15 per cent of the youth population and 3 per cent involved youth of other races who made up 5 per cent of the relevant population.

Minority youth in the UK, especially of West Indian descent are also over-represented in the court processes. An analysis by the Inner London Probation Service shows that, during the 1993-95 period, 647 cases of street robbery were recorded and, of those who were charged, 48 per cent were black, 35 per cent were white and the remaining 17 per cent were either not recorded or given as other. During the same period a quarter of the defendants questioned during the compilation of all reports were black. In all this black persons are clearly over-represented.

Australia's indigenous youth have about 10-15 per cent greater chance of being processed through the courts than their white counterpart suspected offenders (see, for example, Luke and Cunneen 1995). In New Zealand, over half (56 per cent or more) of the cases dealt with in court for which the ethnicity of the young person was known, involved Maori; 32 per cent involved the Pakehas (NZ Europeans) and 11 per cent involved Pacific peoples.

Trends in detention

From 1985 to 1995, the number of youth held in secure detention nation-wide in the US increased steadily by 72 per cent, from 13,400 to 23,000 (Lubow 1999, p 16). This had no direct relationship with actual trends in crime rates. The rate of incarceration increased both when the crime rate was going up and when it was going down. The percentage of youth held in overcrowded centres rose from 20 per cent to 62 per cent during the decade, 1985-95.[5]

The US passed a major threshold in 2000 when it recorded more than two million people behind bars, a significant proportion of which were young. This places the US way ahead of most of the rest of the world when it comes to locking up their population. In fact, the closest rivals were the old Soviet Union and the old South Africa, both now out of business. The real source of the staggering growth in the percentage of America's population in jail is the wave of punitive legislation and law enforcement policy that has spread across America (Adolph Reed, Jr 2000).

Research shows that, relative to their proportion in the referral population, white youth are generally under-represented while African-American youth are over-represented in the detained population. The over-representation of minority youth increased from 43 per cent to 56 per cent during the same period. The 1997 figures illustrate this vividly. An estimated 326,800 delinquent youths were detained in that year. Of 66 per cent of the white youth referred to juvenile court, a smaller percentage (53 per cent) were locked up in detention facilities. Conversely, a larger percentage of African-American youth referred to juvenile court were locked up in detention facilities: 31 per cent referred, 44 per cent detained. This pattern of disproportion was across all offence categories but was most dramatic among drug offence cases.

An Office of Juvenile Justice and Delinquency Prevention 1999 study reported that on 29 October 1997 there were 105,790 young people in juvenile detention facilities prior to adjudication or committed to state juvenile correctional facilities following adjudication. Minority youth represented almost two-thirds (63 per cent) of this number although they represent only about one-third (34 per cent) of the total adolescent population in the country. Nationally, 204 white youth were in residential placement on that day for every 100,000 youth in the population compared to 1018 African-American youth, 515 Latino youth, 525 Native-American youth, and 203 Asian youth. Custody rates for African-American, Latino and Native-American youth were 5.0, 2.5, and 2.6 times higher than those of white youth respectively (Building Blocks for Youth 2000).

The United Kingdom's undifferentiated custodial population, including untried, convicted unsentenced, detained under sentence in a young offender institution, and detained under s 53 of *Children and Young Persons Act* 1933, increased from 1995 to 1997 but has been on a marginal decline since. The female custodial population commenced an upward movement since 1997 and has not abated.

Table 4.5 Custodial population of 15-17 year-old offenders in England and Wales, 1995-99

	1995	1996	1997	1998	1999
Male	1626	2024	2408	2387	2336
Female	49	69	71	79	86
Total	1675	2093	2479	2466	2422

Source: Constructed from *Criminal Statistics*, Home Office.

About 80 per cent of all young male offenders who were jailed during the 1995-99 period had at least one previous conviction. In the categories of 1-2, 3-6, 7-10, and 11 and over previous convictions, the largest proportion had 3-6 previous convictions.

In Canada, the number of custodial dispositions of youth cases showed no steady pattern between 1994 and 1999. In proportion, however, this form of disposition rose slightly from 33 per cent in 1995 to 35 per cent in 1999 (Table 4.6).

Table 4.6 Custodial disposition of youth cases in Canada, 1994-99

Year	Custodial disposition	% of all dispositions
1994-95	25212	33
1995-96	24312	33
1996-97	25278	34
1997-98	25669	34
1998-99	25169	35

Source: Constructed from *Statistics Canada*. Online:
          <http://www/statcan.ca/english/Pgdb/State/Justice/legal>

In Australia, the number of persons in juvenile corrective institutions per 100,000 of the 10-17 year old population increased from 577 in 1992 and has stabilised around 780 since 1996. Table 4.7 illustrates the variation between the jurisdictions in Australia in relation to juvenile incarceration. The number of persons held on remand, as a percentage of the total number of persons in juvenile corrective institutions, also increased from 21.4 per cent in 1981 to 42.6 per cent in 1998 (Carcach and Muscat 1999).

Table 4.7 Rate of juveniles (10-17 years) in Australia's corrective institutions, 1992-98

Year	Rate per 100,000 relevant population								
	NSW	Vic	Qld	WA	SA	Tas	NT	ACT	Aus
1992	38.88	10.34	20.06	46.49	33.25	8.79	127.06	26.80	28.55
1993	46.40	10.23	22.68	51.59	38.45	15.83	102.71	16.15	32.19
1994	54.77	12.89	24.93	64.31	36.42	17.59	57.45	24.27	36.89
1995	57.83	14.87	35.06	49.33	24.44	17.51	74.78	37.77	38.33
1996	49.33	13.98	34.44	50.41	51.64	45.38	56.14	18.91	37.66
1997	51.39	14.11	24.94	51.97	47.83	40.20	89.38	43.75	37.11
1998	48.01	13.22	33.61	62.65	30.93	33.52	103.53	30.39	37.01

Source: Carcach and Muscat (1999, p 12)

The national rate of incarceration among indigenous young offenders declined from 538.2 per 100,000 in 1993 to 406.6 in 1998. Compared with the rates for non-indigenous youth (20.66 in 1993 and 21.99 in 1998), however, this decline does little to dent the mountain of over-representation for Aboriginal young offenders in custodial corrections. The seasonally adjusted data for the last quarter of each year within this period show that the over-representation ratio in fact changed from 16.2 in 1993 to 18.5 in 1998 (Carcach and Muscat 1999, p 24). Census of persons in juvenile detention taken on 30 June 1998 shows that the rate of Aboriginal young detainees ranged from 7.8 in the Northern Territory to 31.8 in Western Australia (Ferrante, Fernandez and Loh 1999, p 118).

A key feature of the indigenous youth custodial trend is the declining age at which some of these young people are incarcerated. During the 1990s, age at entry tended to get much younger than in the previous decades. In Queensland, for example, 56 per cent of all 13 year olds and 81 per cent of all 14-year olds detained were Aborigines (Lincoln and Wilson 2000, p 211). These figures were less in the previous years and, more significantly, they show an increasing proportion of persons incarcerated in this age category. Populating our jails with children under 15 years does take us back to the pre-child saving movement era and goes against contemporary international standards as discussed in Chapter 3.

In New Zealand, the total number of cases involving a young offender which resulted in a custodial sentence more than halved when the CYP&F Act was introduced. The total number of custodial sentences imposed has remained at a lower level since then. Despite the lower number of cases resulting in a custodial sentence from 1990, a slightly higher proportion of proved cases has resulted in a custodial sentence since the introduction of the Act. Even with this, it is remarkable how the New Zealand diversionary scheme drove the detention rate downwards when the Western Australian scheme did not have a similar impact (see Table 4.7). In fact, New Zealand closed all but one of its secure institutions for young offenders in 1990; it found that 'saving money by closing juvenile institutions [has] great appeal' (Strang 2000, p 25).

Trends in victimisation of young people

Often, the focus on youth crime overlooks the criminological fact that young people are the most likely group to become victims of serious crime (including robbery, theft, physical and sexual violence) compared to adult groups (Halstead 1992). Put differently, it is not a complete criminological story to state that young people commit crime disproportionately. They also suffer from it disproportionately. Between 1987 and 1992, violent victimisation (rape, robbery and assault) was highest among the 12-24 year olds in the US (Howell 1997, p 57). The National Crime Victimization Survey shows that juveniles age 12 to 17 were nearly three times as likely as adults to be victims of violent crimes in the mid-1990s (Sickmund et al, 1997).

When the British Crime Survey (BCS) questioned 12-15 year olds in 1992, nearly 20 per cent reported having experienced a crime in the previous six months. The Audit Commission showed in 1996 that young people were more likely to be victims of personal crime than adults. According to this 1996 BCS, young people are generally at greater risk of all types of violence than older people, with almost 21 per cent of men aged 16-25 reported being victims of violent crime, as against 4 per cent of men aged 26 or above. Eleven per cent of women aged 16-25 years old reported being the victim of some kind of violent crime, but less than 3 per cent of women aged 26 or above did.

Canadian and New Zealand data show similar victimisation experiences for young people. In Canada, for instance, young people tend to victimise others who are about the same age and who are known to them. Six in 10 victims of violent crime were acquaintances of the accused young person. More than half (52 per cent) of the victims were youths themselves. Only 2 per cent of victims of youth crime were aged 55 and over in 1998 (*Juristat: Youth violent crime* Vol 19, no 13).

During the 1993-97 period, 15-24 year olds consistently had the highest victimisation rate for personal crimes in Australia. In 1993, the rate was 7.9 per 100 persons, about 75 per cent more than the next rate of 4.5 for the 25-

34 year olds (Mukherjee and Graycar 1997, p 26). In 1997 the rates range from 0.75 per 100,000 population (for manslaughter) through 326.17 (for sexual assault) to 2765.04 (for assault) (ABS 1999). The victimisation prevalence rate for 15-19 year olds was the highest at 10.6 per cent, with males in this group having a rate of 12.3 per cent and females 8.7 per cent (Mukherjee 2000, p 55). The 1998 crime and safety survey shows that young males aged 15-24 years had a relatively high prevalence of victimisation for robbery: 22 out of 1000 males in the 15-19 years bracket and 12 out of 1000 males in the 20-24 years bracket (McLennan 2000, p 306)

An Australian case study of homicide victims and offenders by Carcach (1997) found that over a seven-year period (1989-96), 28 per cent of the 2415 victims of homicide incidents were aged below 25 years. The male victims outnumbered females by around two to one. The 18-24 year olds had the highest risk of becoming victims, mostly from 'stranger homicides'. One sixth of the victims had a previous criminal record and about a third of the victims had high levels of blood alcohol at the time of their victimisation. Other notable findings of this study include:

- Most youth victims of homicide belong to the same racial group as their victimisers.
- Most young people become victims as a result of altercations/ revenge homicides and in the course of other crimes such as robbery, sexual assault and arson.
- Many victims died from homicide incidents at their homes and pubs or related environments.
- Youth involvement in homicide, as victims and offenders, is remarkably the result of lifestyle and routine activity patterns, involving high risk places.

It is important to note that much of this victimisation of youth by homicide arose in conditions characterised by intense social exclusion. Evidently opportunities for meaningful participation have been diminishing for our youth over the past 10 years so that 'living' seems pointless and risky lifestyle becomes attractive. The tragedy of a socially induced victimisation of our youth is that 'the killing of a young person represents the loss of many years of potentially productive, active life'.[6]

Reflections on trends in youth crime and victimisation

A full picture of youth crime and victimisation may never be obtained. The barriers to this are many and difficult to surmount. Crime statistics at best reveal the 'business' in the juvenile justice system – what gets reported to the police, what offences are cleared by police, and what matters get dealt with by way of cautions, court appearances and official corrections. Further, there is much youth crime that is probably unreported and hence unrecorded, in which young people are frequently the victims of crime. However, there are some inferences that we can draw in so far as available data allow.

Significantly, court processing and incarceration of young people in the countries studied generally increased when arrest trends were declining. Assessment of over-representation shows higher rates of minority than mainstream youth at all levels of the criminal justice system, especially in relation to incarceration. In the US, for instance, it was estimated that one in 64 white males would be taken into State custody before his 18th birthday, compared to one in 13 African-American males. Overall, minority males have a higher probability rate of incarceration before age 18 than their white peers (Roscoe and Morton 1994).

In terms of types, generally youth crime is non-violent in nature; it is more likely to be directed at property and disorganised. The vast majority of young people who are arrested in the western world are arrested for property crimes and other less serious offences. The prevailing view among researchers who study juvenile violence trends is that guns have been the most important factor that has increased the lethal nature of juvenile violence (Cook and Laub 1998; Zimring 1998). The increase in juvenile homicides in the US, for instance, can be attributed to a sharp increase in gun homicides; non-gun homicide rates has not changed much. As OJJDP's recent report to the Attorney General, entitled *Promising Strategies to Reduce Gun Violence*, makes clear, gun-related violence is an issue of particular concern in the US. The report notes that in 1996, 34,040 people died from gunfire in the US.

The impact of gun violence is especially pronounced among juveniles. A teenager in the US today is more likely to die of a gunshot wound than from all the 'natural' causes of death combined. Of the 2100 juveniles murdered in 1997, 56 per cent were killed with a firearm (Snyder 1998). Furthermore, no other age group in 1997 had a higher proportion of firearm homicides than juveniles aged 13 to 17. Most of the offenders and victims of the school shootings in Pearl, Mississippi; West Paducah, Kentucky; Jonesboro, Arkansas; Edinboro, Pennsylvania; and Springfield, Oregon during the 1991-98 period were juveniles. As will be seen in Chapter 6, one of the most significant partnership projects examined in this book deals with the reduction of guns in a US jurisdiction.

Any critical discussion of the increasing level of violence in youth crime in the US must acknowledge the gang factor as well. There has been a rapid proliferation of youth gangs in the US since 1980 (Howell 1998). In 1980, there were an estimated 286 jurisdictions experiencing gang problems and more than 2000 gangs. By 1996, there were about 4800 jurisdictions with gang problems and more than 31,000 gangs. A recent survey of eighth graders in 11 cities found that 9 per cent of the students were currently gang members and 17 per cent reported having belonged to a gang at some point in their lives (Esbensen and Osgood 1997). Research clearly indicates that adolescents who join street gangs are more involved in delinquent behaviour than are adolescents who are not involved in gangs. This is especially true for serious and violent offenders (Thornberry and Burch 1997). Gang-related crime is violent, with homicides and other violent crimes accounting for about 50 per cent of all gang incidents (Curry, Ball and Fox 1994).

Over 70 per cent of all States in the US have enacted some form of legislation relating to gangs, mostly to enhance penalties and sentencing for gang activities such as drive-by shootings, graffiti, gang extortion and gang member recruitment. In 1999, new categories of legislation specific to gangs included carjacking, expert testimony, law enforcement training, and school dress codes/uniforms. Further, public nuisance laws around the US are increasingly noting gang activity as a factor in determining a nuisance. In one interesting move, Indiana has defined real estate/dwellings as 'psycho-logically affected property' if they are the location of criminal gang activity. This factor must be disclosed, by law, in real estate transactions (Institute for Intergovernmental Research 2000).

Most of the other western countries examined in this book have their own share of the gang phenomenon. Youth gang violence was already a source of concern in the UK (especially in Manchester and Salford) during the 1860-1914 period (Davies 1997). In the 1990s, gangs or organised criminals in all major UK cities were said to involve young people in the drug and cheap cigarette businesses (Scotsman 1998). In 1999, the Solicitor General of Canada, the Minister of Justice and Attorney General of Canada, and the National Crime Prevention Centre co-sponsored a national forum on the problem of youth street gangs. Announcing the forum to the annual conference of the Canadian Association of Chiefs of Police, the Solicitor General said:

> Youth is a priority for this government, as is dealing with young offenders. I know many of you are concerned about youth gangs and that your members include police who are finding innovative solutions. The forum will focus on prevention, enforcement and intervention with youth gangs and will highlight the work of the police, in partnership with others, in dealing with the problem.

Commenting on gangs – a relatively new phenomenon – in New Zealand, Steve Macko, Editor of *New Zealand EmergencyNet NEWS Service*, states that the Devil's Henchmen, Satan's Slaves, the Headhunters and the Grim Reapers represent 'gangbangers' on the streets of New Zealand. As he observes:

> Gangs are reported to be on the rise in one of the most unusual and remote places in the world. Their gang names and insignias seem to be patterned after their American counterparts. They even conduct drive-by shootings – just like you'll find on the streets of Los Angeles.[7]

According to the NZ police, there are about 70 major gangs in the country with about 4000 hard-core gang members: 'if you include associates and prospective wanna-be members, that number grows to about 11,000'. Of the three gang categories identified by the NZ police, real growth has been seen in the youth gangs, especially on the North Island. The other two are the ethnic gangs and motorcycle gangs. One politician told the NZ parliament, 'these are not packs of hooligans who occasionally rough up a pub and occasionally pillage a small town. This is organized crime. It strikes at the very heart of civilized society'.

Australia does not, as yet, have the youth gang problem. However, 'the presence of large groups of young people on the street, or young people dressed in particular ways or with particular group affiliations' seems to convey to the adult population and, perhaps, criminal justice agencies the idea that Australia does have this problem (see Chapter 1). In any case, recent research about 'ethnic gangs' warns that 'the pre-conditions for more serious types of gang formation are beginning to emerge in the Australian context', namely:

- patterns of unemployment;
- immigration and social marginalisation;
- attempts to engage in alternative productive activity (such as the illegal drug economy) and alternative consumption activity (in the form of dealing with lack of consumer purchasing power by taking the possessions of others);
- attempts to assert masculinity in a period where traditional avenues to 'manhood' have been severely eroded for many young men; and
- trends toward ghettoisation and social polarisations (White, Perrone, Guerra and Lampugnani 1999)

Drugs constitute another significant factor in the character that youth crime takes. I will illustrate this with the US and UK experience. In 1997, the 'Monitoring the Future' study measured the use of alcohol, tobacco and other drugs by US youth since 1975. It found that drug use among 12th graders peaked in 1981, with approximately 65 per cent reporting past use of an illicit drug. This figure dropped to a low of 41 per cent in 1992. In 1993, the downward trend began to reverse and, by 1996, 51 per cent of high school seniors reported having used illicit drugs (see Dickinson and Crowe 1997). While drug use among adolescents has since levelled off, there is still far too much drug use by high school students and this is showing in the a high proportion of youth violent crimes (Johnston, Bachman and O'Malley, 1997). More significantly, there is evidence that young people are using mood-altering substances at increasingly younger ages (Dickinson and Crowe 1997).

A new wave of drug use hit UK youth in the late 1980s and, by 1995, the drug economy had burgeoned. Together with 'techno' music, it lured several young people into rave parties and other settings controlled by 'Britain's violent underworld [and] vicious criminals who had no interest in the scene and the culture beyond the profit it could generate' (Turner 1998). These underworld people turned young lads into scary guys with guns and operating as gangsters. Predictably, this activity increased the level of violence in crimes associated with these young people.

Across the western world, youth crime has been declining for a while, contrary to what politicians and the media say. Clearly, factors such as guns, gangs and drugs have increased the level of violence in this crime. It is, however, unjustifiable that court-processing and incarceration have generally escalated out of kilter with the general trend in youth crime.

Costs of traditional response to youth crime[8]

While the personal and social costs of youth crime constitute very significant issues in their own right, the focus of this section is on the official costs or fiscal outlays (capital and recurrent expenditures) for processing and punishing young offenders. As yet, no formula to determine exactly such outlays has been devised (Greenwood, Model, Rydell and Chiesa 1998). The fact that most countries in this study do not provide identifiable information on how states, shires, provinces or territories spend money in the juvenile justice area compounds the situation.

The ways of estimating the outlays that are currently used are all relatively crude. One method is to take the total expenditure on law, order and public safety, including juvenile processing and punishment, and to divide that by the proportion of juveniles in the total population of the country. To get an estimate for each of the States or Provinces, you then divide these figures by the proportion of the youth population that lives in that jurisdiction. The validity of this method is seriously flawed because proportionately greater resources are directed at responding to adult crime since juvenile crime is generally regarded as less complicated, less serious and more likely to be detected than adult crime. Ironically, though, the costs of incarceration for juveniles are higher than those for adults in general.

Another method of obtaining a gross figure for the cost of juvenile justice is to add, as far as possible, the relevant amounts spent by individual departments on youth crime. For instance, one can use budgeting for detention, police youth departments, insurance, security and other easily measurable outlays. Again, there is no easy way of distinguishing how much of these departments' resources was spent in relation to juveniles and how much was spent in relation to adults. One crude measure is the percentage of juveniles in offences handled by the departments. Even then, this will be compounded by the fact that the level of resources departments need to dispose of youth crime may be far more than what they need for crimes committed by adults. For example, it is more expensive to detain a young offender than to imprison an adult.

Despite the methodological limitations of these two methods, most of the available data on the costs of criminal justice have been generated using them. I have drawn on the methods here principally to illustrate the range of financial expenditures by governments in this area.

Global overview

The US criminal justice system costs billions of dollars to operate each year, and the cost is growing rapidly as police, courts and prisons are added. In

1965, the justice system cost taxpayers $4.6 billion, about six-tenths of 1 per cent of gross domestic product (GDP). By 1993 the cost had grown to about $100 billion, 1.57 per cent of GDP. The number of justice system employees grew from 600,000 in 1965 to nearly 2 million in 1993. States reported juvenile justice expenditures of $2.6 billion for fiscal year 1994, with residential placements accounting for the largest portion at $1.7 billion nationally. Community placements total $591 million, delinquency prevention programs total $211 million, and post-residential care totals $89 million.

The total juvenile justice expenditures rose to $4.2 billion in 1998, an increase of 65.4 per cent over the 1994 figure. Significantly, this increase occurred when juvenile crime generally declined by one-third since 1993 (National Association of State Budget Officers 1999). The combined local, State and federal budget to maintain the prison population alone was $24.9 billion in 1990 and reached $31.2 billion in 1992.

Despite these increases in spending and personnel, the fear of crimes remains high[9] and the number of violent crimes reported to the police is at an all-time high. This is one clear piece of evidence that the more resources governments apply to the war on crime by way of intensifying traditional criminal justice approach, the less effective they seem to be (National Centre for Policy Analysis 1994). In fact, California, Florida and other States spend more on corrections than on higher education. The average cost of incarcerating a juvenile for one year in the US is between $35,000 and $64,000. In contrast, the current cost of the *Head Start* intervention program is $4300 per child a year, and the annual tuition cost of attending Harvard University is under $30,000 per student. The Rand Corporation notes that by the year 2002, if current spending trends continue, about 20 per cent of some States' budgets would have been spent on corrections, and less than 1 per cent on higher education (Calhoun 1998).

In the 1994-95 financial year the operating cost of the criminal justice system in the UK was more than £10 billion (Crawford 1998, p 34). About £7290 million was spent on the police alone in 1997-98 – a rise of 33 per cent in real terms since 1988-89, most of which went to pay staff costs. In 1997-98, expenditure supporting criminal work in the Crown Court was about £179 million and in the magistrates' courts about £287 million. About £321 million was spent on the Crown Prosecution Service in 1997-98.

The capital and operating expenditure on the UK Prison Service in 1997-98 was £1740 million. Of this amount, the operating costs (£1460 million) represent an increase of 7 per cent in real terms since 1993/94. In 1997-98 the average net operating cost for a prisoner was £23,940 per year (Home Office 1998). The Audit Commission's report in 1996, *Misspent Youth: Young People and Crime*, estimates that the cost of dealing with offending by young people was around £1 billion a year. It concludes that UK's youth justice system was both inefficient and expensive.

Australia's justice system was costing $2.5 billion annually in the early 1990s (Walker 1996), rising through $4.8 billion in the mid-1990s to about $6 billion by 1998-99 (Table 4.8).

Table 4.8 Expenditure on justice by all Australian governments, 1994-99

Agency	1994-95	1995-96	1996-97	1997-98	1998-99	Real average annual growth rate
	$m	$m	$m	$m	$m	%
Police	3252	3451	3596	3636	3971	5.1
Courts (criminal)	354	356	336	361	383	2.0
Courts (civil)	344	362	414	416	449	6.9
Corrections	891	947	1012	1091	1174	7.1
Total justice system	4842	5115	5359	5504	5977	5.4

Source: Adapted from ABS (2000) *Report on Government Services*, p 506.

The most expensive component of the justice system was police services, which accounted for approximately 67 per cent of the total justice-related expenditure covered by the report. Corrective services accounted for a further 19 per cent and court administration accounted for the remaining 14 per cent.

In 1987, the Australian Institute of Criminology estimated that a global figure of $510 million was spent in Australia on the administration of juvenile justice, most of this going to the detention of young people (see Potas, Vining and Wilson 1990). The costs of incarcerating young people far exceed the costs of the adult system. In 1980s, the average cost per year for a young person in detention was approximately $54,000. In the 1990s, this figure rose to about $70,000.

Over 80 per cent of the juvenile justice budget in New South Wales, for instance, is expended on detention centres. This expenditure directly affects the amount of money which is available for the supervision and organisation of non-custodial sentencing options. Considered in another light, about 7 per cent of court outcomes are detention orders, yet the bulk of departmental resources are directed into this area (Cunneen and White 1995).

In the 1990s, governments in Canada spent an estimated $10 billion on the criminal justice system annually (National Crime Prevention Centre 1998). It is hard to say how much of the police, courts, prosecution and legal aid costs were incurred in responding to youth crime. However, as Table 4.9 shows, on average about 21 per cent of the expenditures on corrections went on 'correcting' young offenders. When the shares from the other sectors are added, it is reasonable to conclude that Canada, like other Western countries, spends substantially on traditional criminal justice responses to crime.

Table 4.9 Justice Spending in Canada, 1992-97

	1992-93	1993-94	1994-95	1995-96	1996-97
			$ millions		
Justice spending[1]	9555	9623	9,944	9966	9996
Police[2]	5717	5790	5784	5809	5856
Courts	867	852	838	847	857
Prosecutions	x	x	257	261	265
Legal aid	602	594	646	622	536
Youth corrections[3]	489	508	526	508	513
Adult corrections	1880	1879	1894	1919	1969

x   Data unavailable, not applicable or confidential.

1.   In order to allow annual comparisons, court expenditures for 1993-94, and 1995-96 are estimated, based on the average between the reporting years immediately preceding and following the reference period. Prosecution expenditures for 1995/96 were estimated in a similar manner. Note that these estimates are included in the totals. Prosecution expenditures for 1992-93 and 1993-94 are not included in the totals.

2.   Most municipal police forces report on a calendar year, all other data represent fiscal year reporting.

3.   Youth corrections costs are estimated. The figures likely underestimate total costs.

Source: Statistics Canada, Catalogue no 85-002-XIE.

Conclusion

All the relevant data examined in this chapter suggest that the 'ticking time bomb' prediction about youth crime in the western world, based on movements in demography, is unduly alarmist. It is true today as it was 20 years ago that crime levels of any description may be one step too high, especially for victims. However, this is a far cry from the perception that our society is in the midst of a dramatically rising epidemic of crime committed by young people. Despite the difficulty in accurately determining trends, it is safe to say that youth crime statistics reflect the activities of the criminal justice agencies as much as the activities of young people themselves.

It is not obvious why the cost of administering the criminal justice response to youth crime keeps going up at a time when this crime (in all its categories) has been in decline. Given that citizens' feelings of safety have not increased over the same period, the verdict must be that the traditional criminal justice responses have not produced value for money. Recent studies demonstrate that processing young offenders through the formal system leads to more crime, higher detention costs and increased violence. With the waiver mechanisms to send some young offenders to adult prisons in most western countries, as we saw in Chapter 3, the prospect of 'waived' youth recidivating more and expressing greater violence in the process can only increase.

The search continues for crime prevention programs that work and are cost effective. It is now conventional wisdom that early intervention programs that try to steer young people from wrongdoing can prevent as much as 250 crimes per $1 million spent. In contrast, investing the same amount in prisons would prevent only 60 crimes a year and diminish the prospect of redeeming more young people from criminal impulses within their societies (Greenwood et al 1998). The challenge is to mobilise the criminal justice juggernaut for a more productive contribution to nation-building in its dealings with young people.

Notes

1   See also Walklate (1998, p 7).
2   This section draws largely on some of my contributions to Sercombe, Omaji, Drew, Cooper and Love (2000).
3   While not every criminal incident results in arrest, such outcome remains the best official indicator of crime level in a country.
4   See *Juristat: Youth violent crime.* Vol 19, no 13.
5   See Census of Public and Private Juvenile Detention, Correctional and Shelter Facilities, 1985-1995.
6   Dr Adam Graycar, Director of Australian Institute of Criminology, in Carcach (1997).
7   *New Zealand EmergencyNet NEWS Service* Friday, 31 May 1996 Vol 2 - 152.
8   Readers should note that the monetary figures in this section relate to the currencies of the countries with which they are mentioned and that the values of those with the same name (dollar) differ significantly.
9   Wilber (1999) observes, 'Americans feel no safer now than 10 years ago'!

5

Towards partnership:
changing perspectives in criminal justice

Several writers of different theoretical persuasions – the realist, the institutionalist, the radical, etc – have used the distressing news of increasing crime and arrest rates, overwhelming backlog of court cases and expanding prison populations to tell the story of the failure of the criminal justice system (Immarigeon 1991; Israel and Sarre 1999). The prognosis is that criminal justice agencies' 'lack of effectiveness at a pragmatic level destines them to a degree of futility' (Sutton 1997, p 17), notwithstanding the fact that their symbolic power makes them seem essential. Curiously, while the prospect of becoming futile looms large, the conservative crime control ideology that has put the system on the path to futility has not abated. Its catch cry of 'get tough, crack down on criminals, lock'em up and throw away the key' still sounds loudly across the western world especially during election periods.

Interestingly, the media propaganda which feed this conservative ideology not only construct the fear of crime; they also fuel public despair over the failure of the criminal justice system. In both instances, they lead politicians, justice officials, criminologists, public interest groups and the like to despair about 'what is to be done' (Omaji 1997). The convergence of politicians seeking an electoral issue, the wider public expressing punitive pre-dispositions, the media sensationalising news to enhance ratings and the professional proclivities of the crime control establishment towards public relations gives rise to policy dynamics in more ways than one (Surette 1996). This has partly been demonstrated in the preceding chapters.

Critically, though, the heightened awareness that increasing police power, prosecutions and prison capacity alone are neither sufficient nor even effective in stemming the perceived tide of crime has raised the expectation that things have to change. Reliance on the failed traditional criminal justice approach has also led to the burgeoning budgets of the criminal justice system – now appropriately called the 'incarceral archipelago' (Foucault 1977) – as we saw in the previous chapter, and further underscores the expectation for change.

For most of the last decade in the 20th century, the traditional methods of crime control were a predominantly reactive, repressive and costly joke unleashed upon the society. It is not surprising that stakeholders would seek an entirely new way of tackling the problem, 'one that does not wait for the crime to be committed but intervenes to stop the crime before it occurs' (O'Malley 1997, p 255); one that is resource-efficient; and one that delivers on the 'promise of crime prevention' (Grabosky and James 1995). Thus far, this search has pointed towards the partnership approach.

Even the most ardent critic of the traditional criminal justice approaches to crime would acknowledge that the relevant agencies have not remained static in their perspectives. The many changes that have taken place in the policy contexts within which these agencies operate, meant that they had to adapt. Thus, beyond further underscoring the failure of the traditional approach, this chapter highlights the perspectival shifts[1] that underlie the trend towards partnership or collaboration as a more promising crime-prevention approach.

Failure of the reactive model, universally acknowledged

The state and its apparatuses of justice would be judged to have failed their duty in relation to crime prevention where a citizen who became an offender 'emerged at the end of his or her prison sentence the same or worse than he or she was at its commencement' (Page 1950, p 22). Failure would also be recorded where a far greater number of offenders is sent to prison because of lack of effort to find alternative treatments, because the custom of instant committal to prison of defendants unable to pay their fines continues and because there is a lack of facilities to replace the grim reformatories and industrial schools of earlier years and their contemporary substitutes. On all these counts, most governments in the western world have achieved less than a pass mark.

In addition to serving as a monument to their failing, the low faith in prisons, aptly expressed by the American Friends Service Committee below, makes infatuation with prisons more intriguing:

> If the choice were between prisons as they are now and no prisons at all, we would promptly choose the latter. We are convinced that it would be far better to tear down all jails now than to perpetuate the inhumanity and horror being carried out in society's name behind prison walls. Prisons as they exist are more of a burden and disgrace to our society than they are a protection or solution to the problem of crime. (quoted in Hudson 1987, p 49)

John Braithwaite, one of Australia's foremost criminologists, observed in 1996 that few sets of institutional arrangements created in the west since the industrial revolution have been as great a failure as the criminal justice system. He describes how, despite its theoretical claims to just and proportionate corrections that deter, the system in practice fails to correct or deter, just as often making things worse as better. It is a criminal injustice system that systematically turns a blind eye to the crimes of the powerful, while imprisonment remains the best funded labour market program for unemployed and indigenous peoples. Braithwaite emphatically states that 'all Western criminal justice systems are brutal, institutionally vengeful, and dishonest to their stated intentions'. With regard to juvenile justice, he observes that 'see-sawing between retribution and rehabilitation has got us nowhere. If we are serious about a better future, we need to hop off this see-saw and strike out in search of a third model' (Braithwaite 1996).

In the same year, Laura Murphy, Director of the American Civil Liberties Union, submitted a statement to the Congressional Black Caucus Brain Trust bemoaning the current state of the juvenile justice system in America. Her assessment captures the widespread observation that the American juvenile justice system has continued to fail. The system has become captive to haste and 'political expediency, rather than thoughtful deliberation':

> [I]n our zeal to address the problem we have hastily resorted, once again, to the failed 'lock em up' philosophy … At the urging of social conservatives, our nation has turned to an ever increasing punitive approach to solving its criminal justice problems with little success. In the last decade, we have doubled the prison population in our country, resulting in such noteworthy accomplishments as unprecedented prison construction and imprisoning over one million adults, including ever increasing numbers of juveniles. These efforts have produced only slight effects on the crime rate. (Murphy 1996)

The juvenile incarceration rate has far exceeded the juvenile justice system's capacity to house and provide even minimal standards of care for the children who are incarcerated. Today, more youth than ever are confined, despite the fact that over the past two decades the juvenile population nationwide has dropped. Fiscal constraints in State budgets have severely impacted on the quality of services provided by public defenders' offices and legal aid services. The increased use of incarceration for juveniles has failed to rehabilitate them, while it has increased corrections costs (Gatewood 1993).

Beside massive overcrowding, many juvenile facilities lack adequate schooling programs, substance abuse treatment, medical and psychological care. The failure to provide basic services unique to the needs of the juvenile offender should be enough for us to re-examine the entire system.

Like the argument earlier in Chapter 3, Murphy saw it as part of the utter failure of the juvenile detention system that many children who have been housed in state institutions, detention facilities and adult jails have been subjected to some of the most inhumane treatment that violate common standards of decency at the hands of governmental authorities:

- children housed in adult facilities have been raped and physically assaulted, sometimes causing the child to commit suicide;
- children housed in detention facilities have been beaten by staff, tied down by restraints and held in deplorable conditions; and, finally,
- children housed in state institutions have been hogtied, handcuffed, injected with 'aversive' drugs and denied special education.

'Despite the futility of these policies in curbing adult crime', Murphy notes, 'public policy makers are proposing that even more incarceration is necessary to stem the supposed gigantic pending juvenile crime wave. Indeed, they seem eager to unleash the failed policies of the adult system on our children by enacting laws that make it easier to transfer increasingly younger children into the adult system and incarcerate them in adult jails' (Murphy 1996).

One hundred years after the juvenile court was introduced in the United States in 1899, many Americans, including local, State and federal policy makers, are questioning the value of the juvenile justice system and asking if it effectively serves children and protects society. Today, largely in disregard, the original principles that motivated the US juvenile justice system (especially the Illinois reform) were:

- that children, because of their minority status, should not be held as accountable as adult transgressors;
- that the objective of juvenile justice is to help the youngster, to treat and rehabilitate rather than punish;
- that disposition should be predicated on analysis of the youth's special circumstances and needs; and
- that the system should avoid the punitive, adversary, and formalised trappings of the adult criminal process, with all its confusing rules of evidence and tightly controlled procedures (Siegel and Senna 1988, p 330).

A further clear indication of the failure of the system is the fact that many States began to respond to the increase in juvenile violence during the early 1990s by enacting legislation to expand the use of transfer mechanisms. These mechanisms not only allow juveniles charged with serious and violent criminal behaviour to be tried in criminal court, but also predispose the system to use imprisonment more widely for these juveniles (Bilchik 1999). This is happening in spite of the common knowledge that the massive US experiment in the use of incarceration in the past two decades has been extremely expensive in both human and fiscal terms.

In addition to proving to be a massive failure in controlling crime, the system has also intensified the underlying conditions of disconnection and alienation that breed crime. It is a reactive system in which victims, offenders and community members are all caught in a downward spiral in which more crime leads to greater fear and increased isolation and distrust among community members, leading to even more crime (Clark 1994).

The impact of this failed system has been greatest on minorities. As Murphy (1996) observes, one in three young black men is in prison or jail, on probation or parole on any given day; African Americans are imprisoned at five times the rate of their counterparts in apartheid South Africa. Nationally, in 1980, African American and white juveniles were arrested for drug offences at approximately the same rate. After declaring a 'War on Drugs' in America in the mid-1990s, black youth were being arrested at nearly five times the rate of white youth, even though their levels of substance abuse were identical. The pervasive criminalisation of black youth is analogous to the slave owners' practice of hobbling or crippling young male slaves to prevent them from escaping to freedom. Sounding rather exasperated, Murphy calls upon her nation to act: 'We must abandon such cruel and futile policies because we are on the verge of incarcerating a generation of our nation's youth'.

The US currently spends over $1 billion per year on the prison population. This cost is set to spiral as the system increases the rate at which the agencies incarcerate children. The raft of legislation across the country to put children as young as 14 in adult-like prisons until they are 24, and then release them back into the community, means that the manufacture of more violent criminals is virtually guaranteed for years to come.

The failure of England's criminal justice system is also remarkable:

> Despite the massive investment by successive governments in 'law and order' – through considerable legislative changes and a cost of the criminal justice system to the Treasury which exceeds 10 billion pounds – we appear to be 'losing the fight against crime'. The traditional institutions of policing, prosecution and punishment appear powerless to make a significant impact ... [They have failed in their] own terms, lost direction and become an increasingly crippling financial burden (Crawford 1998, pp 1, 35)

In 1996, an independent monitoring agency, the Audit Commission, had endorsed in its poignantly titled report, *Misspent Youth*, the prevailing view about the failure of the UK traditional criminal justice responses to youth crime. Noting that resources could be used better, the Commission says:

- the youth court process takes four months, on average, from arrest to sentence;
- the process costs around £2500 for each young person sentenced, amounting to £1 billion per annum;
- half the proceedings against young people are discontinued, dismissed or end in a discharge;
- the many different agencies involved do not always agree on the main objectives; and
- monitoring of reoffending after different sentences is rare (Audit Commission 1996).

Analysing the situation as 'the crisis of the nation-state', Taylor (1999, p 20) holds that in the last years of the 20th century, there was the widespread feeling that different institutions of the state guarding social peace – that is, the police and other criminal justice agencies – are failing to deliver. The Keynesian welfare state, Taylor says, has been relatively powerless to prevent random outbursts of violent crime. This conclusion echoes an earlier observation that 'the failure of penal policy to reduce crime became allied to public alarm over increasing poverty, and to disillusion engendered by the failure of Victorian capitalism to sustain the economic growth' (Hudson 1987, p 6). It was Nicholas Tilley (1994) who argues forcefully that this economically contingent failure of the traditional responses led to the shift towards multi-agency crime-prevention policies in the UK.

The UK juvenile justice system has been intensely criticised because of its failure to reduce offending and because the concept of *parens patriae* has been neglectful of the victims of crime (Wakefield and Hirschel 1996). By the 1980s, youth justice in England was a mess:

> It was a system which was locking up more and more less difficult children and young people. This was forcing older juveniles up into the adult system where they were placing enormous strains on a prison system which was itself at a bursting point ... Government spending [was] perceived to be spiralling out of control and this was acutely embarrassing for [the] administration. (Pitts 1999, p 2)

Table 5.1 The 'hopeless recidivist' in the United Kingdom

Date	Offence	Sentence
1914	Obtaining bicycle by false pretences (9 similar cases considered)	6 months
1914	Desertion from HM forces	Returned to army
1917	Larceny of 3 motor cycles	6 months
1917	Larceny of motor cycles (3 similar cases)	18 months
1919	Larceny of motor 2 cycles (10 similar ooooo, 28 cycles, and cash)	5 years
1927 (17 years)	3 cases of house breaking (12 cases taken into consideration – TIC)	12 months probation
1927 (17)	2 cases of garage breaking	3 years borstal
1929	Forgery, false pretences (68 similar cases)	7 years
1929 (19)	3 cases of house breaking (50 cases TIC)	2 years hard labour
1930	Burglary and larceny	18 months
1931	Larceny	3 months
1931	Taking motor car	2 months
1932	2 cases of burglary and larceny	3 years
1935	House-breaking and larceny (23 cases TIC); Burglary and larceny (9 cases TIC)	3 years
1936	Larceny of 3 motor cycles; Habitual criminal (29 other cases)	5 years preventive detention
1939	House-breaking and larceny	5 years
	Being habitual criminal (41 cases TIC)	5 years preventive detention
1943	Larceny of 3 cycles	12 months

Half a century earlier, Page (1950) had written about the failure of the English juvenile justice system which had evolved during the preceding 100 years. He notes that almost all the young men whose stories are told in his book are failures of the approved school and Borstal systems. Page was critical of the principle of deterrence – 'that single harsh canon that if criminals were made to suffer sufficient pain and degradation in their punishment they would not sin a second time' (1950, p 21) – which dominated the English penal system at this time. For him, it was so merciless that the administration of the criminal law enforced the same hard practice 'against mere children' (1950, p 21).

In 1938, there were 10 borstal institutions in England with an approximate population of 2250 inmates. Barely 10 years later, there were 17 borstal institutions in 1949 with 21,000 inmates. Page illustrates the failure of the system with one classic case of a 'hopeless recidivist' (Table 5.1 opposite). He was born in 1890 and went on to be convicted of more than 160 crimes of dishonesty.

The situation in Australia, Canada and New Zealand was not different. *The Criminal Injustice System* (Zdenkowski et al 1987)[2] basically sums up the consensus that began to emerge in the 1980s about the Australian criminal justice system. The verdict of the observers was that the system, from police interviewing to the sentencing of offenders, was not delivering justice. Warner's (1987) contribution to this work presents one of the early views about the failure of the juvenile court system. The physical settings and facilities were 'cold' and 'barren' (metaphorically and in reality). The court procedures were ridden with delays and insensitive to the special needs of children defendants. They offered little that could possibly reduce the disposition towards reoffending.

In June 2000, the failure of one Australian juvenile justice system was illustrated starkly by the case of a teenager dubbed by the media as 'Western Australia's worst juvenile criminal'. Commencing his life of crime at the age of eight, he clocked more than 374 convictions by the age of 22. He began his detention or jail experience at the age of 12. As Table 5.2 shows (following page), his case stands in the same, if not higher, league as the UK's most 'hopeless recidivist' of the early part of the 20th century. The severity and intensity of this Western Australian teenager's violent offences escalated as the years went by.

The judge who sentenced him in 2000 heard a psychiatric report that showed this young man 'suffered personality deficits, drug and alcohol problems, and ingrained anti-social behaviour' but 'hoped the man would be able to "give a lie" to the predictions by rehabilitating himself' (*The West Australian*, Saturday 24 2000, p 1). Like other personnel of the criminal justice system before him, this judge could only hope in vain. Although the judge said that the court would not give up on him entirely, there was no indication that the system could do more than apprehend, convict and punish. The editorial of the newspaper echoed this systemic disability: 'the courts can only make findings of guilt or innocence and hand down sentences – they cannot directly influence personality and behaviour patterns'.

Table 5.2 Australian counter-part of the 'hopeless recidivist'

Year	Offence	Sentence
1986	Break and enter	Dismissed as first offender
1989	Unlawful use of a car	Not known
1990	Assaulting a police officer	Jailed
1992 (April)	Driving a stolen car; manslaughter (2 counts)	3 years, 7 months
1992 (September)	Staged a roof-top break out from detention centre	Detention increased by unknown number of years
1992 (November)	20 offences on his escape from detention	Indefinite sentence, under the *Crimes (Serious and Repeat Offenders) Sentencing Act 1992*
1994 (November)	Breaking curfew	Sent back to jail
1995	Escaped from remote community service placement	Released on bail into parents' custody
1998	Sex attack and armed robbery of a woman while on home detention	Trial and judgement deferred
1998 (December)	Criminal damage and assaulting a prison officer	Jailed for 2 years in November 1999
1999	Aggravated burglaries, attempted armed robbery and assault	8 years in prison
2000		9 years with no parole + indefinite imprisonment for the sex attack and armed robbery in 1998

What an abject failure! 'That [the system] has failed (the man) is not quite so tragic as that it has failed society as a whole ... This system robs us all of what talents the individuals it ensnares might have and makes us all the poorer for that theft. Locking people away from all that is good in the world from such an early age cannot possibly make them better people' (ibid).

As Forget (1998) summarises the Canadian experience:

> More and more Canadians are dissatisfied with our criminal justice system and its inability to meet the needs of victims, communities and offenders. Those working within the justice system are becoming disillusioned and frustrated. Canada's incarceration rate, the second highest among western democracies, has produced costly and overcrowded prisons, and our current practices fail to provide lower crime rates or a sense of safety for Canadians.

In New Zealand, crime, and particularly violent offending, remains of great concern. Few feel safe in their homes or on the streets. Many believe the government's failure to address the causes of crime is responsible for this reduced feeling of safety and call for a return of the justice system 'to its proper purpose of protecting people and their property; and to reduce crime so everyone can feel much safer on the streets and in their own homes' (ACT 1999).

Why the failing machine ticks on

The 1970s demonstrated the uselessness of imprisonment; the 1980s demonstrated the failure of social reintegration in prisons. However, the effect has not been to reduce the number of detainees or the prison-building program. Responses to insecurity in the 1980s and 1990s have been marked by disappointment with prevention efforts, by an increase in the number of detainees and by the unprecedented development of private expenditure by companies and individuals to prevent crime or repair the damage done. It is the case of a blacksmith who keeps missing the anvil. People are now asking more vociferously: are we doomed to keep the machine going simply because we do not know how to convert those who operate it to other tasks, its parts to other functions, its production system to other markets?

The failing machine ticks on because the theme of 'law and order' has been a popular one in politics during the last two decades of the 20th century. While in its early forms it was likely to be connected with the agendas of conservative parties, recent events in the USA and Australia indicate that even parties traditionally identified as at the left of the political spectrum have apparently decided that they must be ready to 'out-law-and-order' the conservatives. In the early 1990s in the USA, a Democratic Congress and a Democratic President passed heavily repressive national crime legislation with an emphasis on expansion of capital punishment and extension of the 'three strikes and you're out' regulations which assure long institutional sentences for repeat offenders.

From the 'New Deal' of the 1930s to the 'Contract with America' of Mr Newt Gingrich in the 1990s, most political campaigns featured both major parties attempting to 'out tough' each other in their support for repressive legislation such as three strikes. In Australia, repressive juvenile legislation was passed under a Labor Government in Western Australia in 1992, very similar to that of conservative governments in the Northern Territory, Queensland and Victoria (Polk 1997, p 496).

The rise of the fundamentalist parties or groups of the Right has increased the bidding even further. In Canada, for instance, apart from the separatist resurgence of Quebec, the traditions of political liberalism which recognised the plurality of Canadian society were being questioned and undermined by the rise of the Reform Party which in the general elections of 1996 became the official Opposition (Taylor 1999, p 28). In Australia, the One Nation Party under Pauline Hanson, with a similar agenda, polled over a million votes – enough to sound some warning to the major parties (Liberal, National, Labor and Democrats)[3] during the 1996 federal elections.

In this political climate, the instrumentalist perspective continues to overshadow or, in fact, undermine the normative perspective. Whereas the former relies on the punitive regime as the primary mechanism for controlling crime, the latter emphasises the role of the legitimacy of the social system. Where the system enables people to invest socially, economically and psychologically, the people would not risk their investments by committing crime. Both adult and juvenile justice systems in the West have been driven by the instrumentalist response to crime and offenders; hence the lingering of the failed repressive system.

Shifting thoughts among criminal justice agencies

As I mentioned in the Introduction Chapter, one of the two remarkable phenomena in the criminal justice field of the late 1980s is the shift in attitudes about responses to crime. Although the wheels of the 'old' system continued to turn, there was evidence that criminal justice agencies had needed to shift paradigmatically and in praxis.

Police: towards a community and problem-solving model

Although the description of the police as gatekeepers of the criminal justice system invokes a static imagery for them, it is evident that changes have taken place among this agency of justice at perspective, policy and operational levels. In the heyday of reactive policing, especially during the post-Vietnam War era, concepts from the general systems theory were applied to policing. Quick police response to reports of crime, with scientific investigations and presentation of evidence in the courts would lead to the conviction of offenders, who after their rehabilitation would lead productive lives in the community. Under this dominant utilitarian and deterrence approach to crime prevention, there was a strong argument for increasing police numbers to support rapid response rates and to make the apprehension of offenders certain (Wiatrowski 1996, p 123).

However research, particularly in the US, found that neither the density of police patrol operations nor rapid response affected the fear of crime and the levels of criminal victimisation (Kelling, Pate, Dieckman, and Brown 1974). The failure of the principles of the professional model to suppress crime led the police to develop alternatives, many of which took the form of community policing, especially after the pioneering work of Goldstein in 1979:[4] the 'police working with the community to define and deliver police services that were demanded by the residents' (Wiatrowski 1996, p 125). Reflecting on the experience of the change in policing, the Deputy Chief of Police in Fort Worth Texas said: 'There has been a sea change. Once people made obscene gestures at my officers, and now they wave. They've seen the work we can do together, getting some of the violent off the street, ... starting youth programs and the like' (quoted in Calhoun 1998).

Originating from an evolving understanding that contemporary methods of policing are ineffective in substantially reducing crime and coupled with a belief that community-based disorder poses a serious threat to public safety, community policing initiatives throughout the country were attempts to reduce disorder, combat fear, and involve members of the community in identifying and solving problems plaguing their community. Neighbourhood-oriented policing programs became the flavour of the time (Goldstein 1990).

Most of such programs rely on a collaborative problem-solving approach that analyses neighbourhood problems, develops and implements tactics to address the problems and reviews the effectiveness of the tactics. More significantly, the programs represent a fundamental shift in which police officers, whose role within the criminal justice system had been constructed solely as restricted to investigation and prosecution of offences, 'will be tasked with the provision of services to young people in trouble and their families' (NACRO 1999).

Courts: towards a therapeutic model

When Judge Julian Mack declared the purpose of juvenile court in 1909 as 'not so much to punish as to reform, not to degrade but to uplift, not to crush but to develop, not to make him a criminal but a worthy citizen' (Mack 1909, p 107), he was describing a therapeutic ideal, albeit based on sentimental generalisations about childhood. As the discussion in Chapter 3 shows, this agency has hardly approximated this ideal in its century-long existence. It has see-sawed between retribution and rehabilitation, but in both cases it has made the youth more of a criminal than a worthy citizen.

In recent times, there appears to be a rediscovery of the potential of the juvenile court to adopt an approach that contributes to preventing youth crime. In an article titled 'How the Courts Can Help Fight Delinquency and Neglect',[5] Judge Eugene A Moore – Chief Judge of the Probate Court, Oakland County, Michigan and past president of the National Council of Juvenile and Family Court Judges – stresses the role of every juvenile court in preventing 'denominators' of juvenile crime from occurring. This role would thereby keep youngsters out of juvenile court and develop treatment programs that deal with these denominators, thereby rehabilitating youngsters who have been adjudicated in a juvenile court.

He enumerated some standards ('the Moore Standards') that every juvenile court should follow to ensure that this goal is accomplished:

1. A voluntary delinquency prevention program sponsored by the court, the schools and the municipality. The court must be an active sponsor to ensure full community support.

2. A runaway shelter that provides protection from exploitation of youngsters on the streets, and counselling for the youngster and family.

3. In-home detention with daily monitoring by community volunteers.

4. Effective court probation with case loads of no more than 40 youngsters per worker.

5. A volunteer one-to-one program to ensure that every youngster who comes into court will have a constructive, loving, caring adult who can provide a model for the youngster and help that youngster develop self-respect and self-esteem.

6. Community services programs to ensure that youngsters who appear in court can repay the community for injury thereto by serving that community, without being paid, thereby learning accountability and developing self-esteem and self-respect through helping others.

7. A job placement program to ensure that each youngster who comes into the juvenile court can find a part-time job. Again helping to develop self-esteem and self-respect.

8. Parent effectiveness training where every parent of an adjudicated juvenile can receive skilled training on how to be a better parent.

9. Individual and group counselling to ensure that each youngster can better understand how to deal effectively with their own behaviour.

10. A diagnostic clinic to help develop a treatment plan to meet the needs of the child, family and community.

11. Adequate rehabilitative foster care, group homes, half-way houses and institutions whose primary goal is to teach youngsters self-esteem and respect for others through concerned staff who care about youngsters and provide a positive role model.

12. A restitution program that ensures the victim will be reimbursed in part for the injury.

13. Alternative day care education program to improve basic skills and help develop pre-trade skills.

14. A co-op program to help youngsters learn good work habits.

15. A dedicated judicial officer who recognises his responsibility can ensure these services if he or she is fully committed to these standards. (See Judge Moore's article as per note 5.)

A frank assessment of the current approach of the youth court must conclude that, all too often, inadequate attention is given to changing offending behaviour. This is not the fault of individuals working within the system. It is encouraged by the court's very structures and procedures. The purpose of the youth court must change from simply deciding guilt or innocence and then issuing a sentence. In most cases, an offence should trigger a wider enquiry into the circumstances and nature of the offending behaviour, leading to action to change that behaviour. This requires in turn a fundamental change of approach within the youth court system.

No doubt punishment is necessary to signal society's disapproval when any person, including a young person, breaks the law and as a deterrent. However, if the youth justice system is to fulfil its aim of preventing offending by young people, disposals should focus on changing behaviour as well as on punishment (Home Office 1997).

Thus, reform of the youth court is needed to effect the Moore Standards by providing:

- speedier decisions on guilt or innocence, much closer to the date of the offence and with less tolerance of adjournments;
- a system which is more open, and which commands the confidence of victims and the public;
- a stronger emphasis on using sentencing to prevent future offending;

- more efficient arrangements for the scheduling and management of cases; and
- processes which engage young offenders and their parents and focus on the nature of their offending behaviour and how to change it.

Advocates of the change towards this therapeutic orientation advise that when a young offender goes to the youth court, the process must seek to involve the young person and his or her parents directly. This will require a system-change:

- to encourage training for magistrates to emphasise the value of talking directly to both the young defendant and his or her parents during court proceedings, even where the young person has legal representation;
- to remove any obstacles in the Magistrates' Courts Rules, which may prevent or discourage magistrates from questioning defendants about the reasons for their behaviour, before reaching a final decision on sentencing; and
- to encourage youth courts to consider changing the physical environment of the courtroom to promote proceedings which involve the young person directly and are less adversarial. This might involve (except where the security constraints were overriding) all participants in the case, including the magistrates, sitting around a single table.

Several jurisdictions have adopted the diversion strategy as a first step towards the required fundamental change. The New Zealand Family Group Conferencing[6] and Western Australia's Juvenile Justice Teams[7] are some examples of this strategy. In the UK, under the *Youth Justice and Criminal Evidence Act* 1999, the government included a diversion strategy in the youth court operations so that in its wider inquiry into the reasons for a young person's offending behaviour, the court must refer first-time young offenders (ie those aged between 10-17) who plead guilty to newly established youth offender panels, unless the court thinks an absolute discharge or custody is appropriate. This panel will be made up of people recruited from the local community, who have an interest or expertise in dealing with young people. The Panel will also include a member from the local Youth Offending Team.

The panel will agree on a contract with the offender and his or her family aimed at tackling the young person's offending behaviour and its causes. This contract will set out clear requirements that they will have to fulfil. These might include an apology and some form of reparation to the victim, carrying out community work, taking part in family counselling or drug rehabilitation. In fulfilling these contracts young persons will have to face both what they have done and its consequences. If they fail to agree or breach the terms of a contract, young persons will be returned to the court for sentencing for the original offence.

The *Young Offenders Act* 1994 (SA), *Young Offenders Act* 1997 (NSW) and *Juvenile Justice Act* 1994 (Qld) have provided for similar diversionary schemes. In the past few years also a number of jurisdictions (eg several in the US, and NSW and WA in Australia) have created specialised drug courts as a further step in orienting the court system towards therapeutic jurisprudence. Many observers have credited these courts as being pioneers in developing a problem-solving approach to case processing and developing a new role for judges. Such courts, by using their coercive powers to link substance abusers with treatment programs, have demonstrated an innovative path by which courts can collaborate with community agencies to achieve new solutions to long-standing problems.

Corrections: towards constructive custody

Juvenile corrections have the responsibility through various correctional modes to reduce the frequency of delinquent acts of those children assigned to them. This thinking represents a shift in emphasis beyond traditional offender-management practices. It also leads to the realisation that corrections must move towards encompassing 'a wider vision of involvement in community partnerships to achieve crime prevention, community safety and the effective rehabilitation of offenders within a restorative justice framework' (Moore 1998).

A reform strategy for New Zealand in the 1980s recommended that prisons form partnerships between distinct cultural and ethnic groups in the country and provide both secure containment and rehabilitation. This strategy outlined at least four levels of participation in the partnership process: corrections administration, prisons, habilitation councils, and habilitation centres. In light of the overwhelming evidence that the overriding culture of prisons is punishment and that habilitation in the prison environment is not effective, the strategy recommended that therapeutic programs for offenders be developed that are separate and distinct from the traditional prison system.

Habilitation centres were to offer inmates realistic opportunities to make permanent changes in their lives and to stop criminal activities. Habilitation programs must be based on a social learning model rather than a medical model of treatment, emphasising the reinforcement of socially acceptable behaviour, and be coordinated with available community resources. The selection of inmates for habilitation programs must be guided by a principal consideration of placing them as near their home area as possible so that family support could be accessed (New Zealand Ministerial Committee of Inquiry into Prisons System 1989).

This New Zealand example conveys the message that partnership with the community has the potential to make 'coercive' institutions humane places. For, as Jerome Miller argues from his experience of reform of the US juvenile custodial institutions, reform of institutions in vacuo can never make them humane 'no matter what money, staff, and programs are pumped into them' (Miller 1991, p 18).

Searching for the grail:
paradigm shift towards 'partnership'

The foregoing discussion demonstrates that criminal justice agencies have had to face a profound 'change era'. The main question became – in which direction should the agencies be heading? The ensuing discourse about the institutional response to crime in the 1990s put a spotlight on the shift towards the 'partnership' framework in criminal justice policies and practices that had crystallised in the 1980s. For instance, the Cornish Report to the Home Office in Britain had recommended in the early 1980s the setting up of 'crime prevention panels' by the police in order to form wider networks within communities and to encourage support for crime prevention within given localities (Crawford 1998, p 33). The French Bonnemaison model in the mid-1980s had highlighted the need for a coordinated inter-agency approach. So also was the Dutch *Society and Crime* policy in 1985 which, drawing on the Roethof Committee's recommendation, directed that 'cooperation with municipal agencies and the voluntary sector' be emphasised (van Dijk 1997, p 101). However, it was the UK Home Office's Safer Cities Program and its publication, *Partnerships in Crime Prevention* in 1989, that provided the clearest signals of the emerging currency of this approach to crime.

Although still unclear about the role of 'partners' at this stage, the UK saw the 'partnership' approach as 'a promising and systematic way of mobilising the support of relevant agencies in the fight against crime' (Bright 1992, p 87). In 1990, the Home Office released Circular 44, *Crime Prevention – The Success of the Partnership Approach*, and a 'good practice' booklet. The latter identified six elements – structure, leadership, information, identity, durability and resources – that the Home Office considered essential 'for any effective crime prevention project' (see Crawford 1998, p 37). This was followed by its *Safer Communities: The Local Delivery of Crime Prevention through the Partnership Approach* (Home Office 1991), produced by the Morgan Committee. This report not only tried to broaden the definition of 'crime prevention beyond the role of police' but also strengthened the case for a multi-agency approach. Later, the Office launched its 'Partners Against Crime' initiative in September 1994 to fully endorse the 'new way'. Against this backdrop, the UK's largest police service, the London Metropolitan Police, began to develop an extensive program of preventative partnership with the community.

In October 1994 Crime Concern claimed there were over 200 genuine multi-agency crime-prevention partnerships in England and Wales (Crime Concern 1994). A more recent survey of local authorities in England and Wales found that 62.6 per cent of authorities have been involved in independent, multi-agency partnerships; 48.3 per cent are involved in local authority based approaches and 44.9 per cent in facilitating approaches whereby the local authority 'signposts' and refers the public to community safety projects – such as crime-prevention panels and neighbourhood watch – and encourages the public to take community safety measures.

With the statutory duty on local authorities and the police to form community safety partnerships since the last two years of the 1990s, there has been a significant increase in the number of such arrangements. Notably, the UK *Crime and Disorder Act* 1998 introduced a new multi-agency approach emphasising early intervention with young offenders, especially those exhibiting known risk factors. At the heart of the strategy are the new steps to ensure that every local Crime & Disorder reduction partnership (there are now about 400 in England and Wales) and police force is performing to its maximum potential. This will involve both establishing clear arrangements for performance monitoring and providing effective support. One of the key aspects is the target that the police and local authorities (through the Crime & Disorder reduction partnerships) will set themselves to reduce vehicle crime, domestic burglary and robberies.

The *Crime and Disorder Act* has also placed a duty on local authorities with social services and education responsibilities to establish a Youth Offending Team(s) (YOTs) as a partnership with the other relevant local agencies in their area. In particular, it places other key agencies – the probation committee and the police and health authorities – under a reciprocal duty to participate in YOTs, in accordance with government guidance. YOTs are to work with agencies such as the courts and the prison service and alongside complementary inter-agency groups such as the new community safety and crime reduction partnerships.

At the operational level, YOTs are to include social workers, probation officers, police officers, and education and health authority staff. They might also include people from other agencies and organisations, including those in the voluntary sector. The most important requirement is that YOTs should have the right blend of skills and experience and that all team members should have a common approach to youth justice, focused on addressing offending behaviour. YOTs' functions include:

- assessment and intervention work in support of the final warning to young offenders by the police;
- supervision of community punishments for young offenders;
- provision of 'appropriate adult' services, bail information, bail supervision and support;
- placement of young people on remand in open or secure accommodation;
- court work and the preparation of reports;
- throughcare and supervision of youngsters who have been released from custody; and
- preventative work taking account of the work of local authority youth services (including, where appropriate, supervising parenting and child safety orders).

The publication by the US Bureau of Justice Assistance, entitled *Working as Partners with Community Groups* 1994, underlines the positive view about partnership, especially among law enforcement agencies, in that country. It states that:

> [L]aw enforcement officers are showing that working in partnership with community members and groups is an effective and productive way to address [crime]. This effectiveness can translate into less crime, less fear of crime, and a greater sense of community power and cohesion.

The need for partnership, the Bureau recognised, is fundamental in achieving results in arresting youth crime. A strong system of intervention requires effective partnerships between law enforcement, courts, corrections and community services. To this end, the Office of Juvenile Justice and Delinquency Prevention funded and evaluated the demonstration of this approach in three communities (Oakland, California; Baton Rouge, Louisiana; and Syracuse, New York).[8] These communities formed partnerships among community residents, faith organisations, law enforcement agencies, the media, schools, and families to reduce juvenile gun violence – focusing on strategies related to access, carriage and use of guns by juveniles as three critical aspects to the problem (Hedges 1997).

In a keynote address to the First Annual Conference of the New York Campaign for Effective Crime Policy titled 'New Beginnings', Mr Travis, the then Director of the US National Institute of Justice, emphasised the significance of the partnership movement:

> To be more effective, I believe that ... components of the criminal justice system must view the community as a co-producer of justice. Al Blumstein, one of our foremost criminologists, stated that we now live in a 'pre-Galileo, prison-centric' universe, where our conceptions of how to achieve justice revolve around incarceration. I share his belief that we need to conceive of a post-Galileo world, where both safety and justice are achieved through a thousand complex interactions, and the agencies of the traditional criminal justice system explore new possibilities for defining their missions, operations, and expectations. (Travis 1996)

He explained the view of community as a full partner in producing public safety to mean to 'listen to the people you serve, ask them what they think is important, value their priorities, explore their capacities to provide solutions'. For the police this has obvious short-term benefits of providing intelligence about criminal activity, which can be generated through community involvement and the credibility of the organisation. In the long run, it positions the police to become a catalyst in communities that care for their young people and to promote the infrastructure of community life that reduces crime and fear and disorder. 'If it is part of the mission of the modern day police department to prevent the next crime – then the police must think differently about the dynamics of crime and about the best ways to prevent crime' (ibid).

That partnership has since permeated the criminal justice thinking in the US is evidenced by many such projects. For example, under the School Based Policing program, police and school communities in the US are working together to reduce crime by developing open lines of communication between police and young people. The program seeks to reduce anti-social behaviour within school communities and provide a safe and supportive environment which promotes cooperation and care (Ranger and Hall 1999).

For the prosecutors who are now exploring a similar interaction with the community – the beginnings of a community prosecution movement – the approach offers opportunities to provide safety counselling to the community. This is designed to build the capacity of community groups to make their community safer and minimise the need for criminal prosecutions. The courts can harness partnership with the community to develop 'community impact statements', similar to the victim impact statements, as part of the sentencing process. They can also involve the community directly in sentencing and monitoring functions.

Travis (1996) writes about a domestic violence court in Dade County, Florida, that has set out to reduce the level of violence within the families that came before the court and to ameliorate the impact of that violence upon the children. Significantly, this court has brought the medical community into full partnership with its operations. Travis also recounts the decision of the Connecticut Department of Correction to reduce gang violence and influence, both within correctional institutions and in the community at large. In collaboration with other community groups, the Department developed a highly successful program of breaking up the gangs, breaking the hold that gang membership had over young people, renunciation of gang identities, and creating alternative, positive peer-group involvement

These projects or initiatives clearly demonstrate that the criminal justice system can:

- take as its objective to ensure that defendants entering the system are, on the whole, less likely to commit further crimes against the public when they leave the system (a bona fide crime-prevention mission); and

- build partnerships with their host communities to achieve such an outcome.

When crime prevention finally crept into Australia's political and social radar in the late 1980s, the compelling force being economics not idealism, the pioneering effort of South Australia's *Together Against Crime 1989* emphasised the idea of partnership. Several police jurisdictions in Australia have since indicated in their mission statements that they are committed to working in partnership with their respective communities to create a safer and more secure society.

The development of national crime-prevention strategies in Canada and New Zealand in the 1990s also demonstrates how an interest in partnership model has also entered the criminal justice thinking in these two countries. As Presdee and Walters (1997, p 201) observe, these strategies 'pivot on the central place of government coordination and community partnerships as the means by which community-based crime prevention can be achieved'. The Royal Canadian Mounted Police developed the view that, to achieve the desired crime-prevention goal, 'there will have to be an increased and effective use of partnerships and community involvement ..., we will require an integrated cooperative approach involving all facets of the criminal justice system, community services and the community' (Muirhead 1996, pp 3, 8).

The New Zealand Police similarly declare in their mission statement that they are community oriented: 'We involve the community in crime prevention and crime control ... We work in Partnership with local communities to identify and resolve community problems related to law and order'. A planned approach to crime prevention in New Zealand actually began in 1987 with the publication of the Report of the Ministerial Committee of Inquiry into Violence (the Roper Report) which recognised that the responsibility for crime prevention lies with the community as a whole. Over the next three years, the government worked on a crime-prevention strategy based on the French 'Bonnemaison' model.

In July 1990, the government announced a pilot community crime-prevention program based on the establishment of four safer community councils. These were established at Manukau City in Auckland, Wairoa, Christchurch and Ashburton. Following an evaluation of these four councils in 1993 the Safer Community Council model was adopted. The Crime Prevention Unit was established in September 1993 and the New Zealand Crime Prevention Strategy was released in October 1994. Partnership became fashionable thereafter.

Conceptual debates and perceptions about the partnership approach

Although greeted with enthusiasm when it became prominent in the 1990s, the concept of 'partnership' carries within itself seeds that can potentially confuse. First, there are terms, such as multi-agency, cross-agency, inter-agency, cooperative approach, coordinated strategy, and federated initiative, that appear to mean the same thing as partnership. Further, there are questions as to whether partnership is anything more than a code name for paternalism, out-sourcing, net-widening or responsibility displacement by criminal justice agencies in the era of economic rationalism (see, for example, Hannah-Moffat 2000).[9] It is therefore pertinent to clarify the concept of partnership before providing a substantive analysis of its application in reality.

Partnership has been used in several contexts to suggest several meanings. For our present purposes, two of these usages will be examined. The UK Home Office (1993) operationalises partnership as an association between a number of individuals, groups and agencies to pursue a common goal. Realising that 'many of the measures that contribute to prevention are not within the remit of any one agency', the Home Office posits that many different agencies' preventative actions can only be effective when 'coordinated by a formal partnership'. This involves the partnership sharing and mobilising resources, generating commitment and enabling the contributions of individual agencies to be targeted to best effect. Partnership has also been defined as a dedicated community coalition of citizens, private businesses and public agencies that can direct a collaborative effort for crime prevention (Omaji 1993; Sterner 1994). Both definitions reveal at least two critical aspects of partnership.

First, it shows that partnership is not just an arrangement between government agencies, but the coming together of agencies from different sectors of the mixed economy of crime prevention (Sutton 1997). Thus, the arrangement is as much inter-sectoral as it is inter-agency. The National Anti-Crime Strategy (1996, p 9) in Australia recognises this distinction when it says that preventative 'whole-of-government' approaches to crime, on one hand, 'require cross agency coordination, co-operation and implementation' and, on the other hand, that 'specific crime prevention issues should be addressed using inter-sectoral approaches' involving stake holders such as business and industry, local government, the non-governmental welfare sector, community and residents groups. The New Zealand Crime Prevention Unit (1994) had similarly distinguished coordination among government agencies from coordination between government agencies and community organisations. The Unit later reiterated this distinction in their *Responses to Crime Strategy* (1997).

Secondly, the definition emphasises or presents the relationship between the agencies in terms of collaboration. This means more than just working together. As Gilling (1997, p 160) argues, 'it has an ideology of unity that hints at a common purpose, and a sense of togetherness in an uncertain world. It also implies a level of effectiveness, if only because two heads are better than one'. Gilling notes from previous works that there is a continuum of collaboration that increases in intensity from communication to cooperation, to coordination, to federation, and to merger. The farther the relationship between agencies moves to the right of the continuum, the more the autonomy of each agency in the association is compromised or lessened. By definition, genuine partnership falls more to the right than to the left of the continuum.

In relation to perception, there is something puzzling about the ascendancy of partnership in criminal justice thinking. Western criminal justice agencies – especially the police, who it is generally believed never share power – have enthusiastically embraced the power-sharing idea of looking beyond themselves and forming partnerships with various community groups to fight crime. It has also been observed that the judiciary is never 'keen to share power with newcomers'. The police are even more reluctant and the corrections are most unwilling (Pratt 1995; Sarre 1997).

Several explanations have been put forward for the sudden apparent willingness of these agencies to share their powers. At one end of the continuum, it is held that agencies opted for this approach because it could produce notably successful and cost-effective outcomes. The Home Office (1993) subscribes to this view when it argues that its Safer Cities Program demonstrated that partnership is 'the most promising way forward' in crime prevention. At the other end of the continuum, partnership is viewed as little more than a legitimation exercise for the criminal justice agencies. The agencies legitimise themselves not only by ensuring quality in their encounters with citizens and rendering their organisations transparent and accountable. They must engage citizens 'as co-producers of crime control and justice in operations designed to help [them] achieve goals that they cannot achieve alone' (Moore 1997). In other words, they must work in community-based partnerships which may involve relinquishing much of the direct control over crime.

Both the varying degree of loss of autonomy in the relationship and ideological implications raise questions about what criminal justice agencies expect to gain from, and are prepared to concede to, any partnership arrangements that they initiate. On these questions, O'Malley (1997) queries whether the police have sufficiently moved away from their paternalistic practices of the previous era to be able to engage in cooperative (further still, 'coordinative') politics with the community – 'as equals, as implied in the partnership model'. Expressing a similar reservation, Sarre (1997, p 76) notes that:

[T]o have the police share some of the roles with the community will be akin to asking them to re-define their entire raison d'etre. It is therefore highly unlikely that there would be a genuine shift to a community partnership for crime prevention without a great deal of reluctance and stalling, if not at the senior management level then certainly at the level of the rank-and-file patrol officer.

This expression is a more recent rendition of the view strongly articulated a decade earlier by Sampson, Stubbs, Smith, Pearson and Blagg (1988, p 491) where they stated that the police are also enthusiastic proponents of the multi-agency approach, but they tend to prefer to set the agendas and to dominate forum meetings, and then to ignore the multi-agency framework when it suits their own needs. Against the backdrop of the possible loss of autonomy and the perceived lack of capacity or willingness on the part of criminal justice agencies, it becomes necessary for concerned scholars to look at these agencies' emerging practices of partnership more closely.

Recalling the general insularity of criminal justice agencies, the ideological implication and the loss of autonomy inherent in partnership which I discussed earlier, it is argued that the adoption of any approach other than the usual reactive and retributive responses (let alone the partnership model) entails a remarkable shift in perspective or paradigm, especially for organisations such the police. The change from reactive policing to community policing and problem-oriented policing since the early 1970s exemplifies this phenomenon (Edwards 1999). Also, the judiciary has had to grapple with its own philosophical orientation. In some cases, especially since the 1990s, this involved relinquishing its die-hard commitment to the adversarial and punitive approach and embracing a shift towards therapeutic jurisprudence. This phenomenon is particularly remarkable because, wherever there is a paradigmatic shift, it meant that the general understanding of historical, empirical or normative realities that the outgoing paradigm has enunciated had to be challenged, de-emphasised, devalued or simply ignored. It is similar to the saying that to call for a new power is to appeal for new concepts and categories of thinking about a given subject (Dilulio 1993) which modify or supplant the old ones.

Another puzzle in the shift towards partnership relates to the notion of 'community involvement'. This issue is illustrated with a Canadian experience. Since 1984, Canada has run a nationwide campaign, sponsored by its Solicitor General, aimed at involving the community in prevention and reporting of crimes. The goals are 'to heighten awareness, broaden the crime prevention partnership and stimulate community-based crime prevention'.[10] The strategies involve cooperation between business people, voluntary organisations, lawyers and other professionals, as well as ordinary citizens – aimed at reducing burglary and vandalism in selected neighbourhoods. People are encouraged to take part in a wide variety of activities: co-learn about crime rates in their areas, report suspicious occurrences, participate in Garbathons (marathon pick-ups of litter), and lend their homes for police radar traps to be set up to catch dangerously speeding drivers. There are special awards given to businesses that have helped promote crime prevention and individuals who have worked in various volunteer centres dealing with diverse crime problems, including delinquent teenagers. 'Secure your home but recognise that security also comes from a closely knit community' is the overarching message.

The argument about this aspect of partnership revolves around the motive for the involvement. Is it to contribute to the development of more closely knit communities as the Canadian example suggests or a pragmatic response in the face of the rising social and economic costs of crime? This question underlines the prevailing crucial and central ambiguity about further community involvement in the control of crime. It is unclear whether community is being proposed as a means to an end, that is, as a new resource for tackling the problem of crime, or whether the creation of better community feeling is itself the end that is being pursued. Are we seeking reduced crime or increased community spirit? There is a political gulf between those on the right who wish to draw on public support to help the forces of law and order and those on the left who seek rather to empower the disenfranchised in the community so that they can confront existing institutions and hierarchies as a way to bring about genuine crime prevention (Nelken 1985). Thus, the debate is not only real, it has manifest ideological bases.

Edwards and Hughes (2002, p 5) aptly recognise the complexity of the debate about the objectives of community involvement in crime-related governance; hence they advise that:

Rather than reducing an explanation of community governance to either the reformulation of sovereign authority or making private citizens more responsible for their self-government or the search for a new model of associative democracy or a more economical government of crime etc, it is better to see these objectives as coterminous.

Conclusion

From the late 1960s onward, police, courts and youth corrections underwent the wrenchings and twistings associated with such policy trends as decriminalisation, diversion and de-institutionalisation (Polk 1997, p 491). By the early 1980s, it was no longer possible to hide the abject failure of their traditional approach to crime control. Their predominantly reactive orientation was found to be particularly unsuitable for youth crime as it did nothing to tackle the underlying crisis in the social system.

Although the failed criminal justice approach was sustained inordinately for so long by inertia, political opportunism and by its usefulness to a post-Fordist society, there was little doubt that it would unravel. Whether it was for self-preservation or a bona fide reconstitution of thought, agencies did review their orientations and saw the need to change direction. The tilt towards citizen or community involvement probably did little to affect the crime level or its perceived seriousness, but it certainly represents some reaction to an era of centralisation, bureaucratisation and professionalism that failed to take society closer to killing the dragon in crime. Whatever the motivation, the search for the partnership approach was arguably earnest.

As the next chapter shows, the ensuing community-police collaboration came to stand in contrast to an age of police in radio patrol cars, cut off from the community, responding to calls for service issued by a central dispatcher. Similarly, community courts emerged as a step beyond centralised, high volume criminal courts, dominated by the need to manage caseloads and dispensing 'revolving door justice'. Corrections as warehousing came to be seen for what it is – a criminogenic practice. More significantly, the capacity of this institution to be constructive has re-emerged in criminal justice thinking, despite the abolitionist and postmodernist arguments to the contrary.

The 'partnership' approach that the criminal justice agencies began searching for is not easily accessible conceptually. Further, it has failed to disclose a clear ideological stance for the criminal justice agencies. Nonetheless, it seems to have provided a way of escape from a destiny of futility for which their traditional approaches had positioned them.

Notes

1   These include: the changes from reactive policing to community policing and problem-solving policing since the early 1970s, the philosophical shift in the judiciary from a die-hard commitment to adversarial/punitive process to therapeutic jurisprudence since the early 1990s, and the movement from 'destructive prison' to 'constructive prison', and

from views of prisoners as enemies to prisoners as citizens capable of reform in the correctional field.

2   The editors, George Zdenkowski, Chris Ronalds and Mark Richardson, titled the work as such because it attempts to capture the prevailing disillusionment of the public and academics about the system's failure and lack of fairness in its operations.

3   Particularist and tribal political movements, such as the Front National in France led by Le Pen, the Northern Leagues in Italy and the Freedom Party in Austria led by Jorge Haider, are similarly disposed. They appeal crudely to the public's fear of crime and, by so doing, pressurise the main political groupings to display their credentials on 'toughness' about crime.

4   Goldstein (1979). He later developed this theme in his book titled: *Problem-oriented policing*. New York: McGraw-Hill.

5   See *A World of Prevention* at <http://www.tyc.state.tx.us/prevention/howcourt.html>.

6   See Alder and Wundersitz (1994) for a comprehensive description of this strategy.

7   This strategy is discussed in greater detail in Chapter 6 of this book.

8   Details of one of these projects – Baton Rouge – are provided in Chapter 6 of this book.

9   In this work, Hannah-Moffat shows how recent policy changes in Canadian women's imprisonment, as part of neo-liberal strategies of penal governing, involve a reconfiguration of the responsibilities of state and civil society. Although the stated aim of these changes was to provide 'empowerment' to indigenous Canadian communities in crime prevention, the partnership strategy led mainly to 'responsibilisation' whereby policy makers and correctional officials shifted crime-prevention responsibilities to the communities without providing them with extra resources.

10   See *Partners in preventing crime and good neighbours report*. Programs branch, Ministry of the Solicitor General, Ottawa: 1 March 1994.

6

Criminal justice partnerships:
selected experiences

This chapter uses a case study approach to examine selected 'partnership' projects so as to illustrate recent criminal justice practices of collaboration for crime prevention in the western world. Most of the primary data used to develop this chapter was collected around the mid-1990s. This was before many of the now well known legislated and large experimental juvenile crime-prevention schemes, such as victim-offender mediation in North America and 'conferencing' in Australasia, became prominent in intellectual discourse (see Strang 2000). The data relate mainly to those schemes that have been initiated or substantially led by criminal justice agencies (see the Introduction Chapter).

In the end, the projects that have been selected are those considered to be sufficient for the purpose of this book, namely to underscore the paradigmatic shift in criminal justice towards partnerships and to use the characteristics of such partnerships as a basis for constructing a model of partnership that can effectively prevent youth crime. The wealth of literature that has developed since the mid-1990s, especially in relation to the shift towards restorative justice (see Bazemore and Umbreit 2001; Daly and Hayes 2001), confirms rather than contradicts the general orientation of the projects described in this chapter.

As the reader will notice, the details of the projects selected for this exercise vary significantly. This is because the amount of information available at the time of writing was different for each project. This, in turn, was due mainly to the fact that the projects were at different stages of development and implementation. Beyond adapting the information to a pre-determined format, I have presented here the findings as closely as possible to their original descriptions.

Although the focus in this book is on the criminal justice agency-centred model, I have included a few projects from the 'local authority-centred' model, in which criminal justice agencies played a significant role, mainly to introduce some diversity in the partnership characteristics that are discussed in the next chapter. It is pertinent to note here that these two models are part of a much broader typology that the UK Morgan Committee identified after reviewing some national developments. The five basic models of partnership that the committee identified reflect differences in coordination, structure and resourcing:

- the 'independent' model, with an independent coordinator;
- the 'local authority based' model;
- the 'police centred local' model;
- the 'police centred headquarters' model; and
- the 'indeterminate' model, with no clear leader, coordinator or strategy (Home Office 1991).

To this list Liddle and Gelsthorpe (1994) have added a sixth model, the 'corporate' model, with no 'lead agency'. Here the coordination, decision-making and implementation of work are regarded for the most part as being the responsibility of the partnership group as a whole. The *Crime and Disorder Act* 1998 creates a slightly different model whereby the 'leadership' is shared between the police and local authority. On the whole, the models attempt to identify the existence or absence of a clear dominant party within a given partnership. This is important in itself for, as we shall see, power relations represent the central dynamic in the study of inter-agency relations. And yet, in doing so, these models tend merely to reflect the self-proclaimed image of a partnership and its organisational location rather than the more subtle nature of relations between the agencies. For example, Coleman, Sim and Whyte (2002) saw a project established under the UK *Crime and Disorder Act* 1998 (the Safer Merseyside Partnership) as a mechanism for extending the reach of government into new spheres of influence. They describe this as 'local hegemony building, in particular, with respect to policing' (p 98).

To some extent it is the standard of Liddle and Gelsthorpe's 'corporate' model that most partnerships aspire to reach. The next chapter, which applies analytical and interpretive frameworks to the descriptive presentations here, will comment on the dominant orientation in these projects.

Criminal justice agency-centred partnership model

Baton Rouge Partnership for the Prevention of Juvenile Gun Violence, LA (US)[1]

Background

During the 1990s, Baton Rouge experienced dramatic increases in the number of youth involved in violent crimes. The January 1998 Rev Dr Martin Luther King Day parade shootings, at which an eight-year-old girl died and several others were injured, clearly illustrate the level at which gun-related violence had afflicted this area. Between 1992 and 1996, the number of juveniles (under 16 years of age) arrested annually in East Baton Rouge Parish increased 61 per cent, from 2931 to 4716. Sixteen per cent of these juveniles had committed a total of 940 violent crimes, including 14 homicides, 51 armed robberies and 132 aggravated assaults; and 122 juveniles committed 192 weapons violations. Of the 71 homicides in Baton Rouge in 1996, 13 were committed by youth under the age of 21 and 18 involved a young victim.

Baton Rouge is like many American cities that have seen an increase in violent crimes among young people in recent years. Though law enforcement has had some success in dealing with the problem, it was clear that the police alone could not address all the underlying issues and causes. What was required was a broad coalition of intervention and prevention services, grassroots groups, residents and the youth themselves.

In response, law enforcement, city officials, community agencies and grassroots volunteers joined together, supported by funding from the Office of Juvenile Justice and Delinquency Prevention, to form the Baton Rouge Partnership for the Prevention of Juvenile Gun Violence. These interests came together with local, State and federal law enforcement in 1997 as equal partners in shaping a plan of action. The result was a multifaceted approach that has shown some positive results in addressing juvenile gun violence in the city. Although the partnership grew in strength and number, the goals and the comprehensive approach to achieving them remained the same. As it turned out, this comprehensive approach and the ability of the partners to stay focused on it is one reason for the success of the partnership.

The partnership targeted multiple-offender youth up to age 21 from two high-crime ZIP code areas. Because the effects of juvenile violence are felt by the entire community, the partnership felt that solutions to the problem must involve a community-wide effort by a collaboration of agency and community stakeholders. No single organisation or agency could address all the risk factors associated with juvenile violence.

The organisational structure of the Baton Rouge partnership emerged from the project strategies that were developed during several programs development workshops involving law enforcement, the courts, the juvenile justice system, community service providers and the faith or religious community. The structure of the partnership is simple and informal, consisting of two standing committees with specified decision-making responsibilities: the Executive Committee (program policy or planning) and the Judicial Advisory Committee (legal advice and planning). These committees used several task forces – Enforcement, Intervention and Prevention – to make operational decisions in carrying out the comprehensive plan.

Strategies

The partnership designed a comprehensive strategy with four specific goals. First, it developed a multi-agency law enforcement (suppression) strategy to reduce gun-related and other violent crimes by juveniles and older youth. The partnership sought to reduce juvenile gun-related and other violent crimes through a three-pronged suppression strategy:

(1) identify and monitor, through intensive probation and law-enforcement surveillance, the small group of serious, violent and chronic young offenders who have committed multiple felony offences;

(2) reduce access to illegal guns and the incidence of juveniles carrying illegal guns by identifying and closing gun-distribution sources; and

(3) expedite the judicial response to those offenders involved in gun-related offences, including expedited prosecution in federal courts when possible.

The most noticeable suppression activity was called Operation Eiger. The Eiger strategy is a high-intensity probation and parole effort that targets an identified group of young people who are chronic violent offenders known as Eigers.[2] Three-member police/probation pilot teams make regular and intensive contacts with the 'Eigers' and their parents. Additionally, Operation Eiger teams contact an identified group of 'non-Eiger' youth who are at risk of becoming serious, habitual offenders. The strategy facilitates an immediate response to delinquent behaviour when it occurs. As of September 1998, 311 Eigers had been identified, 198 juveniles and 113 young adults. A total of 9570 home visits were made by Operation Eiger teams during their first year with the monthly average number of contacts per Eiger ranging from 3.3 in the first month of implementation to more than six during the last three months of the reporting period.

The second strategy was to implement an intensive intervention program to reduce the risk factors for the highest risk youth, their families and the community. The partnership's gun violence intervention strategies sought to address risk factors that contribute to the violent behaviours of the identified Eigers through a three-pronged approach: (1) provide intensive intervention services for the Eigers to address their alienation and rebelliousness, propensity for violence, association with peers who engage in high-risk behaviours, academic failure, unemployment and lack of social and interpersonal skills; (2) strengthen the Eiger families to instil moral values and support for their children by intervening in family conflicts and dysfunctional relationships, and alcohol and drug abuse; and (3) build resiliency in the community by intervening to address risk factors that include attitudes and conditions favourable to drug use, gun violence, community disorganisation, low neighbourhood attachment and economic deprivation.

To achieve these objectives, the partnership implemented case-management and intervention services. These services were initially designed to facilitate the reintegration of Eigers into the community. However, during the first year only a small number of Eigers were targeted for prerelease strategies because so few of them were incarcerated in local facilities. (Most were incarcerated elsewhere in the State.) A decision was made to shift the focus from prerelease/aftercare to intervention services for the entire Eiger population. The partnership thus sought to identify specific risk factors for all of the Eigers. A case-management specialist developed individual service plans (ISP's) that address factors identified in the risk and needs assessments. Individual needs assessments were completed for 138 juvenile Eigers and 106 young adult Eigers.

Intervention services in the first year included substance abuse evaluations and treatment, a chemical awareness clinic, an anger-management clinic, a crime-prevention clinic, psychological evaluations and counselling, family counselling, pre-employment job skills training, and job training and placement. These programs included the following:

- Mentoring program. Seeks to provide at-risk youth with positive messages on how they can turn their lives around. Mentors are largely drawn from the faith community and the 100 Black Men organisation. This has allowed some Eigers to be paired with neighbourhood-based spiritual mentors.

- Job training/placement program. Identifies existing employment training and job skills programs suitable for the Eigers and formalises a strategy for involving neighbourhood businesses to provide jobs.

- Family education program. Enables family members to deal more effectively with the Eigers and other central family issues. The initiative also identifies specific needs and gaps in family services. There is a minimum of one contact per week by probation officers with parents of Eigers.

- I-CARE: School-based services. As part of the prevention initiative, the partnership identified younger siblings of Eiger youth to be referred to school-based services and other relevant service programs. By the end of the first year, 87 siblings had been identified and referred to the I-CARE program for coordination of access to school-based services.

- Juvenile diversion program. A 40-week program, run by the Boy Scouts of America, one of the partnership's member agencies, provides an alternative to incarceration for first-time offenders to facilitate positive character development and prevent recidivism. Two groups of about 20 youth participated in the first cycle of the program, which began in January 1998.

- Youth Services Resource Directory. A comprehensive directory has been created listing programs, organisations and services throughout the city for targeted youth, their siblings and other at-risk youth. This compilation includes 1578 businesses, 183 churches, 67 schools, family service agencies in 69 categories, health services groups in 74 categories, and more than 400 other programs and services.

Last, the partnership mobilised the community at the grassroots level to address the problems of hard-to-reach families and the highest risk youth. They did this by (1) involving youth and families in identifying and helping resolve gun-violence issues in their neighbourhoods and encouraging accountability at the street level; (2) identifying organisations and resources that individuals and families in the target area can turn to for help in dealing with their respective risk factors; (3) addressing residents' negative attitudes about what they perceive as law enforcement's lack of interest and involvement in solving neighbourhood crime; and (4) implementing a public information strategy to raise community support and publicise positive outcomes of grassroots initiatives.

Activities included community fora, community surveys, community help/hotspot identification phone line, media coverage on program activities and school presentations. The partnership members increased their visibility in the target communities. For instance, the Chair, who was the Baton Rouge Chief of Police, attended many community fora and several police officers maintained a presence in the targeted communities. Further, the partnership members collaborated with local civic groups to sponsor community fora and respond to community-defined problems. Community members were encouraged to identify hotspots and individuals engaged in criminal activities as part of the suppression efforts. As part of an overall public awareness program, the partnership devised an anti-gun violence public information campaign. It established strong relationships with local newspaper and radio stations and cooperated to provide information for a number of articles and announcements about violence-related issues.

Outcomes

External evaluation conducted by COSMOS Corporation Bethesda showed that the number of homicides in Baton Rouge dropped 17 per cent from 1996 to 1997, from 71 murders in 1996 to 59 in 1997. Of these, 10 (17 per cent) involved a suspect under the age of 21, and 14 (24 per cent) involved a victim under the age of 21. The number of aggravated assaults dropped 43 per cent (to 1,135 incidents), with 995 involving firearms. One hundred and sixty-nine youths were involved in these firearm-related aggravated assaults, down 30 per cent from the previous year. The percentage of Eiger contacts in which no violations were reported increased from 56 per cent in September 1997 to 71 in September 1998.

Although Operation Eiger does not aggregate data by type of violation, it is estimated that 80 per cent of violations were for curfew violation, disobeying parents, failure to notify a parent of whereabouts, and truancy. The remaining 20 per cent were for more serious infractions such as failing a drug screening, associating with prohibited persons and committing a new offence. Through the first quarter of 1998, 14 Eigers (9.5 per cent) were incarcerated on new adult offences – a figure considerably less than the expected recidivism for this group of repeat violent offenders. Preliminary data for 1998 suggest significant reduction in firearm-related crimes. There were 34 homicides and 399 firearm-involved aggravated assaults through September 1998. Only 50 youths were involved in these firearm-related assaults. These reductions in homicides, aggravated assaults and other firearm-related crimes were attributed to the cumulative impact of a comprehensive, multi-pronged approach of the partnership.

Maple Ridge Youth Conference Project (Canada) [3]

Background

The British Columbia police initiated this partnership project in 1994 as a diversion scheme for simple first offenders. The institutional framework for the project involves the police, probation service, and schools on one hand and, on the other hand, local businesses and welfare or charity organisations. The project aims to help young offenders to understand the impact of their actions on the victim, families, community and themselves so that they can choose to avoid offending behaviour in the future. To achieve this aim the project uses tools such as victim impact statements, parental statements, volunteer work in a drug and alcohol treatment centre, a visit to a secure facility, referrals to cadet corps, as well as restitution and volunteer work with local people. Drawing on community resources, as a way of involving the whole community in addressing youth crime, the program develops one-on-one mentoring for the offenders, using volunteers as mentors. Volunteers with a variety of life experiences are drawn from agencies including businesses, churches, and charitable organisations for this mentoring.

Strategies

The management strategy involves incorporating a Board of Directors in order to keep the project on track. The Board set up an Intervention Committee that holds meetings in private with parents and the offenders and, where necessary, with the victims, with a view to deciding appropriate consequences for the crime. At the end of all deliberations, the parties sign a voluntary contract which may include restitution, apology, writing an essay, volunteer service work, attending counselling and visiting a secure facility. Following the signing of a contract, the committee assigns a member to monitor each case and report the progress. Where a youth is sent to a business, church or community organisation, the committee requires the organisation to provide supervision, mentoring and a report on progress. The successful completion means that no record is kept against the offender. The success and the 'no record' outcome of the process have made the program score high marks with both parents and young offenders who say that this gives them a fresh start on a new life on the right side of the law.

Outcomes

One year after it commenced, the verdict of the Maple Ridge community was that the project had had a successful start. This positive assessment has been maintained ever since. Regarded as the first of its kind to be introduced by any municipality in Canada, the program is said to represent a welcome departure from the 'lynch mob screaming for blood or arguing every young offender be locked up and the keys thrown away'. As an alternative to the formal court processing of young offenders, the project has succeeded in keeping about 90 per cent of its clients away from the stigma and the trap of the court system. This result is achieved mainly by getting the young offenders to accept accountability for their behaviour and re-connecting them to the community.

The factors that were shown to be most critical to the success of the project include one-on-one mentoring, the quality of the volunteers, the time limits in getting young people before the committee, the accountability process of the committee, and the involvement of the community which raises a sense of ownership and provides outlets for a deeper and meaningful contact with young offenders.

Western Australian Juvenile Justice Teams (Australia)

Background

During early 1990s, it was felt that an unacceptably high number of children were being apprehended by police and charged before the children's courts in Western Australia. Most were being processed for minor offences. After consultation with key agencies and the Aboriginal community and an analysis of several justice systems, the State Government Advisory Committee on Young Offenders recommended in 1994 the continuation of the Juvenile Justice Teams (JJTs) that were established in Western Australia as a pilot initiative in 1993. Their establishment was a recognition of the 'need for a higher level of involvement of families and the Aboriginal community as a whole in providing appropriate responses to young people who offend' (Cant and Downie 1998, p 30).

The teams approach was formalised under law (the *Young Offenders Act*) in 1994. The aim was to divert early and minor young offenders away from the formal justice system in a manner that recognises the importance of family in helping the young person to stop offending and provides the victim with an opportunity to be part of the process of redressing their victimisation and addressing the offending behaviour (Omaji 1997b).

Cant and Downie (1998, p 33) observe that the teams 'represent an attempt at a true inter-agency approach to establishing a diversionary alternative to court processes for juveniles'. Together with the Ministry of Justice, the police played a significant role in setting up the scheme. To extend the partnership to other major players in the life of a young person, the law provides for the Education Department and the Aboriginal community or other relevant communities to be represented on the teams.

JJTs take whatever individual cases have been referred from police officers, prosecutors and the Children's Court. The child and the responsible adult must agree to the matter being dealt with by a team and the child must accept responsibility for the offence before referral can be made by any of these agencies. As far as practicable, victims must be given an opportunity to make submissions or participate in the proceedings as the teams see fit.

Strategies

JJTs adopt a strategy founded in the 'restorative justice' philosophy. Once a matter has been referred to the teams, a member of the team will contact the young person and his or her family. The victim, where identifiable, will also be contacted and be advised about the plan to hold conference on the matter. After full discussion of the relevant issues, the team, together with all the parties, will determine the most appropriate outcome in the cir-cumstances. This outcome will be outlined in an action plan which may involve getting the young person to undertake community work, providing recompense to the victim by apology, restitution and/or reparation, and reinforcing the consequences already imposed by the parents.

The legislation that established JJTs stipulates that the intervention by the Teams should be culturally appropriate, both in terms of the time frame to which young people can relate, their level of maturity and responsibility, and the way of life of their ethnic backgrounds.

Outcomes

The evaluation of the pilot stage of this program showed that some 95 per cent of young people successfully completed their action plan. While this outcome tells us little about how many of these young people went on to reoffend, it certainly indicates that, unlike the formal criminal justice process where the penalty generally sets up convicted offenders to fail, the teams were successful in facilitating appropriate action plans that young people could complete without breach (Jones 1994). In the more recent evaluation, it was found that 92 per cent of offenders interviewed were satisfied with the way that they had been dealt with by the teams; 90 per cent of parents were satisfied with the JJTs approach and outcomes; and 83 per cent of victims expressed an overall satisfaction with the process (Cant and Downie 1998).

The factors that were considered to be most critical to the success of this program include a sound philosophical basis, an interactive and inclusive management style, a clear process of goal setting, and the collaboration between the Ministry of justice and the police. Regarding the collaboration, Cant and Downie (1998, p 37) observe thus:

> [A]lthough largely taken for granted in any discussion about the Juvenile Justice Teams, the fact that the Ministry of Justice and the police service have worked to collaboratively establish and maintain the teams must be identified as a major strength. A Juvenile Justice Team without one of the parties would be a poorer model.

As with other initiatives of this nature, the implementation of the project has experienced some difficulties, especially with regard to the composition of the Teams, the referral process, the administration and the resourcing of the Teams.

Mt Roskill Police Community Approach Project (New Zealand)

Background

In early 1994, juvenile offending and junior gang affiliation occurring in the Wesley–Morrie Lang area of Mt Roskill was highlighted in the media and the 'unsafe' nature of the district was emphasised. The particular area identified as a trouble spot has a relatively high Maori and Pacific Islander population compared to other parts of the Mt Roskill ward. In July 1994, Youth Aid constable, Nick Tuitasi called a community meeting to introduce a comprehensive five-prong preventative approach to reducing youth offending. The *Community Approach* is one of these prongs. The aim is 'to engage in preventative strategies against criminal offending in the community by empowering family, "whanau", "hapu" or "iwi" in Maori, through networking with government and community agencies'. More specifically, the project seeks to break the cycle of recidivist offending and to reduce crime among young people between the ages of 13 and 17 (Police National Headquarters Youth at Risk of Offending Evaluation Team 1998).

The project's aim follows the research wisdom that the defining characteristic shared by serious and repeat youth offenders is the level of disadvantage experienced in their lives and claimed that, for most, personal and social disadvantage has become entrenched. It also embodies the spirit of the 1989 *Children Young Persons and their Families Act* under which juvenile offending in New Zealand is dealt with. The principles of this Act are to avoid criminal proceedings in the court and to institute measures that strengthen the family and family group of the child or young person concerned.[4]

The project takes an ecological approach to youth offending, placing the young offender in the context of both family and community. The model, therefore, locates the focus of intervention with both family and community, instead of focusing on the offender. This does two things. First, it 'externalises' the offending and, secondly, it becomes a family and community issue instead of only an individual responsibility, as in the alternative Youth Justice model. Most importantly, it looks to structural causes of family deprivation.

Strategies

The strategy is to empower families through networking with government and community agencies. After studying offenders' files and visiting their homes, the staff of the project identify areas of immediate need, ascertain what should be done, work with the families to set specific goals and introduce agencies to corresponding immediate needs and social environment. The staff then work out a prevention plan which is acceptable to the families. Having established a public contact between the clients and agencies, the staff arrange a weekly visit to see if the prevention plan is running smoothly.

The project is collaborative, systematic and goal directed (Worall 1996). Conceived to foster inter-agency collaboration with education, employment and recreation to meet the need of the youth, the police officers responsible for the project work closely with several government and welfare agencies. Different sets of agencies are brought into the partnership to address different clients and their different needs. For one client, the project may involve the school, Housing New Zealand and the Best Training agency. For another, the partners may be Graffiti Busters, Children, Young Persons and their Families Service, Pacific Island Drug and Alcohol Service, and Hillsborough Baptist Church.

Outcomes

Evaluation shows that this program was successful. There was a record of 132 offences against the families at intervention point but, since involvement with the project, only two minor offences had been committed and these were by the same client. More significantly, over 50 per cent of these families had started to 'put back' into their communities in the form of church work, prisoner support work, voluntary assistance and general participation in events in their communities.

The factors most critical to the success of this project included:

- the commitment to a vision by the project's initiator;
- the energy, hard work and dedication of the project staff;
- the coordinated approach using a case-management model;
- proper targeting of the clients (focusing on the 'kernel families');
- the long-term involvement with families ('as long as it takes');
- being accessible, small and parochial enough to generate a sense of ownership within the community;
- linking and networking with agencies for information, resources and assistance, adopting an ecological approach (the youth together with family and community); and
- a culturally sensitive approach that meant 'a dignified way of treating other human beings'.

The staff adopted a collegial management style and holistic perspective of the clients thus recognising not only the physical, intellectual and social dimensions of their needs, but also the spiritual component of their struggles. Funding was initially difficult to secure. The first project officer had to work in the first six months in a voluntary capacity. Following a television documentary about the success of the project, an anonymous donation was made to support the project. Later on, the New Zealand police approved funds to support the salary of the coordinator and further funds had to be secured from the Pacific Islander community to employ a Family Work Coordinator. The financial analyses for the 1997-98 year and the 1998-99 year show an improved position, most of the income coming from the Crime Prevention Unit/Police funding (Police National Headquarters Youth at Risk of Offending Evaluation Team 1998, pp 19-20).

Midtown Community Court, New York – An Alternative for Involving Citizens and the Community in the Justice Process Project

Background

The public generally believe that the judicial system has failed to respond to the problem of crime in their communities. Thus, research reveals that, although the judiciary has great confidence in the courts, the public consistently rates the courts lower than other public institutions (American Judicature Society 1994). One reason for this is that 'since the beginning of the twentieth century, courts have lacked a natural and easy affinity with the community they serve' (Memphis Shelby Crime Commission 1999). This, in turn, arose from court reformers focusing on the development of a new type of court system – one consolidated in a central location with specialised branches to address newly evolving, complex legal problems. Their concern was that there appeared to be an uncontrolled growth in the number and variety of courts resulting in a lack of co-ordination and an increase in inefficiency, along with increasing concern about the link between these courts and local political machines. Thus, the court unification they advocated emphasised the need for specialisation and professionalisation of the law.

The experience of the city of Chicago illustrates what these reformers achieved. In 1931, 556 courts served the citizens of that city and, by 1991, the city was served by a single court with a main courthouse and 10 satellite locations. As this pattern of consolidation was replicated throughout the metropolitan areas of the United States, it resulted in the estrangement of the courts from their communities. Increasingly, courts, and their processes, became less visible to the community and its members:

> To most people, the term 'courts' conjures up an amorphous image of the judicial branch in which local, State, and Federal jurisdictions merge without distinction. Courts are remote and mysterious and while police chiefs are known in the communities, the chief judge is not. Furthermore, the organisation he or she heads consequently lacks a human face. Lack of knowledge about what the courts do and about which court does what is pervasive. (ibid)

As Chapter 2 showed, the mystique is even greater for young people. Overall, analysts have identified a number of propositions relating to the estrangement of courts from their communities. Centralised courts focus resources on serious crimes and devote insufficient attention to quality-of-life offences. Both communities and criminal justice officials share a deep frustration about criminal court processing of low-level offences. Community members often feel shut off and isolated from large-scale centralised courts. Low-level offences, to which the courts fail to pay sufficient attention, erode the quality of life and create an atmosphere in which serious crime flourishes.

These types of concerns led in 1991 to the formation of a joint effort in New York to develop a community court, the Midtown Community Court, where meaningful community service sanctions were introduced as a punishment for quality-of-life offences. The court became the product of a unique private-public coalition of criminal justice officials, corporations, community leaders, residents, social service providers and local government leaders. Corporations, private foundations and public sector agencies provide funding for the court.

In developing the court, planners designed the project to do more than simply re-create at the neighbourhood level the 'business as usual' routine case processing of low-level crimes. The court departed from conventional courts in several respects (described under Strategies below). Specific attention was directed at establishing a program that would address problems prevalent in the location of the community court: a high concentration of quality-of-life offences, broad community dissatisfaction with court outcomes, visible signs of disorder and clusters of persistent high-rate offenders with serious problems, including addiction and homelessness (ibid).

Working in collaboration with community groups, criminal justice officials and representatives of local government, the planners aimed for a project that could 'make case processing swifter, make justice visible to the community, encourage the enforcement of low-level offences, marshal local resources and help restore neighbourhoods that are victimised by low-level crime' (ibid). Project planners were influenced by an emerging body of criminal justice research and policy literature, especially in relation to community policing.

Midtown Community Court planners believed courts could also participate as a partner in developing constructive solutions to community-based problems of disorder by designing community service projects to eradicate local 'hot spots' and 'eyesores'. Moreover, planners believed the court could build on the imagery of the community policing movement; a humanised court which combined a small scale community focus with intimate local knowledge produced by incorporating the voice of the community in identifying local problems and developing collaborative solutions (ibid).

Strategies

Planners for the court focused on developing an innovative model that would have both a 'carrot' and 'stick' approach – one which encouraged voluntary engagement by defendants with service providers.

After dialogue with the community, social service providers, criminal justice experts, the police, victims and former defendants, the court adopted a new agenda that both punishes and helps defendants. This new agenda was based on simple ideas and common sense: If a defendant pays back the harmed community and at the same time receives help solving problems that can lead to crime, justice in low-level cases can be both restorative to the community and constructive to the defendant.

The court pulled together two trends to address these goals, favouring the local adjudication of low-level offences and building new bridges between courts and communities. In meeting its objectives, the court project introduced a number of innovative features:

- a coordinating team, working in partnership with court administrators, to foster collaboration with the community and other criminal justice agencies; to oversee the planning, development and operations of court-based programs; and to develop ideas for new court-based programs;

- an assessment team, operating between arrest and arraignment, to determine whether a defendant has a substance abuse problem, a place to sleep, etc;

- a resource coordinator, stationed in the well of the courtroom to match defendants with drug treatment, community service and other sanctions;

- innovative technology, to provide immediate access to information needed to inform judicial decision-making;

- space for court-based social service providers to address underlying problems of defendants;

- community service projects specifically designed to 'pay back' the community harmed by crime;

- a Community Advisory Board to keep the court abreast of quality-of-life problems in the community, identify community service projects to address these problems, assist in planning and provide feedback about the court;

- court-based mediation to address community-level conflicts, rather than just individual disputes; and

- a court-based research unit, to analyse information on case processing and case outcomes, and to suggest outcomes.

Outcomes

A comprehensive and rigorous evaluation research of the court was completed in 1997 (see Jones, Berman, Dodson and Hodos 1997). The research involved both a process analysis and an impact analysis of the project. At the end of 18 months of operation, evaluators found clear evidence that the project had achieved its operational goals. Justice was dispensed more swiftly at the court than in the centralised courts. Arrest-to-arraignment time averaged 18 hours at the court compared to 30 hours at the central courts. Moreover, staff in the community court achieved a 'same-day' or 'next-day' start for 40 per cent of defendants with community service sentences. In fact, some defendants were arraigned, sentenced and community service sentences recorded on the same day (Sviridoff, Rottman, and Curtis 1997).

The court made justice substantially more visible to the community. Community leaders participating in focus groups and individual interviews expressed high levels of awareness about the court and its processes. The existence of the court encouraged enforcement efforts against low-level offences by taking quality-of-life crimes seriously. The formation of a relationship between local police and court personnel resulted in enforcement of low-level warrants and the growth of partnership directed at developing responses to these crimes for which traditional methods had proved ineffective.

Court staff assembled nearly two dozen community-based partners to provide a broad range of social services and to supervise neighbourhood-based community service projects. The court worked closely with community groups to identify local problems and to develop various approaches for addressing these problems through community restitution. The court increased awareness of the way communities are victimised by low-level crime and made extensive use of community service projects that were designed to 'pay back' the community where crimes occurred. The evaluation also found an additional benefit of the court – the community advisory group kept the court informed of changing neighbourhood conditions and problems and court-based mediation was often able to resolve various conflicts between community groups.

Evaluators found substantial impact in all areas that the project planners had targeted as goals. It demonstrated that a community-focused court could indeed change traditional practices, affect 'going rates', promote defendant compliance with community service orders and help make a difference in neighbourhood conditions. The project served to demonstrate that courts can develop closer links to communities and become active partners in solving local problems. Overall, the court served to spark broad recognition in both local and national-level conversations of the role that community-focused courts can play in developing constructive responses to quality-of-life offences (ibid).

Local authority-centred partnership model

Safer Slough Enterprise Partnership (UK)[5]

Background

Slough is a town of approximately 106,000 inhabitants, 34 kilometres to the west of London, England. It is a mixture of industrial and residential areas, with nearly a third of its population being ethnic, of which the majority are Asians and Afro-Caribbeans. Some areas of Slough are affluent whilst other areas are impoverished. Crime in Slough had risen by over 70 per cent in five years: from 12,422 recorded offences in 1987, to 21,155 in 1991. Approximately 47 per cent of all offences in Slough were committed by young people aged between 15 and 23.

Following the Morgan Committee Report in 1991,[6] which recommended the implementation of safer communities as a multi-agency approach to crime reduction with local authorities playing a leading role, Inspector Clive Doyle, of the Thames Valley Police Community Liaison Department, approached Slough Borough Council in 1992 and suggested setting up a safer community project, the *Safer Slough Enterprise* (SSE). He was encouraged by his Area Commander, Superintendent Tom Morrison, and the Chief Constable of the Thames Valley Police, Charles Pollard.

Doyle proposed that SSE should have a Steering Committee, or Strategy Group, to formalise the commitment to, and impart ownership of, the departments and organisations involved. It should also appoint a full-time coordinator who would be the focal contact point and a facilitator for the Enterprise. It was thought that the public would respond more positively if the facilitator was neither from the council nor from the police, even though both organisations would play leading roles.

In addition, the Enterprise should have sub-committees to address specific aspects of the partnership focus. Thus, the Management & Advisory Team (MAT), whose members would include representatives from the Police (Chair), Probation Service (Vice-Chair), Community Education Service, Education Welfare, Fire Brigade, Local Press, Slough Borough Council, Slough Council for Voluntary Services, Slough Retailers Group, Social Services, Youth & Community Services and the coordinator, would *assess* local crime problems. It also would coordinate the work of the Action Groups, set up to give a coordinated approach to specific problems (eg auto-crime, women's safety and substance abuse) These Action Groups, with members coming from all parties/agencies interested in the target matter, would look at ways to reduce opportunities for crime, support victims and tackle root causes of crime. The Strategy Group would include representatives from Slough Borough Council (Chair), industry (Vice-Chair), Police and Slough Council for Voluntary Services, plus the Chair of the Management & Advisory Team and the coordinator. The role of the Group would be to produce a business plan, appraise resource implications, and monitor the progress made by the coordinator.

The MAT would provide a forum for issues identified by the Action Groups, or by the Strategy Group and would analyse threats to the community, opportunities for improvement and weaknesses in the program. At the community level, 'Community Forums' would provide an opportunity for the community to tell SSE of its perceptions of crime-related problems. The Forums would enable local discussion of local problems, suggest possible solutions and provide a community-driven focus for SSE. The Forums would engender a greater sense of community spirit, and accept ownership of community problems. Membership of the Forums would consist of any interested party.

SSE was officially launched in June 1992. The press were very supportive and an excellent rapport was established with the local radio stations. SSE also benefited from positive publicity on local and national radio and TV stations, and through exhibitions. Posters and leaflets on the Enterprise were produced and widely distributed.

Finance for SSE came from the Berkshire Probation Service, Motorola, Slough Borough Council, Slough Social Fund and the Thames Valley Police Authority. Money was also raised by selling Match Up Kits (described under Strategies below), personal attack alarms and ultra-violet marker pens for marking property. All projects were self-funding.

Citroen supported the Police for six months by lending a car to be used exclusively by SSE to publicise vehicle security, and to visit clients. A local bus company had several of its buses covered for free with messages about community safety, while ICL donated a computer. Cellnet donated a mobile phone, along with call costs and air time.

SSE conducted various seminars to discuss methods of reducing crime committed *by* young people. One seminar was on inter-agency training aimed at ensuring each of the statutory agencies knew how the others worked with a view to closer cooperation and improved working practices between them. Plans were made between several agencies to have further meetings to explore ways of improving their services, and to interchange personnel, giving staff the chance to gain hands-on learning experience of how other agencies worked.

Thames Valley Police deserve the highest praise for their attitude and support, which included the secondment to SSE in May 1993 of a full-time police officer. Slough Borough Council gave much material and financial support, including an office and furniture. Much time was spent by many of the elected members and the workers at the council in helping the Enterprise. The agencies were willing to support the Project and to attend meetings, and made very useful contributions. However, their own workloads often prevented them from more participation.

Strategies

The Enterprise organised its crime-prevention activities around several targeted projects, a few of which are described here. The Action Motor Project, Slough (AMPS) aimed to divert youngsters committing auto-crime offences into legitimate activities with motor vehicles. Their participation was compulsory by order of the courts. Leadership, team spirit and attitude enhancement were encouraged. It was not intended that the offenders be given privileges for their misdeeds, but it was a serious attempt to reform misguided youth into responsible members of the community. The project did not come to fruition as intended due to problems with sponsorship and in finding premises. Long-term sponsorship was not forthcoming and the project coordinator was absent on sick leave for several months. The project was to be reviewed to consider its running through a service agreement with appropriate organisations.

Match Up aimed to reduce vehicle theft. By bonding a small plastic frame to the screen of the vehicle anyone, but particularly the police, can tell at a glance if an unauthorised person was driving the vehicle. One side of the frame has a unique graphic symbol that cannot be removed. Authorised drivers of the vehicle have a matching symbol that they slip into the frame when using the vehicle and take out of the frame when they leave it. Any vehicle seen by police moving without the match is subject to a spot check. Each individual Match-Up kit has a unique design with three matching cards supplied.

In the Thames Valley Police area it is estimated that about 4,000 Match-Up kits had been sold before 1994. Only one vehicle fitted with Match-Up had been stolen by early 1994 – and that was abandoned after 100 yards. In 1993, vehicle thefts in Slough fell by 1000 over the previous year.

SSE and Sergeant (now Inspector) Mark Hogarth (Thames Valley Police, Southern Traffic Area) established a Casualty Reduction Scheme to improve safety on the roads through education, deterrence and enforcement. In December 1993 a Mobile Exhibition Unit was obtained, and has been widely used. It can be adapted to any road safety topic. So successful was the campaign that the Thames Valley Police created a new post of Casualty Reduction Officer to deal with community safety, with special emphasis on speed, accident black spots, safety campaigns and exhibitions.

A full-time coordinator was employed by SSE to service Business Watch. A paging system was introduced enabling participants to warn each other of any suspicious activity or of attempted break-ins and this resulted in several arrests. Better publicity was introduced through a regular newsletter, and several security/safety exhibitions were organised, as were training programs on security. By 1996, Slough Estates, a property company, had taken over the running of Business Watch.

The Town Centre Scheme involved the installation of closed-circuit television in the town centre, and with the completion of the control room there is the opportunity to establish a community business development program which looks at many aspects of community protection. Security improvements in the main town centre car park led to a drop in crime in the period January to June 1994 of 90 per cent compared with the same period in 1993.

SSE produced a package entitled Elderly Persons Home Watch designed by SSE and the police for distribution to about 900 elderly and socially disadvantaged persons, all of whom had been identified by Social Services. The advice contained in the pack included fire safety and prevention, plus personal and home security.

Mobile Watch is a form of Neighbourhood Watch on wheels that involves any company whose vehicles are fitted with telephone/radios. Drivers of these vehicles keep a look out for suspicious activity in the community and phone through to the police control room to report any incident. The police make only one phone call to each participating company to get information to many people. They may ask, for example, that drivers keep a look out for a missing person, or a stolen vehicle. Despite very good publicity, the scheme was not a great success. SSE omitted to include the police control ROOM at Slough in its early discussions about the scheme. When the time came to be involved, the control room was presented with a *fait accompli* which they did not appreciate and hence made virtually no effort to cooperate.

SSE linked up with Positive Prevention Plus and supported it in its Parenting Skills for Prevention Scheme. It provided parents of pre-teens and teenagers with the information and skills necessary to get their child safely into adulthood, and to help them recognise signs that their children were getting involved in anti-social activities.

'You're OK! I'm OK!' was a totally new project. Utilising the talents of the Learning Through Action Trust, the project worked on the basis that children pick up their life-time habits and thoughts at an early age. Through role play, the project aimed to raise the self-esteem of youngsters and reduce bullying, and to get them to respect other people and their property. A complete week was taken out of the curriculum at Lynch Hill School to accommodate the project and parents were given the opportunity to participate, though very few took advantage of this.

As a result of this pilot project, two national charities offered to provide funding for further projects, as did Marks & Spencer, if it went nationwide. SSE, however, could only participate in projects taking place in the borough and within days had received requests from seven schools for the same project. The initial project was jointly funded by SSE and the Thames Valley Partnership (a safer community organisation covering the whole of the Thames Valley Police area), while the later projects in Slough were funded by SSE alone.

Schools Police Liaison Activities for Summer Holidays (S.P.L.A.S.H.) was aimed at diverting youngsters from becoming involved in petty crime and vandalism, often the start of a greater involvement in crime. Participants were given the opportunity to become involved in activities in which they would not normally have the chance to take part, nor which they would usually be able to afford. SSE funded a pilot S.P.L.A.S.H. scheme in a small area of the town with a high crime rate and in an area of high social deprivation and unemployment. The scheme was conducted three afternoons per week for five weeks. Activities included canoeing and rock climbing. Statistics showed that vandalism at the local school fell dramatically in comparison with the same period in 1992. The scheme has now expanded to other areas of Slough.

Outcomes

Evaluation of SSE's projects in the early days was non-existent and a project was often undertaken on a 'feel-good' basis. During the summer of 1993 the coordinator undertook a course run by Crime Concern, a national crime-prevention organisation, learning how to implement and monitor evaluation techniques for community safety projects. Thereafter, any project undertaken had an evaluation process built into it.

An assessment of the Steering Group and the MAT showed that they did not work as they should have, often due to personality clashes, and it was left to the coordinator to do their work. In its evaluation of SSE, Crime Concern stated that:

> [T]he capacity of agencies to participate in the partnership should be developed. Experience has shown that the induction and training is an important way of increasing understanding of the respective roles of different agencies, raising their commitment, and empowering them to work together effectively. It should be offered to all those expected to manage the partnership or involved in Action Groups. (Crime Concern 1994)

Crime Concern also recommended that there should be a fundamental review of the organisational structure of SSE. There is a need to clarify the role of the Trustees and decide whether there is a real need for a MAT (ibid). Further, it recommended that 'a more strategic approach should be adopted towards the definition of the work program' and that action is needed to ensure quality control of projects. Projects should be required to prepare a project plan that includes an option for appraisal and evaluation arrangements. The number of 'live' projects should be reduced to a level that the coordinator can manage effectively.

Action Groups worked well, while Community Forums had varying degrees of success with many problems resolved on behalf of the public. The main concerns were parking, lighting and speeding traffic. In one area, there was concern over the lack of youth facilities. Discussions with the Youth & Community Service led to a youth club opening one night a week, with extra nights being added later.

Superintendent Roger Herbert of the Thames Valley Police wrote that there was a small reduction in the volume of crime in Slough during 1993 and inferred that safer communities were having an effect. He further stated that SSE 'has grown in stature and relevance as an influence in Slough' which has 'enabled diverse and innovative projects to be undertaken' (ibid).

Observers generally believe that the establishment of SSE was worthwhile and had remarkable success in its first few months of existence setting a clear example for other communities to follow. It represents a model multi-agency approach to crime reduction and raising community spirit in England. It has shown that the statutory and voluntary agencies can work together and with commerce, and that they really can work for the good of the community.

An anticipated advantage with SSE was that because it is an independent body the public may trust it more if they did not trust the council or police. Sometimes this was the case, but more often people contacted SSE after they had failed to get satisfaction from either the council or the police. The disadvantage of being an independent organisation was that the coordinator had constant concerns about project funding and running costs. In addition, whilst it was relatively easy to talk to a member of the council, not being an employee of the council itself meant facing consistent obstacles and no authority to ensure recommendations were followed.

Cairns Community Safety Project, Queensland (Australia)

Background

As one of Australia's best known tourist destinations with a transient and predominantly young population, a large public housing estate and a high per capita alcohol consumption, Cairns has a constellation of all variables 'identified in criminological literature as being linked to higher crime rates' (Boorman and McMillan 1998).[7]

In 1994 Cairns experienced slightly higher than average levels of crime in Queensland including crimes against the person and 'break and enters'. That year, the then-Mulgrave Shire Council commissioned research into crime and the fear of crime in the shire. The report, *The Crime of Fear: Attitudes, Perceptions and Community Safety,* identified a number of strategies which the community could adopt to address issues of local concern.

Council's first response was to establish what was then known as the Mulgrave Community Safety Consultative Committee, representing the first series of partnerships for a safer community. From the outset, this committee attracted high level support from key stakeholders in the community. This support enabled it to be an extremely focused, action-oriented and successful committee.

In January 1995, the Mulgrave Shire Council employed a Community Safety Officer to work with the Community Safety Consultative Committee and the council on a series of community safety initiatives. In March of that same year, the then Cairns City Council employed a Safety Action Project Officer as part of a model designed by Griffith University to replicate the Surfers Paradise Safety Action Project in regional centres.

A local government amalgamation in March 1995 resulted in the merger of the Mulgrave Shire Council and Cairns City Council and, as a consequence, the Community Safety Consultative Committee and the Safety Action Project Steering Committee, also merged. The resultant Cairns Community Safety Consultative Committee (later renamed the Cairns Community Safety Committee – CSC) assumed an ongoing responsibility for overseeing the work of both the Community Safety Officer and the Safety Action Project Officer.

The CSC includes high level representation by a number of 'traditional' partners including the Cairns City Council, the Queensland Police Service, the Chamber of Commerce, indigenous representatives and representatives from a wide range of government agencies. It also includes a number of non-traditional partners including a night-club manager, a representative of the development industry and a media manager. The Community Safety Committee created a number of discrete, but directly linked and accountable, sub-committees which assume responsibility for identifying and addressing issues within specific sectors. The dynamic and cooperative nature of this structure also enables much cross-sectoral work to occur.

The sub-committees include:

- Media Sub-Committee
- Venue Managers Association (night-club managers)
- Community Safety Alert (business people)
- Youth/Education Sub-Committee (and two school-based student groups)
- Alcohol Harm Minimisation Group
- Planning and Development Sub-Committee (urban design issues)

The Community Safety Officer

The work of the CSC and its sub-committees is augmented by the endeavours of the Council's Community Safety Officer. The Officer's position was the first of its kind to be established in Queensland that was fully funded by a local government authority. This officer works with the CSC and all of the sub-committees, though the role differs in accordance with the specific purpose, activities and processes of each sub-committee. The officer also works on council projects and on key issues with local community groups, regularly reporting to both the Community Safety Committee and the Cairns City Council.

Strategies

One of the strengths attributed to the Cairns Community Safety Committee is its ability to attract and maintain a diverse range of partners who share the vision and have the power and influence to act, and to make a difference to community safety in Cairns. This has been achieved through a number of processes including:

1. creative problem solving which encourages the participation of a range of partners including those not traditionally involved in crime prevention;
2. the clear demonstration to all partners of the role that they may play and the links between their areas of responsibility and improved community safety;
3. ensuring the legitimacy and responsibility of partners;
4. avoiding loading partners with 'administrivia' and bureaucracy (ie council assumes responsibility for minute taking, organising meetings etc);
5. structuring meetings and other processes to meet the individual needs of the partners;
6. ensuring that council acts as the 'honest broker' to mediate conflict between partners and when necessary, to circumvent competitiveness between partners and to address 'cultural' differences in approach;
7. publicly sharing, or 'handing over' the credit for achievements;
8. ensuring that costs associated with activities are equitably shared;

9. ensuring that activities are valid and supported by current criminological and crime-prevention research and practice;

10. demonstrating a commitment to monitoring and continuous improvement; and

11. 'leading by example' with council committing significant resources, providing a sound policy framework through policy development and review linked to management systems, staff training and accountability – thus guaranteeing reliable and consistent support and direction.

The committee embarked upon several activities, including four illustrative projects that are described below in some details.

The 'My Place' Campaign: This campaign aimed to overcome the lack of community pride and participation which contributes to a level of apathy regarding crime prevention and which is linked partly to having a highly transient population. It sought to bolster pride and community participation by providing Cairns residents with easy access to knowledge about 'their' suburb in the form of a weekly feature in the free local newspaper and through a series of television and radio community service announcements which focused on the positive aspects of life in Cairns. Each television station undertook to produce a series of 'grabs' of people talking about why they liked their suburb. These 'grabs' were filmed at identifiable places of local significance, for example the corner store, the skate board ramp etc. Each station produced two announcements, with all being given a Community Safety Committee 'tail'. They were aired on all three commercial television stations (at their expense) as a service to the community, and were also complemented by a newspaper campaign. This represented an ongoing commitment to significant 'in-kind' contributions from the Cairns media.

This project has clearly influenced media practice by encouraging the media representatives to collaborate to produce a Community Safety Campaign. The Cairns media, like that which exists generally elsewhere, adheres to the notion that crime sells. Whilst there is some anecdotal evidence that the nature of crime reporting in Cairns has become less sensational since the establishment of the Community Safety Committee and the Media Sub-Committee, the amount of non-sensational information about community safety has clearly increased. The Media Sub-Committee has taken an active role in ensuring that this occurs. Through the 'My Place' campaign the Cairns media have adopted the role of concerned community corporate members. It has also influenced the change in media policy from acting strictly as reporters of the news to 'acting as reporters of the news and as concerned members of the Cairns community' (Boorman and McMillan 1998). The sharing of production costs and other resources among the media outlets was a clear example of the cooperative nature of this project.

The Babinda Crime Prevention Panel Basketball Court: Babinda is a small sugar-farming community approximately 60 kilometres south of the main population centre of Cairns. In 1997, the community was rocked by the deaths of five young people in two single-vehicle accidents in one evening. Following the incident, a local community health worker undertook a survey with young people in the town to ascertain their thoughts about life in Babinda. The survey results clearly indicated frustration at the lack of activities for young people in the community.

At the time of the accidents, the Babinda State High School Crime Prevention Panel had been working on a range of issues in their school including graffiti, inappropriate behaviour at school dances and bullying. This group chose to become involved in actioning some of the recommendations of the above-mentioned survey. An old disused and run down basketball court was identified. The members of the Crime Prevention Panel invited their local government representative to attend one of their meetings and approached him for funds to refurbish the basketball court. With funds from council, the young people set about planning a launch for the court to ensure that young people in the region knew that it would be available again.

The Cairns NBA basketball team was approached to have players attend and to organise basketball drills and games. Local businesses were approached to provide contributions for a sausage sizzle. Local community agencies donated lecterns, PA systems, urns, toilet facilities etc. The Cairns-based Police Citizen's Youth Club attended with their Mobile Activity Centre. Media releases were dispatched and school parades addressed. Invitations were forwarded to prominent local people to attend the launch. The coordinated and cooperative efforts of these young people led to a well attended, well catered and fun launch of what is now a valuable community resource.

The efforts of these young people led the school administration to permit (and encourage) students to become involved in issues beyond their immediate school surrounds, developing a sense of citizenship and participation. The project also sought to involve and coordinate a range of people from both Cairns and Babinda to cooperate for the benefit of young people.

The 'Safe Partying' Coaster: In recognition of Cairns as a 'party town', a sub-committee of the Community Safety Committee, the Alcohol Harm Minimisation Group, developed a promotion to reduce alcohol-related harmful behaviour during the festive season (Christmas to New Year). They developed a drink coaster design bearing 'tips for safe partying'. Coasters were distributed amongst the major four and five star hotels that traditionally host work and club break-ups and Christmas parties. The coasters were designed by the Tropical Public Health Unit. The messages were prepared by Cairns City Council in cooperation with the Road Safety Consultant with the Department of Transport and an officer from Queensland Health. The licensee on the sub-committee obtained funding from Castlemaine Perkins (a Queensland Brewery) to print the coasters. The coasters were distributed by members of the sub-committee and Police Beat Officers. The major hotels agreed to use the coasters. Promotion for the campaign was organised by the Cairns City Council.

Again, council was able to influence the practices of major hotels regarding the provision of safety information to patrons. Council brought together a range of government agencies, with key private sector groups, to seek to reduce alcohol-related harms including violent and wilful damage and driving under the influence which often arise from binge drinking during festive season parties. Anecdotal information provided by hotels indicated that the posters received favourable comments from patrons.

The Community Safety Seminars: Soon after its formation, the Community Safety Alert group conducted a survey to identify the concerns of people who live and/or work in the Cairns Central Business District (where crime in Cairns is most concentrated). Many respondents sought to have better access to information about safety, thus the Community Safety Alert Sub-Committee chose to convene a series of free safety seminars on a bi-monthly basis. These seminars were coordinated using a partnership model:

- the members of the Hotels Association (four and five star) provide the Community Safety Alert with a free conference venue each month;
- Metway Bank prints the fliers for the mail out promoting the seminars;
- the Chamber of Commerce funds 50 per cent of the mail out and a local business funds the remainder;
- all speakers donate their time and expertise;
- the local media promote the seminars; and,
- Cairns City Council handles all bookings, coordinates an evaluation of each seminar, and informs the planning for future seminars.

These seminars were generally attended by between 40-100 people, with the seminars being regarded in many instances as excellent staff training. Again cooperation between apparently unrelated sectors of the community was optimised to the benefit of people who have provided extremely favourable feedback. Stories have related instances in which skills learnt in earlier seminars have been successfully applied in the workplace.

Council and its partners on the Community Safety Committee have maintained a commitment to monitoring and improvement throughout the life of the project. This commitment has enabled the initiatives to remain credible in the eyes of the partners many of whom are from business and government agencies that require the tangible achievement of outcomes as a basic indicator of success.

Outcomes

In March 1997 council invited five key crime-prevention research bodies to submit a proposal to evaluate the early work of the Community Safety

Committee. This evaluation was to complement the Safety Action Project Evaluation which was being undertaken separately by Griffith University, and drew upon the ongoing, albeit ad hoc, monitoring that was being undertaken by the committee and the sub-committees.

The evaluation had as its purpose: to examine the processes, participation, outputs and commitment of the Community Safety Committee and its sub-committees – with a major emphasis on sustainability issues. The evaluation team was impressed by the high level of participation in the review by the key players. This was, in itself, a major indication of their commitment to council's initiative and their preparedness to focus on their role, the concepts of quality and accountability, and the need to address strategies to enhance continuous improvement.

Some of the issues considered by the evaluation team included:

- an assessment of what was possible, given the resources and the time;
- the competing demands within council and within other agencies and businesses especially for those who were volunteering their involvement;
- the limitations which must be placed on those who volunteer, so that their contributions can be sustained and they are not 'burnt out' by their participation;
- the grassroots support within organisations and the community within Cairns for the initiative;
- the success of the inter-agency focus and the development of non-traditional partnerships; and
- the operating environment for the Cairns' initiative within the State and federal community safety and crime-prevention policy context and current/future directions.

One of the key success factors that was evident throughout the evaluation was the continued commitment of the CSC members and the members of the sub-committees to be involved now and in the future. The CSC is chaired by the Mayor with the Deputy Chairperson being the Assistant Commissioner for Police for the region. This high level leadership and involvement have resulted in the continued participation of those who have the capacity to act – to make a difference – either through their positional authority or through their community involvement and influence. Many committees, such as this, commence with high level membership and over time the members are replaced by proxies who do not have authority to commit to action, or to commit resources and then must consult outside of the meeting processes before they can endorse proposals and action. This has not been the case with the CSC and this is a major achievement.

Another success factor in the Cairns partnership model is the support provided by the council to the CSC and to the sub-committees, and to the many volunteers involved in specific projects. There is no doubt that those involved have competing priorities. In the case of some of the volunteers, although they may have a major interest in the project/activity, they may gain additional confidence from being part of a team and from 'on the job' training supported by targeted training workshops. When partnerships are based on volunteers, there must be emphasis placed on minimising burn out and succession planning. The evaluation noted this area as one for further attention – expanding the community development role of the Community Safety Officer to increase the priority on leadership and on workshops and training which can empower more people to undertake planning resulting in sustainable programs, activities and outcomes.

The role of the Community Safety Officer was seen to be a major success factor for the project. This is because this officer provides the linkages and the structure to the appropriately diverse processes of the various sub-committees and also the focus within council for policy and program development and inter-agency approaches. Increasing the co-ordinating and planning role of the CSC should ensure that priorities are developed and that unforeseen issues can be considered within a structured, yet flexible framework. The integrity of such a model at the local level relies heavily on respect accorded to the Officer as an 'expert' and as a facilitator who supports volunteers, and coordinates communications with government and community agencies.

The evaluation team identified a need to increase the level of accountability in a manner that does not superimpose itself over the local processes as an end in itself, introducing a level of bureaucracy which may in itself be off-putting to the involvement of some of the key players. The benefits of measurement and performance indicators are undeniable and provide the rigour which must inform the short-term and longer term planning for the CSC and its sub-committees. Performance indicators can be developed for programs and activities, and can also be developed for processes, for example, CSC planning and operations. The team stressed the need for performance indicators to be measurable and realistic – addressing qualitative and quantitative indicators.

In the three years since its inception, the CSC has realised many major achievements including:

- the development and documentation of local codes of conduct for night clubs;
- changes to town planning Processes;
- preparation and distribution of cartoons simplifying the Queensland liquor legislation;
- convening of community safety fora;
- development of community safety media campaigns;
- publishing of school holiday activity calendars;
- establishment of a Commercial Watch program;
- installation of security cameras;
- coordination of safety audits; and
- extensive involvement in many other projects.

Conclusion

The projects described in this chapter show that criminal justice partnerships come in different shades and sizes. All the projects represent innovation with which criminal justice agencies are now responding to crime generally and youth crime in particular. Although the evaluation of most of them was still rudimentary and tentative in its conclusions, the results sufficiently indicate that this genre of response holds a greater promise of crime prevention than the traditional reactive approach.

The design and implementation of the partnership projects embody an implicit critique of traditional bureaucratic models of societal response and service delivery in relation to crime. In philosophy and praxis, they stand in significant contrast to the lack of systemisation, coordination and integration that produce conflict, friction and institutional gaps in traditional criminal justice systems (Crawford 1998, p 170). Time will tell whether the shift towards partnership, as exemplified in these projects, will significantly result in the correction of the 'system failures' of the old regimen – in terms of cost effectiveness, internal functionality, delivery of genuine crime reduction or community safety and redeeming young people from a life of crime.

Notes

1   The details of this project are collected from 'Profile No 8: Partnership for the prevention of juvenile gun violence' in Bilchik (1999).

2   Eiger is a reference to a mountain of the same name, which is one of the most difficult mountains in the world to climb.

3   The details for this project were gathered from personal interviews and unpublished documents during research visits to Ridge Meadows Youth & Justice Advocacy Association and the British Columbia Police Headquarters in Vancouver, 1997.

4   Maxwell, Kingi, Robertson and Morris (2002) provide a detailed, positive assessment of the application of these principles in New Zealand since the 1990s.

5   Much of the information presented to describe this project derives from Nash's (1998) detailed comparison between this partnership project and a similar project in Townsville, Queensland (Australia) for which he was the City Safe Officer.

6   A Report by a British Government Home Office Standing Conference on Crime Prevention entitled *Safer Communities: The Local Delivery of Crime Prevention Though the Partnership Approach.*

7   The rest of the details of this project presented here is an adapted excerpt from a paper developed by Cathy Boorman of the Cairns City Council and Elizabeth McMillan of the McMillan Management Consulting Pty Ltd, Australia.

7

The partnership benchmark for traditional criminal justice response

The world is changing in ways that make partnerships more important, if not essential, to achieving success in virtually every kind of professional endeavour. Partnerships simply represent a better way to do things ... [They] offer a great potential as a humanising and ultimately liberating force in our society. (Bergquist, Betwee and Meuel 1995, pp X, XIV)

Drawing on specific characteristics of the partnership practices outlined in Chapter 6, this chapter begins to articulate a qualitatively higher point of reference (aka 'benchmarking') for the criminal justice agencies' responses to youth crime. It examines the various key aspects of the partnership projects and assess them as workable crime-prevention responses compared to the traditional criminal justice approach. I have already shown that the underlying justification for the shift towards partnership in the criminal justice endeavour is the belief that this type of response reflects, as far as possible, the multi-dimensional nature of youth crime itself. In the end, it is the capacity of any measures to address the risk and protective factors[1] in relation to crime that determines their utility and status within the prevention discourse. Notwithstanding the implicit superiority of the new approach, the optimism of Bergquist et al (1995) about partnership being 'a humanising and liberating force' demands an empirical verdict.

Comparing key features of the partnership projects to the traditional model

The projects described in the previous chapter highlight key characteristics of the coalitions with which the criminal justice agencies in the western world have responded to youth crime in recent times. First, it should be noted that creating coalitions of any kind is not an easy undertaking. Calhoun (1998, p 2) is right when he observes that building partnerships and coalitions seems 'an "unnatural act committed by non-consenting adults", or a little like screaming fans watching rugby teams exhaust themselves on the field while the real work is to get the playing spectators onto the field'.

The complexity shows up clearly in what moved participants to engage in partnership, what fundamental assumptions they had about the causes of youth crime and about their own roles and capabilities, the level of prevention at which they pitched their interventions, the strategic structures and approaches they adopted, and the nature of community involvement with their projects. These are the issues that are examined in this section.

Motivations

The vast array of stakeholders in all the sample partnership projects – government agencies including the police, Ministry of Justice and Education Department, and community agencies including private businesses and the voluntary or charitable sector – identified central concerns that brought them together. It was to reduce gun violence[2] and youth offenders' recidivism;[3] to divert simple or first offenders,[4] or simply to follow official direction for the design of community safety.[5] The context was one of perceived increasing crime rates, increasing fear of crime and predominance of a generally punitive attitude.

Most of the projects turned on committed and capable individuals, using their personal skills and imagination in discerning the concerns of their communities and devising solutions for them. They underline the fact that the role of a visionary or local champion is critical to the successful formation and implementation of partnership projects.

Each of the participating organisations in all the partnership projects has its own unique motivation for getting involved. For reasons related to the perception of rising crime and declining public confidence, the police have had little alternative but to participate in partnerships. In fact, it has been observed that the promise of greater effectiveness through partnership has had considerable appeal to the police in an increasingly managerialist climate. The New York Midtown project was driven mainly by the need to reverse the image of courts as a disconnected and failed institution.

Community agencies have been enticed by a powerful ideological crusade for active citizenship. Over and above this, private businesses have been encouraged to consider the costs of crime for enterprise, and to consider the benefits of collaboration for publicity and tax deductions. Local authorities and the voluntary sector have been enticed by the availability of additional resources through various special central or State government initiatives, on condition that partnership can be demonstrated (Gilling 1997).

Although most of the criminal agencies personnel involved in the projects showed extraordinary interest in the implementation of the projects, embracing change in that manner is not necessarily evidence of good faith. These personnel may see the partnership projects as convenient tools for them to continue their old practices without attracting adverse judgement from concerned citizens. For instance, evidence suggests that the police in the Western Australian and New Zealand projects refer matters to the diversionary schemes that should have been dealt with by way of straightforward caution. This can result in 'net-widening' which may or may not be the desire of the officers concerned. In other circumstances, the police simply let the partnerships pick up the work that used to be done by them. The situation in the New Zealand project produced this finding: 'there was a strong feeling that Government departments are withdrawing from responsibilities they should still have' (Worall 1996, p 17).

Thus, motivations for partnership have been viewed as either 'benevolent' or 'conspiratorial'. From within the 'benevolent' approach, multi-agency partnership is perceived as a benign development which can only assist in the prevention of crime through greater coordination, systematisation and efficiency. This perspective assumes consensus between the parties. It regards collaboration as a good thing that the criminal justice agencies enter for the benefit of the community under their protection (Gilling 1997, p 170).

By contrast, the 'conspiracy' perspective emphasises the coercive nature of the local state and highlights a sinister interpretation of the multi-agency approach. From within this perspective multi-agency partnerships are seen as both the site of, and a set of, social processes which facilitate the expansion of disciplinary social control into new areas of social life. Through partnerships, it is argued, social welfare and non-criminal justice agencies, as well as community groups, are coupled by criminal justice ones into the multi-disciplinary process, along with their conflicting interests. Partnership is seen largely as a uni-directional process in which control moves outwards from the criminal justice complex into the social body. In this process the former invades and colonises the latter, with the main goal of using collaborative crime prevention to further their coercive ends (see Foucault 1977 and O'Malley 2001).

Crawford (1998) warns that these perspectives not only provide partial understandings, but also 'fall into a trap of juxtaposing conflict with consensus and seeing partnerships as either a wholly good or bad thing'. He suggests that a more accurate perspective is to highlight the ways in which partnerships reflect corporatist tendencies within the capitalist state; to give prominence to the more nuanced 'centrifugal dynamic' and 'osmotic processes' within inter-agency relations and across the public/private sector divide.

> This approach attempts to avoid falling into a uni-directional understanding of power relations, while at the same time refusing to see partnerships as the outcome of pluralistic competition or equal bargaining. Rather, it highlights tendencies towards social closure and monopolistic control as dynamic processes within partnerships. These give prominence to questions about the processes of 'incorporation', which embody the power of exclusion as well as inclusion. (1998, p 185)

The idea of corporatism, as Crawford puts it, 'identifies both the powerful privileges and the regulatory implications of incorporation into partnerships, whereby "included" organisations are given a privileged "public" status which grants them certain powers – including access to policy-formation – while at the same time conferring on them responsibilities – in terms of ensuring the implementation of, and compliance with, public policy' (ibid).

Whether partnerships emanate from benevolent, conspiratorial or corporatist motivations, it is obvious that they represent at least a symbolic departure from the 'go-it-alone' approach of the traditional criminal justice approach. By reaching out to the community, for whatever reason, the criminal justice agencies leave open a window of opportunity for non-government organisations to intervene in the responses to youth crime. In the final analysis the criminal justice agencies' motivation will be only one of several factors that will determine the character of this intervention. Political climate, the health of civil or community organisations, and the media are other essential factors. And, if any combination of these factors leads to reduction in youth crime or redemption of young people from a life of crime beyond the wildest dreams of traditional reactive criminal justice, the partnership approach is vindicated.

Fundamental assumptions

All crime-prevention measures embody assumptions or theories about the causes of crime, the role of the parties and the capacity of these parties to play that role. Aspects of the design, implementation and analysis of a mode of prevention work carry with them commitments to particular models of social explanation and human nature (Crawford 1998, p 7). Chapter 5 has shown that the failure of the traditional response to crime had given rise to a shift in perspective as to how the agencies might do things differently. This section discusses what assumptions informed the partnerships projects that were described in Chapter 6.

First, it is pertinent to see what the projects reveal about the causes of crime to which the agencies responded with acceptance of, and involvement in, crime-prevention coalitions. Some of the partnership projects took as their point of departure the view that youth crime is a symptom of the broader underlying causes of social deprivation and disadvantage. These projects therefore focused on locating the offenders (actual or potential) in their ecological and community contexts in order to understand their offending behaviours. The US Baton Rouge and the New Zealand Roskill projects are particularly illustrative of this approach.

Other projects show the classical view of individual responsibility as the basis for the crime problem that brought about the partnerships. Thus, the Canadian Maple Ridge, the Western Australian JJT and the UK Safer Slough projects concentrated on acceptance of guilt by offenders and target vulnerability as special ingredients for partnership intervention. However, in contradistinction to the traditional criminal justice response, these projects emphasised coordination to improve service delivery by various providers and pro-active intervention to correct criminal dispositions before any crime occurred.

Another assumption concerns the role and capabilities of the criminal justice agencies vis-à-vis the concerns around which the partnerships were built. In most of the projects, it was clearly acknowledged that the agencies alone could not effectively address the crime problem. The sign of the times is the fact that these agencies not only accepted this view but actively promoted it in their communities. Parallel to this view, the agencies emphasised both the need and their capabilities to work in partnership with other organisations in their communities to prevent or control crime.

Still another underlying assumption is that the philosophy and theory of restorative justice provide a better guide in constructing and implementing crime prevention, compared to the punitive philosophy of the traditional response. The New York Midtown community court practises restorative justice. Emphasis is on the ways in which disputes and crimes that adversely affect relationships among community residents can be justly resolved to the benefit of all concerned, including the community at large. The court treats parties to a dispute as real individuals rather than abstract legal entities and uses community resources in the adjudication of disputes. Justice in the traditional court system had become too remote from people living in the community.

Built upon coalitional and restorative principles, neighbourhood justice centres and community courts try to substitute informality, understanding and the perspective of local community opinion for the formal, rigid procedures of the courts and to envision an expanded role for communities victimised by crime in the justice process. Both individual and community restitution are goals; offenders need to pay back victims of crime, become educated about the effect of their actions upon victims and work at reconstructing their lives by participating in rehabilitation programs.

The Western Australian JJTs' Practice Manual stipulates that the scheme is founded upon 'three key principles … of the restorative justice paradigm'. The Canadian and New Zealand projects, which focus on the 'latent strengths of the offenders, the families, and the community, rather than punitive action' (Worall 1996), also represent a major departure from the philosophy that underpins punitive criminal justice and the move towards the communitarian and/or therapeutic paradigm. The outcome, as we shall see later, is that most of the partnership projects combined service-oriented surveillance with social crime-prevention strategies (van Dijk 1997).

Types of preventative intervention

Unlike the traditional criminal justice response that focuses entirely on tertiary crime prevention, most of the partnerships involving criminal justice agencies engage in both secondary and tertiary crime-prevention types. The move to address identified criminogenic conditions, plus their influences that put people 'at risk' of committing crime, constitutes secondary prevention. Criminal justice agencies' intervention to forestall people charged and/or convicted for crime from reoffending forms the core of tertiary prevention. Both differ from primary prevention which, through social, economic and other areas of public policy, including education, employment, housing and recreation, specifically attempts to influence criminogenic situations and the root causes of crime. (See also Omaji 1992).

In addition to targeting persons who have already committed crimes and aiming to prevent those persons from reoffending, some of the partnership projects seek to work with at-risk young persons with a view to preventing them from drifting into crime. Among the projects described in Chapter 6, the Canadian Maple Ridge, Western Australian JJT and New York Midtown projects specifically focus on 'redeeming' young people who have already offended. As the coordinator of the Canadian project put it, 'we want to make sure that first offenders don't become second offenders' (personal communication).

The rest of the projects dwell solely on secondary level intervention (eg UK Safer Slough project) or combine secondary and tertiary programs (eg the New Zealand Roskill project). The latter, while targeting persons who have committed several offences, also identifies the families of such offenders and works with them to reduce the risk of future criminality. It also aims to prevent the children of the present offenders from offending.

With regard to crime-prevention potentials, all the partnership projects described respond to crime in innovative ways. However, those that combine secondary and tertiary elements have a greater chance of reducing total crime incidence in the long run. As we shall argue in the next chapter, there is no reason why criminal justice agencies, through their partnerships, should not participate actively in primary crime-prevention activities. In fact, it is at this primary level that criminal justice agencies can experience the most radical preventive partnerships.

Structural design and administration

All the projects display strategic alliances between several agencies, government and non-government alike. Although the agencies are united in their concern about crime control and criminal justice, the partnership arrangements show that such diverse organisations came with very different cultures, ideologies and traditions, with a tendency to pursue their own distinct aims. For instance, the Slough and Cairns projects created several activity-domains to provide room for the partners to pursue their distinct interests. Research on the parties that sit down together in partnerships has shown that criminal justice agencies have very different priorities and interests, as do other public sector organisations, voluntary bodies, the commercial sector and local community groups (Crawford 1998). Potential partners will come from among those groups directly affected by the current problem, those who must deal with its aftermath or consequences, and those who would benefit if the problem did not exist.

For example, if graffiti is a problem, then those directly affected include business owners and home-owners, other area residents, and highway and park departments. Those who must deal with the consequences include insurers, residents, traffic control personnel, elected officials, and law enforcement. People who would benefit if the problem did not exist include realtors, the chamber of commerce, neighbourhood residents, and school and youth programs that could use funds otherwise spent on clean-ups. All these people are potential partners. Thus, in addition to the obvious deep structural conflicts that exist between these diverse partners, alliances between them would have to contend with the diversity of their interests (ibid).

More significantly, the struggles over conflicting interests and ideologies usually show that not all agencies and groups are equally powerful. Unless properly managed, competing claims to specialist knowledge and expertise, as well as differential access to both human and material resources, tend to overshadow and, indeed, derail the common concern around which partnerships are constructed. Power differentials manifest in certain agencies and have the capacity to:

- dominate the policy and praxis agenda;
- capture crime-prevention goals; and
- prioritise certain forms of intervention against certain types of crime.

In the early stages of the partnership approach to crime prevention, research found that the police, who are often dominant in criminal justice-led projects, were not only enthusiastic proponents of the multi-agency approach, but also tended 'to prefer to set the agendas and to dominate forum meetings, and then to ignore the multi-agency framework when it suits their own needs' (Sampson, Stubbs, Smith, Pearson and Blagg 1988). It is not in all contexts that the police exercise the unequal power relations within partnerships in this way. The degree of conflict and the extent to which 'power differentials' privilege some agencies over the others depend on two main factors: (1) the level at which representatives of the partners are located within the hierarchy of their home organisations; and (2) the level of collaboration between the agencies in the partnership. The hierarchy factor is examined first.

Often the appropriate hierarchical level within organisations at which partnership structures should be located presents an important question to practitioners of community safety partnerships. There is the problem that often decisions struck at a senior level need to be renegotiated at a lower one. In many instances, the implementation of partnerships requires the often ongoing renegotiation of any such agreements at various different organisational levels.

Some practitioners complain that partnerships are set too high within organisational structures and have little relevance for front-line workers. This tends to reinforce a 'top-down' approach to problems and runs counter to a 'problem-oriented' philosophy. One option is to establish multi-tiered partnership structures. This necessitates good quality vertical communication between the structures. However, there are difficulties involved in synchronising the strategic and practice levels in crime-prevention structures. Partnership relations and the influences that shape them can also vary across different hierarchies. A spirit of cooperation at one level might coexist with bitter disagreement at another. Ideally, effective partnerships need to be able to gain the commitment of senior officers and simultaneously affect front-line workers and make them feel involved.

In relation to the level of collaboration, those agencies in a 'multi-agency' partnership generally maintain the boundaries of their operations. By coming together in relation to a given problem, they do not significantly affect or transform the work they do. They merely cooperate with others within a structure that respects the distinct roles of the partners and usually grafts the multi-agency work on to existing practices. They thus encounter less inter- and intra-organisational conflicts.

On the other hand, those agencies that interpenetrate and affect their normal internal working relations with the concerns of the partnership are engaged in an 'inter-agency' relationship. This higher level of collaboration and interdependence at times gives rise to new team structures which may be organisationally distinct from, and physically housed outside of, any of the participating agencies. Usually, these participating agencies second at least one full-time worker to the team structures for a given period to perform functions as part of a team, drawing on their distinct skills, expertise and contacts. In this context, conflict is rife as 'team loyalties may replace or supersede parent organisational loyalties during the secondment period' (Crawford 1998, p 175).

The projects in Chapter 6 lie mostly somewhere between these two polar types. Those that approximate more clearly to the 'inter-agency' model offer greater rewards in collaborative activities, but the problems they generate are equally significant:

> [T]he more that a 'partnership' resembles a collaborative inter-agency approach, the more it is likely to blur the boundaries, as to roles and function, of the participating agencies – and the greater the loss of organisational autonomy. Partnerships, by their nature, blur the boundaries between the roles and functions of incorporated organisations. This can present difficulties for accountability and for the appropriate distribution of responsibilities. Hence, there is a need to maintain clarity of the divergent inputs and their collaborative objectives. (ibid)

The Western Australian and the Canadian projects are predominantly coalitions of government or statutory agencies within structures that respect their distinct roles. They represent the intra-sectoral and multi-agency orientations to crime prevention in which the community plays a very limited role especially in the management of the project. This is more obvious with the Western Australian JJTs which essentially consist of a coordinator nominated by the Chief Executive Officer of the Ministry of Justice and a member of the police service appointed by the coordinator on the nomination of the Police Commissioner. The enabling legislation states that, where practical, the teams are also to include a representative of the Education Department on behalf of the responsible minister, and a member of an ethnic or other minority group where the person to be dealt with by the teams comes from that background.

Clearly, the participation of the Education Department and community representatives is considered less critical and thus made subject to practicality. However, evaluation has shown that this judgement underestimates the importance of the involvement of other government and community agencies, especially given the multi-dimensional aspects of the experience of young offenders. Many of the young people would be experiencing not only welfare problems but education and other problems as well. Therefore, the involvement of key government agencies such as Family and Children's Services, Ministry of Justice, Health and Education in any multi-agency endeavour would be critical (Cant and Downie 1998, p 68).

All the projects show differences in staff independence. The coordinators of the JJTs are nominated from staff of the Ministry of Justice. For the Cairns, Canadian and New Zealand projects, the Coordinators are appointed from the professional bodies in the community. The JJTs' system provides less autonomy and neutrality for staff than the Canadian and New Zealand systems. Invariably, the former experiences multi-agency rivalry more than the latter group.

As the Cairns project suggests, coordination itself is a key feature of a competent partnership. The absence of coordination can be wasteful and ineffective, resulting in a situation in which the 'different interest groups pass each other like ships in the night' (Sampson et al 1988, p 488). Establishing a sense of local ownership of community safety problems among participating agencies can require a 'motivation for involvement' which coordinators are ideally well placed to promote (Lidelle and Gelsthorpe 1994, p 18).

Given the tensions and conflicts within partnerships, the role of an independent coordinator can be instrumental in negotiating conflicts and mediating power differences between the parties. Tilley (1992, p 8), in his review of the first phase of Safer Cities Projects, identified the pivotal role of coordinators who act as 'honest brokers' in the process of overcoming initial suspicion, building trust between agencies and gaining local credibility. In the process, the coordinator creates a virtuous circle 'where trust leads to co-operation which leads to synergism which leads to successful outcomes which leads to resources which increases trust and so on' (ibid).

The success or failure of some of the projects was in large part dependent on the ability of the coordinators, as well as the relationship that coordinators struck with their project steering committees. It would seem to follow, therefore, that the existence or absence of a dedicated coordinator will have considerable implications for the effectiveness of a specific initiative. However, coordination is both labour intensive and time consuming. Many crime-prevention strategies are insufficiently large to be able to afford the cost of a full-time coordinator. Nevertheless, some of the projects are clearly distinguished – in structure and activities – by the presence of a dedicated coordinator.

Strategies of intervention

All the partnership projects adopted strategic processes that set them apart from the traditional criminal justice interventions. First, they all sought to clearly define the crime problem and the target for intervention. For instance, while there were several concerns in Baton Rouge at the time, members of the partnership focused only on the gun-related violence by young people and used official sources to identify both the proportion of youth (the Eigers) involved and their localities. The resulting 'Operation Eiger' built a high intensity intervention around the 'chronic group' of young offenders, their families and community.

The success with which the partnerships strategically identified and structured their interventions derives largely from their commitment to consult widely and purposively with their host communities. The Midtown Community Court planners, before adopting a new agenda aimed at getting the court to participate in crime prevention, sought input from the community. The Cairns Community Safety project rode high on the support of the community which the purpose-directed consultative committee was able to generate through the diverse community-based partners they attracted.

After identifying the issue and mobilising the community, the partnership projects use several methods, including conferencing, case management, and/or mentoring, to address the specific needs of the targeted young people. Where it is considered imperative for all the parties to come together to confront these factors, some of the projects use conferencing, as is evident in the Western Australian project. For an intensive 'wrap-around support systems' approach, some of the partnership projects use the case-management strategy. Thus, the US Baton Rouge and the NZ Roskill projects use 'individual service plans' to target and reduce the risk factors of offenders and their families. Mentoring programs, as the US Baton Rouge and the Canadian Maple Ridge projects show, provide avenues for the partners to re-skill young people with positive messages and healthy relationships with members of their communities.

Poignantly, these partnership projects look beyond the original offending behaviour to see how the underlying factors can be removed or redirected through their intervention and a protracted active involvement in the lives of the young people. Of particular note are those projects, such as the New York Midtown and the New Zealand Roskill projects, that integrate social service provision with criminal justice procedures. Some of these projects also use media campaigns and community education through free seminars (the UK Safer Slough and Cairns Community Safety projects, for instance) to publicise their activities and to enlist more sympathisers for their cause.

Although some of the projects convey community rejection of anti-social behaviour to young people and, in some cases, use shock therapy (eg visits to secure detention), their strategies on the whole contrast sharply with the traditional criminal justice response to youth crime. The contracts they enter with offenders arise out of a mutual understanding of the nature of the problem and the need to address it in a certain way. Further, by linking offenders and their families with community resources, the projects recognise the systemic nature of youth crime and the superior impact of 'problem-solving' approach in contrast to the retributive strategy.

Shortfalls in the existing partnership approach

The philosophical orientations and intervention modalities of the partnership projects show them to be far superior to the traditional criminal justice response to youth crime, in terms of community involvement and productive use of community resources. However, this does not mean that these projects represent all that could ever be desired for effective crime prevention. In fact, a critical examination of the projects will show that several aspects fall far short of the attributes of 'best practice' as I shall discuss later.

Information collected about the origin, operation and impact of most of the partnership projects was woefully patchy and inadequate. I had expected that those projects that had been evaluated at the time of the research would yield necessary and sufficient information not only to allow their cost-effectiveness to be determined, but also to ascertain if and how they could be replicated elsewhere. I was mistaken. The following critique should be read bearing in mind the limited information that was available at the time of the research.

Nature of community and youth involvement

In all the projects, the community is involved in a variety of capacities and roles. Some of the projects look to their host communities to provide grassroots volunteers who could serve in think tanks or as mentors for the at-risk or offending youth. In some cases the community serves as a source of community placements for offenders assigned to do community work or as providers of services to meet particular needs of all of the targeted young people.

However, as highlighted previously in Chapter 5, the way these projects have involved the community has done very little to reduce the ambiguity surrounding the coalitions that criminal justice agencies now form with the 'community' to prevent crime. To start with, the slogan of community involvement which is adopted in certain stages of the criminal justice process means different things in different countries. In Britain and Canada, for example, community involvement refers largely to an emphasis on community policing and neighbourhood crime prevention. In the US attention is focused on experiments in community mediation, quite apart from the community policing ethos, usually after the failure of the criminal justice system to meet the needs of the disputants. And this is presented as an aspect of a community's struggle to settle its own quarrels, to take responsibility for its own social control and its own fate.

Debates have turned largely on the nature of control that communities exercise in their partnership with the criminal justice agencies. Curiously, this nature changes depending on which preposition comes between 'control' and 'the community'.

- If it is 'control *by* the community', the agencies initiate partnerships that aim to give communities a greater role or say in the control of crime which affects them. For instance, police liaison committees or neighbourhood justice centres locate crime as anti-social conduct to be dealt with by the community and challenge the adequacy of the legal solution to the question of who should exercise control.

- If it is 'control *in* the community', the agencies do not necessarily involve members of the community because they need partners, but because they are concerned for instance to keep offenders out of residential institutions where possible. Most coalitions involving halfway houses, probation hostels, diversion schemes, various forms of supervision on licence and community care programs or temporary foster care are founded on this thinking. In the main, they recognise the need to address alienation processes behind crime and the corrupting influence of a custodial response to crime by de-institutionalising corrections without relinquishing control to the communities.

- If it is 'control *for* the community', the agencies tend to see their community partners mainly as beneficiaries. In this regard, the success of the partnership projects is judged by the extent to which they got offenders to recompense the victims of crime through community service, or compensation and restitution orders. While this model permits the criminal justice agencies to see crime as a social problem impairing the quality of life, for which they try to mobilise crime control as an aspect of social defence, it severely limits the involvement of the community to that of a mere recipient of the good services of the agencies.

- If it is 'control *of* the community', the so-called partnership amounts to little more than dispersing or net-widening the existing system of control by the agencies. The agencies merely delegate their current concerns and priorities: it becomes a covert extension of the criminal justice system such as replacing 'empty prisons' with 'the punitive city' (Cohen 1979), rather than devolving crime control to the community.

Why would criminal justice agencies call for community involvement or more of it? Such a call signifies either a failure of some parts of the current system and/or some supposed intrinsic advantages of community involvement. Neighbourhood Watch schemes assist the police: to avoid inordinately high level of policing, they must get the community involved. Community mediation facilities supplement the courts: the spectre of over-loaded courts being clogged up with cases stimulates efforts to introduce community mediation. The scandal of overcrowded prisons must force consideration of alternative or de-institutionalised penalties such as community orders or electronic monitoring. The concern for effective crime prevention in these rationales remains to be seen. They all underline community involvement as a response to the difficulties of the official system. What is going wrong with the system is not examined. This leaves the suspicion that the major virtue of community involvement is that they are thought to save money whilst usefully diverting attention from the failings of existing agencies (Crawford 1998).

Thus, Rawlings (1999, p 177) is cynical concerning the general movement to increase community involvement in criminal justice in Britain. To him, the move to community policing and community corrections is largely driven by criminal justice bureaucrats who do not really value public input. The emphasis on community may be a strategy to avoid or deflect criticism for failing to control crime, and to garner increased financial and political support. 'The community has never been seen as central to the modern criminal justice system so attempts to involve ordinary people have been unconvincing'.

Criminal justice agencies may get away with any pretence of genuine partnership with the community, but they cannot achieve this impression in relation to young people whose behaviours constitute the rallying concern. Although all the projects focus on juvenile offenders, very few involve young people as partners either in the management or in the delivery of services. In *Partnerships to Prevent Youth Violence*, the US Bureau of Justice Assistance (1994) stressed the point that the involvement of young people in community solutions to youth violence problems is essential. By this means young people find a role that will bring them a sense of self-worth and recognition and lead to their developing a stake in their community.

More significantly, research shows young people from diverse socio-economic backgrounds generally desire the opportunity to dispel adult stereotypes of teenagers as shown in Chapter 1 and that this motivates them to get involved in crime prevention. In some contexts, young people run with the challenge: 'prove adults wrong by doing something right'. A 1996 Louis Harris poll found that nine out of 10 teenagers are willing to get involved in activities that prevent crime (Louis Harris and Associates 1996). In fact, according to another 1996 study by Independent Sector, an organisation that supports voluntarism and citizen action, six out of 10 teenagers already volunteer – a larger proportion than adults (Independent Sector 1996). I shall return to this issue later in this chapter and in the next one.

No clear paradigm shift

The most intriguing of all the questions that can be raised with criminal justice partnerships is whether the coalitions represent an actual paradigm shift. A prevailing view is that what actually emerges is a 'mixed agenda' paradigm in which the traditional approach embraces, eclipses and overwhelms the preventive partnership approach. According to Crawford (1998, p 247), these partnerships amount to no more than the 'responsibilisation' strategy based on neo-liberal political ideology. The initiative of Canada's Correctional Services to empower indigenous communities to deal with their female offenders, which allegedly has led to more burden on community resources and no shift in power relations (Hannah-Moffat 2000), exemplifies this view.

This means the state, under the guise that its agencies alone cannot effectively be responsible for public safety and crime control, involves the public not only in these tasks, but 'to take on a greater share of responsibility for personal security and public safety'. With this pretext, partnership with community for crime prevention becomes 'a means by which the state can absolve itself from complete responsibility' (Hughes 1998, p 79). The whole strategy is a renegotiation of state functions that disperses state responsibility and minimises its blame for under-performance in relation to crime prevention. It off loads to the non-state sector – variously described as the community, public and private citizens – the crime-related tasks that have traditionally been performed by state agencies, very much in line with the neo-liberal ideology of marketisation or privatisation of services.[6]

Hughes (1998, p 76) argues that inter-agency or multi-agency crime prevention remains a top-down, neo-corporatist strategy in which there is minimal 'bottom-up' communal participation and minimal popular democratic 'ownership'. To a large extent, this re-echoes the criticism of the first generation research on multi-agency crime prevention, especially in the UK. This research, comprising Blagg et al (1988), Pearson et al (1988) and Pearson et al (1992), found among other things that:

> [T]he police agenda on how to address the question of preventing crime seemed to be dominant over that of other agencies ... Multi-agency cooperation also appeared to seriously compromise the role of other, more welfare-oriented agencies like social work. There also appeared to be little consultation with the communities ... which raised important questions about the appropriateness of the use of the word 'community' to describe what in retrospect may be more accurately designated as 'corporate' multi-agency crime prevention. (Hughes 1998, p 77)

All of this suggests that the partnership approach became another cloak for rearranging the deck chairs on the Titanic without changing the power differentials or underlying forces of crime prevention in any fundamental way. Thus, in the case of law enforcement, the police remained in charge and the community organisations came in as 'servant partners'. The academic critique of the partnership approach to crime prevention, as Hughes (1998, p 86) notes, concludes generally that genuine 'inter-agency' crime prevention which focuses on 'social' as opposed to 'situational' strategies 'remain[s] both marginal to the work of most criminal justice agencies and unproven as a "successful" approach'. Further, multi-agency crime prevention 'has not reduced the trawling capacities of the social control apparatus of the state but rather increased them, thus ensnaring ever-more "deviant" in its nets. [T]he fad during the 1990s for partnerships would be viewed as but one manifestation of the immersion of civil society in the ever-expanding social control machine' of the state (ibid, p 91).

Ground rules for high impact ('dinkum'[7] and effective) partnerships

The foregoing shortfalls notwithstanding, the stint with partnerships reveals at least a twofold lesson in the emerging thinking of criminal justice agencies about crime prevention. First, it shows that these agencies do appreciate that crime and general disorder affect the whole community and have an adverse effect on the lives of real people not abstract numbers. Secondly, they do acknowledge that no single organisation can hope to reduce the incidence of crime and tackle the underlying causes of criminal and anti-social behaviour by itself. The new paradigm of community safety partnerships has been a catalyst in getting criminal justice agencies to take the effect of a wide range of criminal and anti-social behaviour seriously and apparently to turn the criminal justice juggernaut away from a further descent into a dead end.

Although the sample of partnerships examined in the previous chapter demonstrates the potentiality of this new approach to break out of the mould of the traditional response to youth crime, it is evident that they have not dispelled major questions about good faith on the part of those who establish such projects. Nor have they shown themselves to represent 'best practice' as the most effective mechanisms for preventing youth crime. Nonetheless, they epitomise the reality that criminal justice agencies need to work together with local organisations to develop comprehensive solutions which can achieve a viable improvement to the community's quality of life.

Such collaboration must satisfy certain ground rules in relation to good faith and effectiveness, and those rules that the research for this book has uncovered are now discussed.

Intensity of collaboration and the autonomy question

The typology of intensity of multi-agency or inter-agency relationships that Samuel Davidson developed in 1976 is a useful framework for examining the autonomy question in the coalitions that criminal justice agencies now form with community organisations. Davidson (1976) identified a continuum of collaboration in which the autonomy of the agencies involved diminishes as the collaboration intensifies from communication through to merger:

Communication ▶ *cooperation* ▶ *coordination* ▶ *federation* ▶ *merger*

With this continuum, autonomy and partnership do not necessarily 'stand in a highly ambiguous relation to each other' as Crawford (1998, p 175) has argued. The further the autonomous agencies move towards the right of the continuum, the more they lose or compromise their autonomy (Gilling 1997; Kemshall and MaGuire 2001). Where they choose to stay on the continuum would depend on a number of factors, the most significant being the type of partnership they want to form.

In any case, since we know that the 'independent interdependence' has been the bane or 'the weak force' of the criminal justice agencies working together among themselves, it is essential that when these agencies initiate or join partnerships with community organisations they take steps early on to clarify how much autonomy is necessary for each agency to lose or to temporarily forego for the sake of the common concern or goal of crime prevention. To underline the need to resolve these issues, Crawford (1998) reminds us of the tendency of partnerships (particularly of an inter-agency type) to blur the organisational boundaries as to roles, tasks and purpose.

In the first tasks of helping the partners solidify their shared vision of effective community crime prevention, it is critical that they know the level of independence they can retain and use for the partnership goal. Even though partnering groups usually come together because of their commitment to a common cause, there will always be a diversity of the underlying interests among them. Further, partners will differ in their strength or expertise. It is, therefore, important that partners have a clear understanding and articulation of their roles and strengths. Much more than this the partners must understand their own level of autonomy and how to assert it within the partnership before they can harness their differences in creating an effective crime prevention group.

Empowering structures and protocols

To promote joint working and delivery of partnership objectives, appropriate structures, systems and protocols are required to ensure accountability, minimise risks and ensure effective representation and balance of power. Experience suggests that there is no single applicable model for achieving the right structure. The partnership projects investigated in the research for this book demonstrate that local circumstances and the goals of the coalition dictate what structures the partners adopt. Those who initiated the projects appeared to have determined the structures for their respective partnerships.

The relevant ground rule with regard to this matter is that whatever structure is adopted must be acceptable to all the partner organisations and be capable of delivering the partnership's objectives. As we saw in Chapter 6, some of the projects utilised a series of management groups, each with clearly defined roles and responsibilities. Others have one central committee that is responsible for designing and implementing all strategies. In any case, the partnership must agree on appropriate decision-making structures and control of resources for each group and must set targets and timetables for tasks, delegated or otherwise.

There should be good management systems to ensure that partnerships are achieving their objectives. The main focus should be to keep partners well informed on progress and minimising the risk of uncontrolled project development and expenditure. As a matter of principle, systems need to identify problems or failures quickly and recognise opportunities and threats for the partnership. Whether this management is centralised or decentralised, it will have to deal with how it funds the activities of the coalition: across partners or contracting out the process to a single operator which may or may not be a partner.

Next is the ground rule about protocols. Without, for instance, any system to ensure that partners attend meetings regularly or send representatives from an appropriate management level of their organisations, decision-making of the partnership may be delayed or strategies may be undermined as poorly briefed representatives may be unwilling to exercise appropriate powers. In the UK, partnerships are encouraged to use standard Service Level Agreements (SLAs) between partners or adopt standard protocols for inter-agency cooperation. These contracts and agreements have sanctions for non-compliance built into them (see Hiles 2000 for an extensive analysis of SLAs and their applications).

Further, a well designed set of protocols can help prevent partners from 'dumping' on each other, a practice known to be both wasteful and non-productive. Having understood and acknowledged the differing strategic strength and expertise of the partners, there must be a system for allocating workload or responsibilities in a manner that allows the common ground or overall goal of reducing criminal activity and recidivism to be achieved.

Strategically involving young people

The ground rule that is unique to partnerships aiming to effectively prevent youth crime deals with the involvement of young people in a meaningful way. Built upon the dictum: 'by kids with adults for community', and not 'by adults for kids in community', this ground rule prescribes a tripartite framework involving young people, the community and the criminal justice agencies planning and practising together. Ultimately, a significant part of youth crime is a product of their lifestyles. This is one of the messages of Chapter 2 of this book. Thus, it is imperative that young people have a bigger say in the kinds of things on offer to them locally and the decisions made that affect them and their lifestyles.

Because of the centrality of this ground rule to the object of this book, it is pertinent to illustrate it with a concrete experience. In the UK, the Chelmsford Borough Council discovered that what adults think and what young people think do not always match and decided, therefore, that young people needed to be closely involved in drawing up a plan to make sure that services provided for them met their needs as closely as possible (Chelmsford Borough Council 2000). The Council devised a Young People's Action Plan targeting the age group of 13 to 19 year olds. The Plan aims to get these young people involved in decisions affecting them, so they can say what they need and have their needs met. It is 'an Action Plan by, and for, young people'. This means these youth have a say, can be personally involved and be part of the community and, thus, in 'government speak', the aims of local democracy are supported.

The Plan urges all groups working together (in partnership) to look at the best ways to move youth issues forward. In particular, they are to ensure the achievement of the key intentions or aims of the Youth Action Plan which include:

- understanding the needs of young people;
- encouraging the involvement of young people; and
- promoting the positive contribution of young people (ibid).

For each of these aims, the Plan outlines the steps and possible Council actions to achieve them. To encourage young people's involvement, for example, the Plan prescribes the following steps:

1. search out and build on new and existing links with schools, colleges, youth councils and youth organisations to encourage young people to become involved with CBC/community activities;
2. promote links between schools and elected members of the Council so that young people can meet their councillor, understand the Council's role and the democratic process;
3. ensure young people are seen as service receivers;
4. support the creation and work of local youth councils where interest has been expressed;
5. consider how accessible services are for young people;
6. look at ways of producing and giving out CBC news and information to young people;
7. develop a schools information pack to include a full list of Council services and the areas around which officers could provide information/presentations; and
8. develop ways of consulting with young people that work.

To promote the positive contributions of young people, the Plan provides that the Council:

1. continually review issues relating to young people in the Community Safety Strategy and the ways in which that partnership finds out their views on crime and how to prevent it;
2. work with schools to promote the key issues of citizenship and develop activities and presentations that tie in with the aims of the relevant Report;
3. hold at least one inter-school activity each year;
4. work to ensure that young people in the Borough feel they have an involvement and concern with the communities to which they belong, and assist those who may feel they don't fit in to sort out for themselves practical ways of dealing with youth issues; and

5. publicly promote the contributions of local young people through *Chelmsford Borough Life* (the Borough Council's newspaper).

Using this Council's 'participatory' framework, the police went direct to young people 'to canvas their views on what they think of the police and how they would like to be treated'. As well as asking young people a whole host of questions, the survey also extended to parents and professional carers to get a balanced view. The survey revealed that 'the uniformed police officer has a slight image problem among young people and that there are some communication difficulties'. From these findings arose:

- two comprehensive and valuable documents that are being used as the basis of a new collaborative action plan for the Police *Investing in Young People Strategy*; and
- a plan to train police officers in terms of youth issues, their responsibility to be good role models to youngsters and how police can teach themselves to communicate with young people better.

Other criminal justice agencies can gainfully work with this framework. Sensitivity to young people's needs and the way they perceive the world around them is imperative for a successful partnership involving the youth. As one of the Juvenile Justice Decalogue developed in Chapter 3 states,

> Young people should be allowed to have an active role or participation and partnership in all fora including the juvenile justice system, with the right to express their views; they should not be considered as mere objects of socialisation and control. [CROC Articles 12-13; and Riyadh Guideline 3].

Operational imperatives

None of the ground rules outlined in the preceding paragraphs can produce any high impact partnership if there are no operational frameworks to translate them into practical applications. For any partnership to be successful it must, at the very least, satisfy the following 'operational essentials'. There must be:

- a prophetic voice that defines a common goal and helps to keep all eyes on the ball;
- an institutional champion or local crusader (you've got to get someone who gets folks to the table);
- people who commit to specific tasks at strategic operational levels,
- a plan that has short- and long-term goals;
- a resourcing plan that can see benefits way beyond the narrow vision of economic rationalism;
- political saliency; and
- capacity to track and measure achievements (Calhoun 1998).

Very few of the projects examined in Chapter 6 satisfy more than half of these essentials. Unlike these projects, the New Zealand *Strengthening*

Families (Whakakaha Whanau) Strategy has been hailed as a project built upon the frame of the essentials. At the 2000 Australian Institute of Criminology conference in Perth on 'Reducing Criminality – Partnerships and Best Practice',[8] the project was discussed in various fora.

Strengthening Families is a major new strategy that improves the wellbeing of families.[9] It is supported by the Ministries of Health and Education, the Department of Social Welfare and many other agencies involved in, or associated with, providing social services including the police. It involves government and non-government agencies working together, and with their respective sectors, to achieve better outcomes for families at risk. It is inter-sectoral in design with a strong support from the community and is planned to give the task of implementation to local management groups involving representatives from government and local council, Safer Community council, 'iwi', and community groups. Consistent with the ground rules enunciated previously in this chapter, the strategy has developed a protocol for all the agencies working together.

Driven by an institutional champion, Dame Margaret Bazley – Chief Executive Officer of the Ministry of Social Policy – *Strengthening Families* arose from several local and national contributing factors. These included concern about inter-generational cycles of disadvantage, crime and the level of long-term dependence on welfare that some families face. There was also concern about gaps in services at the local level and the recognition by the health, education and welfare sectors that there were many common areas of concern, for example, common clients in common areas of New Zealand. *Strengthening Families* aims to achieve:

- better outcomes for children by helping families meet their care, control and support responsibilities;
- improvements in families' abilities to resolve difficulties and problems, including anti-social behaviours, and maximise the outcomes and opportunities for their children;
- clearer definitions and better collaboration between the health, education and welfare sectors locally and nationally; and
- better use of existing resources.

Organisationally, there are two main areas of work in the *Strengthening Families* strategy: local level coordination and national level coordination. The goal of the local level coordination is to improve local services to at-risk families through improved social service collaboration at a local level. This secondary-level problem-solving intervention is achieved through inter-agency case management which identifies gaps and overlaps in services and undertakes joint initiatives to use resources more effectively.

The local coordination groups, established throughout the country, include frontline workers from the health, education, welfare, justice, housing and employment sectors, and other government and community agencies and *iwi*. These groups are at various stages of development and they are moving towards widespread application of a collaborative case-management process.

The strategy identifies local priority areas in which social service workers make a concerted effort to focus services on children who are at higher risk of experiencing health, education and welfare problems. Local managers will decide on how large a group of children they will initially focus on. It is likely to revolve around primary school children indefinitely suspended from school, children with parents in prison, children of teenage parents and children from families who have been reliant on income support as their main source of income for many years.

At the national level, the coordination focuses on improving the overall cost effectiveness, coordination and accountability of policies and services for families at risk. Thus, the projects under this stream aim to prioritise and realign funding at a national level by:

- setting key goals and targets for improving outcomes for children in families at risk;
- developing a coordinated approach to identify and monitor families at risk in order to improve the delivery and use of services; and
- realigning social services to families at risk to reduce gaps and overlaps in services.

Describing the essential factors in the success of the strategy, Dame Bazley (2000) said it was critical to:

- get a few committed individuals;
- map the problem areas so you know what you are dealing with (eg children in crisis) and where it occurs;
- work in collaboration, not in 'silos' (eg in Whaitaki District, all the School Principals put their suspension money in one kitty to collaboratively deal with 'problem' kids);
- seek not more but to be better with what resources exist;
- give frontline operators freedom to work out best outcomes; and
- showcase a successful outcome to minimise scepticism.

With appropriate adaptation, criminal justice agencies can devise partnerships to deal with youth crime, built upon a similar philosophy and operational framework.

Conclusion

Compared to the traditional criminal justice approach, the examples of the partnership projects we have used thus far are relatively thoughtful and imaginative responses tailored to the specifics of local conditions as these were understood. If they seem so simple in retrospect, it is because of the hard work and imagination of those who put them in place, especially in view of the large volume of costly routine criminal justice practices with no more (and often less) evidence of effectiveness.

This chapter has argued that, while the partnership approach presents a far superior framework for responding to youth crime, none of the projects described in Chapter 6 represents an archetypal coalition that criminal justice agencies could form with community organisations. There is room to remain sceptical about the extent to which the rhetoric of criminal justice-led partnerships is realised. The often-heard ideals of 'partnerships', especially since the last five years of the 20th century, and the reality of its practice are far from co-extensive. Thus, concepts such as 'talking shops' and 'paper partnerships' feature in the literature to underline the view that many partnerships exist merely for the purposes of satisfying funding requirements.

> The development of a partnership approach has fed off managerialist assumptions that crime control needs to be better managed in order to reduce waste as well as limit duplication and friction. In their place a partnership approach appeals to 'coherence, co-ordination and synergy'. Nevertheless, there remain important incongruities between the logics of managerialism and the notion of genuine 'partnerships'. In a variety of ways managerialist reforms have served to exacerbate tensions between inter-organisational and intra-organisational dynamics. (Crawford 1998, p 181)

As indicated at the beginning of Chapter 6, several other partnership projects have come on stream since the data for the chapter were collected. And, some of these newer projects may well display greater superiority. Arguably, though, no other crime-prevention partnership project or scheme currently devised can confidently claim an archetypal status. Judged by the few ground rules discussed here, collaborative crime prevention has a fair way to go to reach an ideal state. The challenge is not to wait for the ideal state to come, but continually to improve preventive partnership projects on the way to this ideal state.

For those tempted to replicate the partnership approach because of the modicum of success so far, it bears emphasising that social phenomena of this nature are context-specific or sensitive. All interventions will not have the same effects in different contexts. It pays to heed Crawford's (1998, p 7) advice that 'it is not just a question of what works or which mechanisms produce what outcomes, but what works where and for whom'. In other words, under what conditions or in what context does the intervention achieve desired effects for the interveners?

Notes

1   For a detailed discussion of these factors, see Howell and Hawkins (1998); National Crime Prevention (1999).
2   The US Baton Rouge project.
3   The New Zealand Roskill project.
4   The Canadian Maple Ridge and the Western Australian Juvenile Justice Teams projects.
5   The UK Safer Slough and the Queensland Cairns Community Safety projects.
6   For further discussion of the broad forms that this process has taken, see Crawford (1998, pp 248-252).
7   An Australian slang for 'good faith' or 'genuine'.
8   31 July – 1 August 2000, Novotel Langley, Perth, Western Australia.
9   The information about this strategy is derived mainly from <http://www.strengtheningfamilies.govt.nz> and the author's notes from the Conference.

8

Criminal justice prevention of youth crime: future directions

The youth are the standard bearers and upholders of a great nation. Don't turn them into the scourge of the future and the harbinger of doom. (Adapted from Brown 1998, p 13)

Why are those who still believe in the essential validity of the basic premises behind the [criminal justice system] in retreat, defending the barricades, rather than out front like drum majors leading a celebratory parade? ... We have been guilty of some self-congratulation and self-satisfaction that is not fully deserved. Like all human institutions the [system] as it developed became careless and complacent in its processes. We believed we always knew what was best ... We fell under the spell of our own rhetoric and ignored the risk in focusing solely on [punitive] ends rather than questioning our means. (Shepherd 1999)

The partnership approach, especially the 1990s type, represents a major shift in the history of crime prevention. Against the backdrop of the failed traditional criminal justice approach, the emphasis in government policy shifted in the mid-1980s from an approach that relies solely on the reactive triumvirate of the police, courts and corrections towards collaboration between statutory agencies. In the last decade of the 1990s, the emphasis shifted further towards proactive collaboration between different sectors of society. This led to what has been described as the 'mixed economy of crime prevention' (Gilling 1997, p 159).

This shift towards collaboration brought a much needed breath of fresh air in what had patently become a toxic conversation about the suitability of the criminal justice agencies in dealing with youth crime. More significantly, it has now provided a window of opportunity for role reassessment by the agencies. Specifically, if young people are a treasured asset or 'the standard bearers and upholders of a great nation', the agencies which possess unique authority to correct derailing youth must seize the opportunity of becoming 'drum majors leading a celebratory parade' towards a great future for all.

Where we have been

In the Introductory Chapter, I argued that crime – especially youth crime – is not a problem we had to have; it is a preventable symptom of an underlying social malady. Yet, the psychologistic and punitive trends in state responses to youth crime continued, apparently oblivious to the socially contingent nature of this crime, culminating in the draconian justice of the early 1990s. This led to further exclusion for young people. The press and the public's voracious appetite for punishing the young remained constant; the ensuing juvenile justice policies and practices denied active citizenship to more youth. Although there has been a philosophical awakening since the 1990s whereby governments have begun to pursue on a larger scale preventive (including partnership) interventions, the traditional exclusionary approach of treatment and control – using the police, courts and corrections – remains the cornerstone of most state policies (Omaji 1997b).

> Alongside the new discourse on crime prevention, the 'old' but resurgent approach of punitive retribution continues to be a central plank of law and order politics in ... neo-liberal societies. (Hughes 1998, p 80)

The 21st century began with this concomitant focus on prevention and punitiveness still in tact. And, as the media and the state intensified their effort to make the society condemn youth more and understand them less,[1] the perception that youth crime was getting worse elevated into a moral panic during the early 1990s. In a totally 'market-driven' project, the state has used neo-liberal economics and philosophy to justify.

- reduction of its responsibilities for providing the benefits of citizenship which ensure full inclusion for all; and
- increase in its control over young people.

Consequently, young people found that 'the pathways to adult status and autonomy are ... replaced with extended forms of dependency' (France and Wiles 1998, p 67). Their experience became one of 'structured dependence and weakened citizenship' (Bloxham 1997, p 2). The rank of youth as a 'surplus population' or a 'human residue' of the economy swelled (Jamrozik 1995). In several western countries, unemployment became much more concentrated among school-leaver age groups – 'precisely the age groups who are most liable to turn to crime out of idleness and boredom' (Walker and Henderson 1991, p 3). Delay in their financial independence greatly enhanced the frustrations normally felt by adolescents anxious to begin life as adults.

Media sensationalisation of youth crime continues to balloon, taking advantage of the ongoing view that 'the potential for community outrage regarding some aspect of the criminal justice system is a subversive sleeper in every election campaign' (Fairall 2000, p 37). As politicians pandered to this media 'cash-in', feelings of insecurity (mainly from fear of crime) increased and private citizens (individual or corporate) responded by creating more 'locations of trust – small bubbles of security in an insecure world'. Such security bubbles further used 'exclusion of those who are believed to be potentially threatening to reduce fear and risk' (France and Wiles 1998, pp 68-69). Young people who bore the brunt of this exclusion felt further marginalised and angry; and some probably responded by intentional delinquency and violence on a larger scale.

The US experience is a case in point. Drug barons took advantage of this situation and inundated young people with hard drugs and guns. This exacerbated the youth crime situation which had become a major concern since the 1970s, with 'guns and violence accompanying the introduction of crack cocaine and the increase in the neighbourhood drug markets' (Redding 1998).

Punitive ideology intensified in several western countries and manifested in:

- extensive use of mandatory sentencing, zero tolerance, and curfews for young people;
- lowering of the age of criminal responsibility: At present, the minimum age for criminal responsibility in NSW and in most other Australian jurisdictions is 10 years. In Tasmania and ACT it is seven years and eight years, respectively. All these are already lower than in New Zealand where a child under 12 years is not considered to be criminally liable for his or her actions (Boni 1999); and
- calls for the abolition of juvenile justice. Again, there is now a growing push in the US for the juvenile justice system to be abolished, and for young people to be dealt with in the same way as adults. The existence of a separate children's court in that country is now 'under the most severe attack it has experienced' since its inception (Wundersitz 2000, p 103).

The turn for the worse in the early 1990s left in its trail more young people with 'no hope, no fear, no rules and no life expectancy' (Macko 1996). In the words of Professor John DiIulio, there emerged in the western world many 'chaotic, dysfunctional, fatherless, Godless and jobless settings where ... self-respecting young [people] literally aspire to get away with [crime]' (ibid). The concept of 'time bomb' entered the discourses of youth in these societies. The response of the state was largely to toughen incarceration terms and law enforcement tactics.

By all preventative standards, the traditional criminal justice response to crime has been a failure. Crime or the perception of it continued to plague the societies as the agencies of criminal justice continued to dip even more and more into the national coffers: 'the costs of crime are breaking the civic wallet' (Calhoun 1998). Even the UN observed that, since the 1970s, the number of reported crimes such as frauds, thefts and homicides has increased dramatically, 'with the most striking increases taking place in the more developed nations' (UN 1991, p 6). Add to this situation the rift that exists not only between the public and the criminal justice system, but also within the criminal justice profession. It should be clear that where we have been in relation to crime control is anything but enviable.

Where we should be heading

The media and the state must generate a greater understanding of the structural and psychological conditions under which youth exclusion and its attendant criminal orientation occurs. Rather than reducing its responsibilities, the state should, as a matter of policy, assist young people to find pathways to active citizenship. Operators of public space and of private space for the public must see young people as bona fide users and agents of advancement who are capable of being 'standard bearers and upholders of a great nation'.

The current level of drug use by young people needs to be rolled back, as the resilience or protective factors need to increase (see, for example, National Crime Prevention 1999). More efforts should be made to remove the criminogenic properties of family, school, work and criminal justice domains that may be damaging to young people's personal development in ways that breed criminal behaviour.

A paradigm shift towards reintegrative or restorative justice must lead to:

- positive measures that involve full mobilisation of all possible resources, including the family, criminal justice agencies, volunteers and community groups, as well as schools and other community institutions, for the purpose of promoting the well-being of young people, with a view to reducing the need for intervention under the law (UN Beijing Rule 1.3); and
- policies that are based not only on responsibility, but also on restoration and reintegration for young offenders.

The benchmark of crime prevention must embody a multi-systemic, family preserving, community-based, intensive wrap-around model designed *for* and in consultation *with* young people. The criminal justice agencies must reject the *new penology* that is focused primarily on narrow community protection (through incarceration) and 'management of the risk associated with particular groups and locales' and, instead, institute a *solidarity project* with a nationwide program of political incorporation and cohesive service provision in partnership with community groups as the centrepiece of their operations.

Britain adopted the *new penology* approach in the 1980s and 1990s, and her reliance on 'market' mechanisms for the allocation of services led to the impotence and withdrawal of youth services. Changes based upon a free market economy encouraged the pursuit of individualism and a morality of 'God helps those who help themselves' offset by small doses of magnanimous philanthropy for the deserving young people. A widening gap between rich and poor, fanned by the flames of commercialism which for many set unattainable targets, gave rise to the social exclusion of a significant group of young people (Pitts and Hope 1998).

Those opting for a counter-culture of street credibility attracted increased measures of control from government through quasi-youth work schemes and intrusive criminal justice practices (Ledgerwood and Kendra 1997, p ii). In fact, New Labour's (Tony Blair government) policy of 'zero tolerance' policing is bound up with an exclusionary targeting of young people predominantly cast as the 'dangerous other'. It is designed to get the homeless, graffiti vandals, aggressive beggars and 'squeegee merchants' off the streets (Hughes 1998, p 113).

France, on the other hand, took the *solidarity project* approach during the same period. Using the philosophy of 'a new relationship between citizen and state', the French central government mobilised resources to link the youth (defined as citizens), the community and the state (Pitts and Hope 1998). Several recreational and support systems were established and criminal justice agencies were encouraged to get involved in the development and use of the systems. In addition to establishing a single cabinet level youth justice agency and a National College for the Training of Youth Leaders, the solidarity project sought to:

- develop community mentoring programs (linking a safe, stable adult with each high risk factor youth);
- provide support services for youth facing loss, grief and post-traumatic stress;
- increase recreation/meaningful pre-employment services;
- increase the number of After School programs;
- promote peer-delivered mediation services; and
- provide effective community reintegration (after-care and transition) programs for young offenders released from detention.

There is a much broader range of players in juvenile justice and one challenge of the 21st century is to be clearer and more strategic in our collective thinking about which members of this broader network should be responsible for the different roles of prevention, early intervention and diversion and the imposition and delivery of sanctions. What should now be crystal clear is that criminal justice agencies have a significant role to play in the vision of a society where responses to young offenders are preventative and reintegrative.

Moving forward with criminal justice prevention partnerships and youth integration

As Barajas (1996) argues, criminal justice agencies 'must address these issues in order to move forward, rather than remaining in a system that is fragmented, lacks a clear mission, and seems to provide little value to the public it is sworn to protect ... What is needed is a paradigm that is non-competitive and non-contradictory; that strives primarily for harmony among the aims of the criminal justice system'. 'Partnership' was the model several western countries adopted to deal with this 'systemic malaise'.

It is now axiomatic to accept that partnership, varied and problematic in meaning as it might be, is a key ingredient for success in criminal justice agencies preventing youth crime redemptively. It has already been shown that the idea of a coalition approach had caught official attention since the 1970s. In fact, the fourth UN Congress on Crime in 1970 started the exploration of the positive contributions of public participation to crime prevention and control. Japan, the host country to the Congress, had applied the civic involvement strategy 'with remarkable success' (UN 1991, p 17). In the end, it became obvious that groups as diverse as police, lawyers, probation officers, doctors and community groups can come together to address youth issues, rather than try to act in isolation.

As the previous two chapters showed, most of the projects that were constructed during the 1990s within the coalition paradigm sit in the tertiary crime-prevention category. Nonetheless, by toying with the philosophies of restorative and therapeutic justice that have been shown to hold good promise of breaking the spiral effect of the punitive system on crime problems, the partnership approach was able to transcend the limitations of the traditional criminal justice system. Admittedly, the existing practices of the partnership approach are not without their own limitations. In fact several basic characteristics of partnerships still cry out for a sustained and systematic investigation, especially to determine the extent to which criminal justice agencies faithfully give effect to the perceived paradigm shifts in their responses to crime.

The best crime-prevention model for all places and for all times may never be found or created. In relation to youth crime in particular, the model that will move the criminal justice agencies forward must be based on at least two pillars: one, a framework of partnership that involves not only criminal justice agencies and community organisations, but also young people, with all parties planning and practising together to provide workable crime-prevention responses; and, two, a reformulation of criminal justice perspectives, policies and legislation to incorporate a developmental understanding of crime, an inclusive construction of the 'other' (particularly the youth category), and the principle of equal co-activity or co-production of crime prevention at all levels of the preventive typology.

Towards 'youth-friendly' partnerships

The biggest challenge for a tripartite partnership framework involving young people is for the adult partners to learn to do other than just rage against and censor young people's cultural preferences. The starting point is for society as a whole, and criminal justice agencies in particular, to declare a 'ceasefire' or 'truce' in this thankless, no-win war with young people. This will create an appropriate context in which to seek to involve youth in a meaningful dialogue and partnership for a common cause. The necessity for involving youth is now beyond question. For, as Calhoun (1998, p 8) perceptively says:

> [W]e can and must bring teens into the social contract, for if they are not signatories to the social contract, they will behave as outsiders. The major policy formulations for teens have either been control (criminal justice

strategies) or repair. Each may be appropriate at certain times. However, teens are often seen as hunks of pathology waiting to explode … Many kids are disconnected … The opposite of disconnection and alienation is not rehabilitation or control. It is involvement – passionate involvement. Said one juvenile murderer: 'I'd rather be wanted for murder than not wanted at all'.

As discussed in Chapter 1, the western world seldom seems to view children as knowing, having and doing but rather as needing, lacking and emerging. Little if any intrinsic value appears to be placed on the state of being young except to justify their exclusion. The liberties we take with young people's active citizenship demonstrate our unwillingness to accept the young for who they are, to recognise their differences and celebrate their distinctiveness. This unwillingness is contrary to several standards of international law (see Chapter 3) and detrimental to the future of the nations.

The social reality experienced by many youngsters seriously infringes upon their rights and sense of responsibility. What we have, then, is a growing number of young people who are suffering because they do not know who they are or where they belong as a result of being unable to engage actively with society. Minority youth are doubly deprived in this regard.

So it is that our children are socially deprived and disengaged. Marginalised and repressed while young, they do not personally appreciate mainstream culture as a concept, a process or a set of products. Hence, they become prey to manipulation as passive recipients of, rather than creative participants in, the larger cultural matrix beyond their limited experience – a retrograde state for any nation, let alone for those so tentative about identity as the nations in the western world.

Research shows that young people who are not involved in their community are more at risk of social isolation, mental health problems and delinquency (France and Wiles 1998). Recognising this connection between non-participation and social problems, a part of modernity's inclusion project was to use productive citizenship, especially employment and adult responsibilities, to contain perceived deviant youth tendencies. The trend in post-modernity, however, is one of an increasing exclusion of 'young people from precisely those institutions which, in modernity, bolstered maturity and reduced youth offending' (ibid, p 70).

A key to promoting better child-adult interaction is support for their enablement rather than containment. In *Surviving as Indians: the Challenge of Self Government*, a powerful book concerned with effecting a just future for Indians in Canada, Menno Boldt (1993) poses five carefully argued imperatives. Four of these are, with adaptation, applicable to a just future for, and productive partnership with, young people in the western world generally:

1. moral justice for children;
2. public policies that treat children's rights, interests, aspirations and needs as equal to those of other distinctive cultural groups in the society;

3. child-focused leadership that is committed to eliminating the colonisation of children and to empowering young people; and

4. assurance of appropriate circumstances for young people to maintain and pursue their cultural traditions with other young people.

How are we to move toward this just future for young people, especially those who offend? First, adults must evidence certain humility with respect to youngsters: what these youngsters experience, what they know, what they have, what they want, what they can best teach themselves and so on. If manipulate we must, then let it be the environment not the youth. In particular, we ought to consider carefully whether our agendas of youth concern and the resultant environments we impose on young people are really in their (and ultimately, then, the societies') best interests (Boldt 1993). The goal should not be to change youth into the mainstream image but to integrate their cultural values and structures into the mainstream means of dealing with crime. This is a *sine qua non* for youth-friendly partnerships that criminal justice agencies must create.

Criminal justice agencies to get involved in all levels of prevention

Our civilisation will have advanced significantly when responses to crime merely for morbid punishment are not the initial justification for criminal justice intervention in the life of young people who break the law. Criminal justice agencies will be greatly aided in their ability to prevent crime when they appreciate that youth crime is not merely juvenile rebelliousness but largely the 'most tangible representation of the marginalisation [or exclusion] and disaffection felt by young people in society' (British Youth Council 1993, pp 19-20).

The first UN Congress on the Prevention of Crime and the Treatment of Offenders, convened in 1955 at the Palais des Nations in Geneva, explored the problem of juvenile delinquency and directed attention to the rectification of social inadequacies that opened the way for criminal behaviour and towards a more holistic understanding of the causes and effects of crime. The fifth UN Congress on the same subject in Geneva in 1975 explored the role of the criminal justice system in the prevention of crime. In particular, it highlighted 'the addition of crime-prevention activities and related social services to the traditional law enforcement roles of police and other law enforcement agencies' (UN 1991, p 17). The Caracas Declaration at the Sixth Congress (1980) extended this connection of criminal justice agencies to 'social responsibility' by stating that 'the success of criminal justice systems and strategies for crime prevention ... depends above all on the progress achieved throughout the world in improving social conditions and enhancing the quality of life'.

Events in the past two decades since this declaration have made a more forceful case for criminal justice agencies to get involved in areas other than their traditional jurisdiction of capturing and punishing offenders. They must, in partnership with community organisations and young people, participate in the design of:

- capitalisation-of-strengths services that help people to learn to cope with difficulties;

- remediation services (the deficit is made good) – services of sufficient power, intensity and duration that have the potential to achieve positive outcomes with 'at risk' adolescents; and

- pre-emptive services (strong mainstream generic services in education, accommodation, health, employment, recreation, personal development and community integration).

Criminal justice agencies must be concerned with policies and practices that address poverty reduction, income redistribution, employment and job-sharing, skills retraining, adequate social housing. These 'activity' areas ameliorate the crime problem; they also generate social justice and empowerment in deprived and marginalised communities (Hughes 1998). For the criminal justice agencies to be able to do so, they need to appreciate that during most of the modern and post-modern periods, state policies and practices have basically created two broad communities in an increasingly dualised society: the 'communities of choice' and 'communities of fate'.

> The particularistic concerns of 'communities of choice' are the development of individual household strategies for income security and utility associated with comfortable, 'safe', convenient, healthy and status-giving private environments, exemplified by the imagery of the gated suburbia. On the other hand, 'communities of fate' are bound together into long-term inter-dependencies because of the lack of opportunities to move, gain access to good education or health care, get decently-paid formal work, or share in the cultural resources of mainstream society (Hughes 1998, p 116)

Criminal justice agencies need to wake up to the fact that most young people from the communities of fate are forced to share certain high-risk lifestyles which include 'informal economic activities, crime and drug use' (ibid). As is now much more evident from the developmental perspective on crime, young people who are at greater risk of demonstrating criminal behaviour are those who experience problems in other domains. For instance, they leave school early with little or no opportunities to gain employment; have poor problem-solving skills; believe aggression is an effective strategy for dealing with stress; have poor social skills and low self-esteem; establish no secure relationships with adults or peers; and do not feel part of their community (National Crime Prevention 1999). When young people experiencing these risk factors are also living in families where there are high levels of stress, substance abuse, family violence and disharmony, marital discord, social isolation and long-term parental unemployment, their predisposition towards criminal behaviour is greatly enhanced.

Additional risk factors at the community level which also add to the likelihood that young people will demonstrate criminal behaviours include: socio-economic disadvantage, population density and housing conditions, neighbourhood violence and crime, cultural norms concerning violence as an acceptable response to frustration, media portrayal of violence, lack of support services and cultural discrimination (Schorr, 1997). At times of transition (for example, when moving from schooling to employment) young people are particularly vulnerable, and undergoing transitional phases in the life course are, in themselves, significant risk factors. It has been well documented both in Australia (Eyers, Cormack and Barratt 1992; Cumming 1998) and overseas (Galton, Rudduck and Gray 1999; Hargreaves, Earl and Ryan 1996) that the transitional life stage of adolescence can be a difficult time for significant numbers of young people. Young people who experience multiple risk factors are less likely to demonstrate resilience and have a significantly enhanced probability of developing criminal behaviours (Howard and Johnson, 2000).

Criminal justice agencies ought to know and/or strategically comprehend a good deal about the key factors which are associated with youth crime. In synthesis, research has confirmed that these key factors include:

- being male;
- being brought up by a criminal parent or parents;
- living in a family with multiple problems;
- experiencing poor parenting and lack of supervision;
- poor discipline in the family and at school;
- playing truant or being excluded from school;
- associating with delinquent friends; and
- having siblings who offend.

If the agencies are to be effective in preventing youth crime, 'they must understand what contributes to it' (McDonald 1992, p 90). The question is: how can the agencies come to this strategic comprehension of the factors? Nothing short of breaking away from their traditional way of doing 'justice' is required. O'Connor (1992, p 138) provides an apt example of this:

> Let us imagine that the court used its powers to 'cause investigations to be made' in a different way. Imagine if the court sought a report on the common social factors that gave rise to the fact that it regularly processed many children for street offences. Imagine if the court sought a report on why so many of the children it dealt with were illiterate. Perhaps the local principal might be called at the time of sentencing to ask why so many children wagged school. What could his school do to remedy the problem of school non-attendance? On another occasion, a representative of local government might be called to explain why there were so few recreational activities for young people in their locality. We should use the traditional processes of the court to inquire into the real causes of local juvenile crime. Such an approach would contextualise juvenile offending. It would call to account not just the individual offender but those whose omissions may have contributed to the context which gives rise to crime. Armed with such information, the court would be in a position to facilitate the prevention of juvenile offending. The court could act as a catalyst, prodding the community and its local institutions to develop responses which could reduce crime.

Further, the agencies ought to know and take a clearly defined stand against the fact that neo-liberal theories of 'marketised' social relations and justice have created deeper marginalisation, inequality and exclusion which, in turn, compound the criminogenc factors listed above and underwrite much of the anti-social activities of young people. The 1990s witnessed 'economic recovery' in several western countries, but it was one without serious new job creation. The ensuing phenomenon of jobless growth – made possible by the labour-saving capacities of the new (computer and other) technologies ceaselessly being developed and improved in the new, competitive circumstances – led many young people to identify themselves, politically and culturally, following the pattern in Britain of the mid-1980s, as a generation with 'No Future' (Taylor 1999, p 14).

The Joseph Rowntree Foundation's Inquiry into Income and Wealth, released in 1995, outlines a steady shift in the distribution of wealth away from the poorest sections of the population towards the better-off in the UK, NZ, Sweden, the US, Japan and Germany. The 'new poverty' has been having a major impact on the lives of the very young and the youthful during the 1980s and 1990s – to an extent not experienced by the young in the earlier post-war period. Invariably, the youthful poor made a visible presence on the streets of these countries (homelessness, public begging, poor health and early mortality).

Thus, criminal justice agencies not only need to cut adrift from neo-liberal market theories, they must become familiar with the more adequate theory of distributive justice which 'must include an analysis of democracy, membership and participation, and hence a theory of social relations which takes account of the ways in which people share their lives as a community' (Jordan 1992, quoted in Hughes 1998, p 117). It is counter-productive to remain wedded to an atomised and punitive ideology of justice which neo-liberalism fosters in the face of the fact that a significant number of young people now live in a pervasively 'depriving, more stressful, more atomised, and less supportive society' (Hughes 1998, p 119).

All those working in the criminal justice system must appreciate a master narrative about life since the last two decades of the 20th century. Essentially, this narrative is about the defence of luxury lifestyles being translated into a proliferation of new repressions in space and movement of those already denied active citizenship. The ensuing architectural and 'law enforcement' policing of social boundaries falls disproportionately on young people whose deprived but nonetheless gregarious lifestyles make them drift into the increasingly privatised public space.[2] While preparing this chapter, I came across an address that the Special Adviser to the Shopping Centre Council of Australia gave at the Western Australian Youth Affairs Conference in November 2000. In this address, she acknowledged that 'shopping centres had become the new town square which privatised what was previously public space'.[3]

Criminal justice agencies must be aware that with restricted access to the now privatised public space, the ensuing conflict between young people who need to use this space and the 'defenders' (public and private police) of the space will drag many of these youth needlessly into the justice system. The essence of the 'knowledges' that have become imperative is that the agencies must reconsider how they imagine youth and get involved in fostering protective factors and processes. These factors may be located within the young person (eg learned attitudes, beliefs); they may be found in the family context (eg caring adults); or the school and the community (eg schools that teach intellectual mastery, local councils that provide recreational facilities and opportunities for young people to socialise etc).

As a first step, the agencies must overcome the paralysis of pessimism or stereotypy and get into what Braithwaite (1996) describes as 'preventing crime through mobilising social movements'. In a sense, this is a call for what Giddens (1990, p 137) calls 'radical engagement'. And, as the Appreciative Inquiry research tool can reveal, those taking a stance of radical engagement hold that:

> [A]lthough we are beset by major problems, we can and should mobilise either to reduce their impact or to transcend them. This is an optimistic outlook, but one bound up with contestory action rather than the faith in rational analysis and discussion. Its prime vehicle is the social movement. (ibid)

This is the crux of the vision articulated in this book. As the agencies bring themselves into the fullness of this vision, their intervention in the lives of young people through partnerships with society at large must be one that is guided by at least 10 key principles which can be distilled from Pinnock (1997) to capture the essence of the foregoing discussions about youth crime and efforts aimed at its prevention. These principles are:

- Empowerment – The resourcefulness of each young person and their family should be promoted by providing opportunities to use and build their own support networks and to act on their own choices and sense of responsibility.
- Participation – Young people and their families should be actively involved in all stages of the intervention process.
- Youth-centredness – Positive developmental experiences should be ensured for young people, both individually and collectively. Appropriate guidance and support should be ensured through regular assessment and action planning which enhances the young person's development over time.
- Family preservation – All services should prioritise the need to have young people remain in the family context wherever possible. It is generally accepted that 'the family of origin not the state is the best parent' and that 'the facilities of the state can never replace the support and socialisation that takes place within the family environment, be it the immediate or the extended family' (Szramka 2001). With this in mind family capacity building and accessibility to a variety of appropriate resources and supports should be of central concern.

- Continuum of care – Young people at risk (and their families) should have access to a range of differentiated services on a continuum of care, ensuring access to the most empowering and least restrictive programs appropriate to their individual needs.

- Continuity of care – The changing social, emotional, physical, cognitive and cultural needs of the young person and their family should be recognised and addressed throughout the intervention process. Additional support and resources should be available after disengagement.

- Integration – Services should be inter-sectoral and delivered by a multi-disciplinary team wherever appropriate.

- Normalisation – The young person and their family should be exposed to activities and opportunities which promote developmental needs from the perspective of normal but culturally appropriate development.

- Rights of young people – The rights of young people as established in various UN standards, especially those articulated into the Juvenile Justice Decalogue in Chapter 3, must be protected.

- Restorative justice – The approach to young people in trouble with the law should include resolution of conflict, family and community involvement in decision-making diversion and community-based interventions, with reintegration as the overriding goal.

Conclusion

In a situation where the vagaries of late or post modernity have intensified the sense of failure by traditional criminal justice methods and responses to crime, the need to work together with community organisations and other state agencies has become inevitable for criminal justice agencies. The growing acknowledgment of the limits of the state alone to address crime problems and the rapid erosion of conventional forms of social control mean that criminal justice partnerships must be constructed within the new forms of control which 'community safety' strategies exemplify.

The proactive and socially oriented approach advocated in this book would lead to crime prevention by criminal justice agencies not being about empty slogans and gestures or placatory political statements but about concrete changes in the institutional philosophies, policies and practices of these agencies (Hughes 1998; Ball and Connolly 2000). Criminal justice crime prevention need not be tantamount to 'putting out flames with gasoline' (Hughes 1998, p 15). To avoid this apparent naivety, the criminal justice agencies must develop competence in knowing about and responding to the social processes that alienate a large part of a whole generation of young people and underwrite their counter-cultural identity formation. The agencies must reconsider their partnership-oriented operations in light of a justice and crime-prevention paradigm that prioritises:

- restoration of the victim losses;
- reconciliation between the victim and offender;
- reintegration of the offender back into his or her family and community networks; and
- reharmonisation of the entire community through healing of the rift caused by the offence.

The overarching goal for criminal justice partnerships must be to develop and apply 'a strategy of social and economic inclusion to reconstruct communities rather than the dominant strategy of penal exclusion which has to date resulted in large detention and prison populations' (Hughes 1998, p 120). The challenge is to 'build a society that is less unequal, less depriving, less insecure, less disruptive of family life, less corrosive of co-operative values' and in which adults and young people alike learn to 'live together in compassionate and co-operative ways' (ibid). The call in this book is for criminal justice agencies to use their enormous power to mobilise young people of all backgrounds as a resource for the building of such a society.

Notes

1   A former British Prime Minister, John Major, had stated that 'society needs to condemn a little more and understand a little less' (*Mail*, Sunday 21 February 1993).
2   The imagery that underpins this point has been fully captured by Mike Davis in his book, *City of Quartz* (1990), which depicts Los Angeles as a 'fortress city' where the wealthy neighbourhoods are barricaded behind walls guarded by gun-toting private police and state-of-the-art electronic surveillance.
3   See the 'Give young shoppers a go: expert', in *The West Australian*, Saturday 28 October 2000, p 10.

References

ACT (1999) 'A Fairer Justice System'. Available at <http://www.scoop.co.nz/ stories/PA9910/S00374.htm>.

Adolph Reed, Jr (2000) *Two Million Behind Bars: Making a Crime of Class*. Labor Party Press Online: <http://www.igc.org/lpa/lpv54/lpp54_ classprison.html>.

Against the Current (2000) 'A letter from the Editors: A war on black children?' 14(6) *Against the Current*.

Akers, R and Hawkins, R (eds 1978) *Law and Control in Society*. Englewood Cliffs, NJ: Prentice-Hall.

Alder, C (1998) *Juvenile Crime and Juvenile Justice: Toward 2000 and Beyond*. Canberra: Australian Institute of Criminology.

Alder, C, O'Connor, I, Warner, K and White, R (1992) *Perceptions of the treatment of juveniles in the legal system : report to the National Youth Affairs Research Scheme*. Hobart: National Clearinghouse for Youth Studies.

Alder, C and Wundersitz, J (1994) 'New Directions In Juvenile Justice Reform in Australia' in Alder, C and Wundersitz, J (eds) *Family Conferencing and Juvenile Justice: The Way Forward or Misplaced Optimism?*. Canberra: Australian Institute of Criminology, pp 1-12.

American Judicature Society (1994) *Results of a National Survey of Strategies to Improve Public Trust and Confidence in the Courts*. Chicago: American Judicature Society.

American Psychological Association (1996) *Is youth violence just another fact of life?* Washington DC: American Psychological Association.

Amnesty International USA (1999) 'The "War On Juveniles": Children and the US Justice System FACT SHEET #1'. Available: <http:// www.amnesty-usa.org/rightsforall/juvenile/factsheet1.html>.

Amnesty International (1999b) Three child offenders scheduled for execution in January: A new Amnesty International report. Available: <http://www. aiusa.org/news/1999/ 220705199.htm>.

Amnesty International (2000) 'Australia: Amnesty International's submission on juvenile mandatory sentencing'. Available: <http:// www.amnesty-usa.org/news/2000/ 31200100.htm>.

Anderson, S, Kinsey, R, Loader, I and Smith, C (1994) *Cautionary Tales: young people, crime and policing in Edinburgh*. Aldershot: Avebury.

Asquith, S (1983) 'Justice, retribution and children' in Morris, A and Giller, H (eds) *Providing criminal justice for children*. London: Edward Arnold Publishers Ltd, pp 7-18.

Atkinson, L (1997) 'Juvenile correctional institutions' in Borowski, A and O'Connor, I (eds) *Juvenile Crime, Justice, and Corrections*. Melbourne: Longman, pp 399-418.

Audit Commission (1996) *Misspent Youth: Young People and Crime (National Report)*. London: Home Office.

Australian Bureau of Statistics (1999) *Australia Now – A statistical profile: crime and justice*. Available: <http://www.statistics.gov.au>.

Australian Bureau of Statistics (2000) *Report on Government Services*. Sydney: AGPS

Australian Law Reform Commission (1981) *Child Welfare*. Sydney: AGPS.

Australian Law Reform Commission (1992) *Multiculturalism and the Law*. Canberra: AGPS.

Australian Law Reform Commission and Human Rights & Equal Opportunity Commission (1997) *Seen and heard: Priority for children in the legal process*. Report No 84. Canberra: AGPS.

Ball, C and Connolly, J (2000) 'Educationally disaffected young offenders: youth court and agency responses to truancy and school exclusion' 40(4) *British Journal of Criminology* 594-616.

Barajas, E (1996) 'Moving toward community justice', *Community justice: striving for safe, secure, and just communities*. March 1996. National Institute of Corrections.

Barman, S (1934) *The English Borstal System: A study in the treatment of young offenders*. New York: Staples Press Ltd.

Bartollas, C (1996) 'United States' in Shoemaker, D (ed) *International Handbook on Juvenile Justice*. Westport, Connecticut: Greenwood Press, pp 301-316.

Bazemore, G and Umbreit, M (2001) *A comparison of four restorative conferencing models*. Washington, DC: Office of Juvenile Justice and Delinquency Prevention.

Bazley, M (2000) 'Strengthening Families Strategy', a paper presented at the Australian Institute of Criminology conference on *Reducing criminality – partnerships and best practice*. Perth, 31 July – 1 August 2000.

Beresford, Q and Omaji, P (1996) *Rites of Passage: Aboriginal youth, crime and justice*. Fremantle, WA: Fremantle Arts Centre Press.

Bernard, T (1992) *The Cycle of Juvenile Justice*. Oxford: Oxford University Press.

Bergquist, W, Betwee, J and Meuel, D (1995) *Building strategic partnerships*. San Francisco, CA: Jersey-Bass.

Bessant, J (1993) *Constituting categories of youth: towards the 21st century*. Melbourne: National Centre for Socio-Legal Studies.

Bessant, J, Sercombe, H and Watts, R (1998) *Youth Studies: an Australian perspective*. Melbourne: Longman.

Bilchik, S (1999) *Juvenile Violence and Juvenile Justice in America*. Prepared for The Japan-US Conference on Juvenile Problems and Violence in a Changing Society Policies and Practices. Available: <http://www.ojjdp.ncjrs.org/about/ spch990226.html>.

Bilchik, S (1999b) *Promising strategies to reduce gun violence*. Washington, DC: Office of Juvenile Justice and Delinquency Prevention.

Blagg, H and Wilkie, M (1995) *Young People and Police Powers*. Sydney: Australian Youth Foundation.

Blagg, H and Wilkie, M (1997) 'Young People and Policing in Australia: the Relevance of the UN Convention on the Rights of the Child' 3(2) *Australian Journal of Human Rights*. Available: <http://www.austlii.edu.au/au/other/ ahric/ajhr/V3N2/ajhr3206. html>.

Boldt, M (1993) *Surviving as Indians: the Challenge of Self Government.* Toronto: University of Toronto Press.

Boni, N (1999) 'Youth and serious crime: directions for Australasian researchers into the new millennium'. Paper presented at the Children and Crime: Victims and Offenders conference, organised by the Australian Institute of Criminology. Brisbane, 17-18 June 1999.

Boorman, C and McMillan, E (1998) 'Partnerships in Cairns: from implementation to activation, evaluation and beyond', presented at the conference on *Partnerships in Crime Prevention*, convened jointly by the Australian Institute of Criminology and the National Campaign Against Violence and Crime. Hobart, Tasmania, 25-27 February 1998.

Boss, P, Edwards, S and Pitman, S (1995) *Profile of young Australians: facts, figures and issues.* Melbourne: Churchill Livingstone.

Box, S (1987) *Recession, crime and punishment.* London: Macmillan

Braithwaite, J (1989) *Crime, Shame and Reintegration.* Cambridge: Cambridge University Press.

Braithwaite, J (1996) 'Restorative Justice and A Better Future', Dorothy J Killam Memorial Lecture. Dalhousie University, 17 October 1996.

Bright, J (1991) 'Crime Prevention: the British experience' in Stenson, K and Cowell, D (eds) *The Politics of Crime Control.* London: Sage Publications, pp 62-86.

Bright, J (1992) *Crime Prevention in America: A British Perspective,* Chicago: The Office of International Criminal Justice, the University of Illinois.

British Youth Council (1993) *Looking to the future: towards a coherent youth policy* . London: British Youth Council.

Broadhurst, R (1999) 'Crime, justice and indigenous peoples: the "new justice" and settler State' 32(2) *Australian and New Zealand Journal of Criminology* 105-106.

Brown, S (1998) *Understanding youth and crime: Listening to youth?.* Buckingham: Open University Press.

Building Blocks for Youth (2000) *And justice for some: minority youth at a 'cumulative disadvantage'.* Available: <http://www.buildingblocks foryouth.org/justiceforsome/jfs.html>.

Bureau of Justice Assistance (1994) *Working as Partners with Community Groups.* Rockville, MD: BJA Clearinghouse.

Butts, J (1992) 'Delinquency Cases in Juvenile Court'. Available: <http://www. ncjrs.org/txtfiles/fs-9418.txt>.

Calhoun, J (1998) 'Making partnerships work', presented at the conference on *Partnerships in Crime Prevention*, convened jointly by the Australian Institute of Criminology and the National Campaign Against Violence and Crime. Hobart Tasmania, 25-27 February 1998.

Cant, R and Downie, R (1998) *Evaluation of the Young Offenders Act (1994) and the Juvenile Justice Teams.* Perth: Ministry of Justice.

Canter, D and Alison, L (eds) (1997) *Criminal detection and the psychology of crime* Aldershot: Dartmouth.

Carcach, C (1997) 'Youth as victims and offenders of homicide' *Trends and Issues in crime and criminal justice.* No 73. Canberra: Australian Institute of Criminology.

Carcach, C and Muscat, G (1999) *Juveniles in Australian Corrective Institutions 1981-1998.* Canberra: Australian Institute of Criminology.

Chan, J (1994) 'Policing Youth in Ethnic' Communities: Is community policing the answer?' in White, R and Alder, C (eds) *The Police and Young People in Australia.* Melbourne: Cambridge University Press.

Chan, J (1994) *Preventing Juvenile Property Crime: A Review of the Literature.* Sydney: Juvenile Justice Advisory Council of New South Wales.

Chan, J (1997) *Changing police culture: policing in a multicultural society.* Cambridge: Cambridge University Press.

Chan, J (2001) 'Negotiating the field: New observations on the making of police officers' 34(2) *Australian and New Zealand Journal of Criminology* 114-133.

Chappell, D (1989) 'Opening remarks' in Vernon, J and Bracey, D (eds) *Police resources and effectiveness.* Canberra: Australian Institute of Criminology.

Chelmsford Borough Council (2000) *Action Plan for Young People can go ahead.* Available: <http://www.chelmsfordbc.gov.uk/actionpl/index.htm>.

Chibnall, S (1977) *Law and order news.* London: Tavistock.

Clark, D (1994) 'Restorative justice is what many communities of faith seek in the criminal justice system', *Crossville Chronicle.* Available: <http://www.crossville-chronicle.com/archive/op00005.htm>.

Clarkson, C and Keating, H (1990) *Criminal Law: Text and Materials.* London: Sweet & Maxwell.

Cohen, S (1973) *Folk Devils and moral panics : the creation of the Mods and Rockers.* London : MacGibbon and Kee.

Cohen, S (1979) 'The Punitive City: Notes on the dispersal of social control', *Contemporary Crises.* Vol 3, pp 339-363.

Coleman, R, Sim, J and Whyte, D (2002) 'Power, politics and partnerships: the state of crime prevention on Merseyside' in Hughes, G and Edwards, A (eds) *Crime Control and Community: the new politics of public safety.* Cullompton, Devon UK: Willan Publishing, pp 86-108.

Commonwealth of Australia (1997) *Bringing them home: Report of the National Inquiry into the Separation of Aboriginal and Torres Strait Islander Children from their Families.* Sydney: AGPS.

Consedine, J (1995) *Restorative justice: healing the effects of crime.* Lyttleton, New Zealand: Ploughshares Publications.

Cook, P and Laub, J (1998) 'The Unprecedented epidemic in youth violence' in Tonry, M and Moore, M (eds) *Youth Violence.* Chicago: University of Chicago Press.

Corrado, R and Markwart, A (1996) 'Canada' in Shoemaker, D (ed) *International Handbook on Juvenile Justice.* Westport, Connecticut: Greenwood Press, pp 34-56.

Crawford, A (1998) *Crime prevention and community safety: politics, policies and practices.* London: Longman.

Crime Concern (1994) *Crime Prevention in Berkshire – Assessing the Partnership Approach.* Final Report. England.

Cumming, J (1998) 'Young Adolescents, Schools and Communities: New Roles and Responsibilities', Incorporated Association of Registered Teachers of Victoria *Occasional Paper* No 55, Jolimont, IARTV.

Cunneen, C (2001) *Conflict, politics and crime: Aboriginal communities and the police.* Crows Nest, NSW: Allen & Unwin.

Cunneen, C, Fraser, D and Tomsen, S (1997) *Faces of Hate*. Sydney: Hawkins Press.

Cunneen, C and McDonald, D (1997) 'Indigenous Imprisonment in Australia: An Unresolved Human Rights Issue' 3(2) *Australian Journal of Human Rights*. Available: <http://www.austlii.edu.au/au/other/ahric/ajhr/V3N2/ajhr3204.html>.

Cunneen, C and White, R (1995) *Juvenile Justice: An Australian Perspective*. Melbourne: Oxford University Press.

Curry, G, Ball, R and Fox, R (1994) *Gang Crime and Law Enforcement Record-keeping*. Washington, DC: National Institute of Justice.

Daly, K and Hayes, H (2001) 'Restorative justice and conferencing in Australia', *Trends and Issues in Criminal Justice*. No 186. Canberra: Australian Institute of Criminology.

Davidson, S (1976) 'Planning and coordination of social services in multi-organisational contexts' 50 *Social Services Review* 117-137.

Davis, B (1995) 'Crimes Against Business: An Overview' 6(4) *Criminology Australia*.

Davis, P (1998) 'Police: students planned a blood bath at Wisconsin high school', *CNN.com*. Available: <http://www.cnn.com/US/9811/16/school.plot.03/>.

Davies, A (1997) 'Youth gangs and urban violence: Manchester and Salford, 1860-1914'. Available: <http://elara.salford.ac.uk/lsi/page21f.htm>

Department of Human Services (2000) 'Community key for young people in custody' *People Focus* September 2000. Melbourne. Available: <http://www. dhs.vic.gov.au/peoplefocus/sep 20/jjcmc.htm>.

Dickinson, T and Crowe, A (1997) 'Capacity Building for Juvenile Substance Abuse Treatment'. *Bulletin*. Washington, DC: US Department of Justice, Office of Justice Programs, Office of Juvenile Justice and Delinquency Prevention.

Dilulio, J (1993) 'Rethinking the criminal justice system: towards a new paradigm' in Dilulio, J (ed) *Performance Measures for the Criminal Justice System*. Washington, DC: United States Department of Justice, National Institute of Justice.

Dodd, V (2000) 'Prison staff jailed for cell attack', *Guardian Unlimited*. Tuesday September 5, 2000 Online: <http://www.guardianunlimited.co.uk/uk_news/story/>.

Duncan, M (1996) *Romantic outlaws, beloved prisons: the unconscious meanings of crime and punishment*. London: New York University Press.

Easteal, P (1997) 'Migrant youth and juvenile crime' in Borowski, A and O'Connor, I (eds) *Juvenile Crime, Justice, and Corrections*. Melbourne: Longman, pp 151-166.

Edwards, A and Hughes, G (2002) 'Introduction: the community governance of crime control' in Hughes, G and Edwards, A (eds) *Crime Control and Community: the new politics of public safety*. Cullompton, Devon UK: Willan Publishing, pp 1-19.

Edwards, C (1999) *Changing Policing Theories for 21st Century Societies*. Sydney: Federation Press.

Ekblom, P (1988) *Getting the Best out of Crime Analysis*, Crime Prevention Unit paper 5, London: Home Office.

Ekblom, P and Pease, K (1995) 'Evaluating Crime Prevention' in Read, T and Oldfield, D (eds) *Local Crime Analysis*. London: Home Office Police Research Group.

Emerson, R (1969) *Judging Delinquents: context and process in juvenile court*. Chicago: Aldine Publishing Coy.

Esbensen, F and Osgood, D (1997) *National Evaluation of G.R.E.A.T. Research in Brief*. Washington, DC: US Department of Justice, Office of Justice Programs, National Institute of Justice.

Eyers, V, Cormack, P and Barratt, R (1992) *The Education of Young Adolescents in South Australian Government Schools*. Report of the Junior Secondary Review. Adelaide: Education Department of South Australia.

Family and Children Services (1990) *An Agenda for Juvenile Justice in NSW: A statement of government policy, achievements, future directions*. Sydney. Family and Children Services.

Feld, B (1977) *Neutralising Inmate Violence: Juvenile Offenders in Institutions*. Cambridge: Balinger Publishing Coy.

Feinberg, J (1965) 'The expressive function of punishment' 49(3) *The Monist* 397-423.

Feld, B (1992) 'Criminalising the juvenile court: a research agenda for the 1990s' in Schwartz, I (ed) *Juvenile Justice and Public Policy: Toward a National Agenda*. New York: Lexington Books, pp 59-88.

Feld, B (1995) 'The social context of juvenile justice administration: racial disparities in an urban juvenile court' in Leonard, K, Pope, C and Feyerherm, W (eds) *Minorities in juvenile justice*. London: Sage Publications, pp 66-97.

Feld, B (1998) 'Juvenile and Criminal Justice Systems' Responses to Youth Violence' in Tonry, M and Moore, M (eds) *Youth Violence*. Chicago: University of Chicago Press, pp 189-261.

Ferrante, A, Fernandez, J and Loh, N (1999) *Crime and justice statistics for Western Australia*. Perth: Crime Research Centre.

Finch, L (1993) 'On the streets : working class youth culture in the nineteenth century' in White, R (ed) *Youth subcultures : theory, history and the Australian experience*. Hobart: National Clearinghouse for Youth Studies, pp 75-79.

Finn, P (1996) *The courts and the vulnerable*. Canberra: Centre for International and Public Law, Law Faculty, Australian National University.

Forget, M (1998) 'Quaker Concern: Book, Vancouver conference highlight new justice options'. Available: <http://calcna.ab.ca/quaker/231justice.html>.

Foucault, M (1997) *Discipline and Punish: the birth of the prisons*. New York: Vintage Books.

France, A and Wiles, P (1998) 'Dangerous Futures: Social Exclusion and Youth Work in Late Modernity' in Finer, C and Nellis, M (eds) *Crime & Social Exclusion*. Oxford: Blackwell Publishers, pp 59-78.

Galton, M, Rudduck, J and Gray, J (1999) *The Impact of Transitions and Transfers on Pupil Progress and Attainment*. Annesley, Nottingham: Cambridge University Press.

Gatewood, D (1993) 'High Cost of Juvenile Justice' 20(3) *Fordham Urban Law Journal* 659-668.

Gest, T and Pope, V (1996) 'Crime time bomb', *US News and World Report*, 25 March 1996.

Giddens, A (1990) *The consequences of modernity*. Cambridge: Polity Press.

Gilling, D (1997) *Crime prevention: theory, policy and politics*. London: UCL Press.

Goldman, N (1963) *The differential selection of juvenile offenders for court appearance*. New York: National Council on Crime and Delinquency.

Goldson, B (1999) 'Youth (in)justice: contemporary developments in policy and practice' in Goldson, B (ed) *Youth Justice: Contemporary Policy and Practice*. Aldershot: Ashgate, pp 1-27.

Goldstein, A (1990) *Delinquents on delinquency*. Champaign, Illinois: Research Press.

Goldstein, H (1979) 'Policing: A problem-oriented approach' 25 *Crime and Delinquency* 236-58.

Gottfredson, M and Hirshi, T (1990) *A General Theory of Crime*. Stanford: Stanford University Press.

Government of South Australia (1989) *Confronting Crime: The South Australian Crime Prevention Strategy*. Adelaide: Crime Prevention Policy Unit, Attorney-General's Department.

Governor's Crime Commission (1996) *The Juvenile Justice System in North Carolina: Past, Present, and Projected Trends*. Online: <www.gcc.state.nc.us/ ss_sum96.htm>.

Grabosky, P (2001) 'Crime control in the 21st century' 34(3) *Australian and New Zealand Journal of Criminology* 221-234.

Grabosky, P and James, M (1995) *The Promise of Prevention*. Canberra: Australian Institute of Criminology.

Graham, I (1993) 'Managing cultural diversity: the New South Wales experience', paper presented at the Australian Institute of Criminology conference on *National Conference on Juvenile Detention*. Darwin, 10-13 August 1993.

Graham, J (1990) *Crime Prevention Strategies in Europe and North America*. Helsinki: Institute for Crime Prevention and Control.

Greenwood, P, Model, K, Rydell, C and Chiesa, J (1998) *Diverting children from a life of crime: measuring costs and benefits*. Santa Monica, CA: Rand Corporation.

Griffith, L, Heilbronn, G, Kovacs, D, Latimer, P and Pagone, T (1993) *Introducing the law*. Sydney: CCH.

Hadfield, P (2000) Review of: *Romantic outlaws, beloved prisons: the unconscious meanings of crime and punishment* (by Martha Duncan), 40 *Journal of British Criminology* 180-182.

Hall, S, Critcher, C, Jefferson, T, Clarke, J and Robberts, B (1978) *Policing the crisis: mugging, the State, and law and order*. London: Macmillan.

Hannah-Moffat, K (2000) 'Prisons that Empower: Neo-liberal Governance in Canadian Women's Prisons' 40(3) *British Journal of Criminology* 510-531.

Harding, R (1993) 'Opportunity costs: Alternative strategies for the prevention and control of juvenile crime' Harding, R (ed) *Repeat Juvenile Offenders: the Failure of Selective Incapacitation in Western Australia*. Perth: UWA Crime Research Centre, pp 137-155.

Harding, R (1999) 'Prisons are the problem: a re-examination of Aboriginal and non-Aboriginal deaths in custody' 32(2) *Australian and New Zealand Journal of Criminology* 108-123.

Hargreaves, A, Earl, L and Ryan, J (1996) *Schooling for Change: Reinventing Education for Early Adolescents.* London: Falmer Press.

Hazlehurst, K (1987) *Migration, Ethnicity, and Crime in Australian Society.* Canberra: Australian Institute of Criminology.

Hedges, M (1997) 'Policy Issues in Responding to Young Offenders', presented at Australian Institute of Criminology Conference on *Juvenile Crime and Juvenile Justice: Toward 2000 and Beyond.* Adelaide, 26 & 27 June 1997.

Hess, K and Wrobleski, H (1993) *Police Operations.* St Paul, Minnesota: West Publishing Coy.

Hewlett, S (1993) *Child neglect in rich nations.* New York: UNICEF.

Hiles, A (2000) *Service Level Agreements: Winning A Competitive Edge for Support & Supply Services.* Brookfield, CT: Rothstein Associates Inc.

Hogg, R (2001) 'Penality and modes of regulating indigenous peoples in Australia' 3(3) *Punishment & Society: the International journal of Penology* 355-380.

Home Office (1991) *Safer communities: the local delivery of crime prevention through the partnership approach.* London: Home Office.

Home Office (1993) *A Practical Guide to Crime Prevention for Local Partnerships.* London: Crime Concern.

Home Office (1997) *No More Excuses – A New Approach To Tackling Youth Crime In England And Wales.* Online: <http://www.homeoffice.gov.uk/cpd/jou/nme.htm#CHAP 5>.

Home Office (1998) *Entry into the Criminal Justice System.* London: Home Office

Home Office (1998b) *Annual Report* and Prison Service *Annual Report 1997/98.* London: HM Stationery Office.

Home Office (1999) *Statistical Bulletin 12/99.* London: HM Stationery Office.

Home Office (2000) *Crime Reduction Strategy.* Online: <http://www.crimereduction.gov.uk/crssummary_1.htm>.

Hood, R (2001) 'Penal policy and criminological challenges in the new millenium' 43(1) *Australian and Zealand Journal of Criminology* 1-16.

Howard, S and Johnson, B (2000) 'Resilient and non-resilient behaviour in adolescents', *Trends and Issues in Crime and Criminal Justice* No 183. Canberra: Australian Institute of Criminology.

Howell, J (1997) *Juvenile justice and youth violence.* London: Sage Publications

Howell, J and Hawkins, J (1998) 'Prevention of Youth Violence' in Tonry, M and Moore, M (eds) *Youth Violence.* Chicago: University of Chicago Press, pp 263-315.

Howell, J (1998) 'Youth Gangs: An Overview', *Bulletin.* Washington, DC: US Department of Justice, Office of Justice Programs, Office of Juvenile Justice and Delinquency Prevention.

Hudson, B (1987) *Justice through punishment: a critique of the 'justice' model of corrections.* London: Macmillan Education Ltd.

Hudson, B (1996) *Understanding justice: An introduction to ideas, perspectives and controversies in modern penal theory.* Buckingham: Open University Press.

Hudson, B (2000) 'Criminology, difference and justice: issues for critical criminology' 33(2) *Australian and New Zealand Journal of Criminology* 168-182.

Hughes, G (1998) *Understanding crime prevention: social control, risk and late modernity*. Buckingham: Open University Press.

Human Rights Watch (1999) *Juvenile Justice*. Available: <http://www.hrw.org/children/justice.htm>.

Hurst, Y and Frank, J (2000) 'How kids view cops: the nature of juvenile attitudes toward the police' 28 *Journal of Criminal Justice* 189-202.

Immarigeon, R (1991) 'Beyond the Fear of Crime: Reconciliation as the Basis for Criminal Justice Policy' in Pepinsky, H and Quinney, R (eds) *Criminology as Peace-making*. Bloomington: Indiana University Press, pp 69-80.

Independent Sector (1996) *Volunteering and Giving Among American Teens*. Washington, DC: Independent Sector.

Institute for Intergovernmental Research (2000) Analysis of Gang-related Legislation. Available: <http://www.iir.com/nygc/gang-legis/analysis.htm>.

Israel, M and Sarre, R (1999) 'The Elusive Nature of Crime' in Sarre, R and Tomaino, J (eds) *Exploring Criminal Justice: Contemporary Australian Themes*. Adelaide: South Australian Institute of Justice Studies Inc, pp 3-29.

Jackson, H (1995) 'Juvenile Justice', a paper presented at the First National Outlook Symposium on Crime in Australia, Canberra, 5-6 June 1995.

James, O (1995) *Juvenile violence in a winner-loser culture: socio-economic and familial origins of the rise of violence against the person*. London: Free Association Books.

James, S and Warren, I (1995) 'Police culture' in Bessant, J, Carrington, K and Cook, S (eds) *Cultures of crime and violence: the Australian experience*. Melbourne: La Trobe University Press, pp 3-15

Jamrozik, A (1991) 'Policy options for young people in the 1990s' 2(2) *Transition: the Journal of the Youth Affairs Network of Queensland* 50

Johnston, L, Bachman, J and O'Malley, P (1997) *Monitoring the Future Study*. Available: <http://www.health.org/pressrel/dec97/10.htm>.

Jones, M and Krisberg, B (1994) *Images and Reality: Juvenile Crime, Youth Violence and Public Policy*. Washington DC: National Council on Crime and Delinquency.

Jones, N (1994) *Juvenile Justice Teams: a six-month evaluation*. Perth: Ministry of Justice.

Jones, S, Berman, G, Dodson, N and Hodos, H (1997) 'Court-Community Collaboration: New Partnerships for Court Improvement' 80(5) *Judicature* 213-218.

Juvenile Justice Advisory Council (1993) *Future Directions for Juvenile Justice in New South Wales*. Sydney: Juvenile Justice Advisory Council of NSW.

Kelling, G, Pate, T, Dieckman, D and Brown, C (1974) *The Kansas City preventive patrol experiment: A summary*. Washington DC: Police Foundation.

Kemshall, H and MaGuire, M (2001) 'Public protection, partnership and risk penality: the multi-agency risk management of sexual and violent offenders' 3(2) *Punishment and Society: The International Journal of Penology* 237-264.

Kirby, M (1995) 'Crime in Australia – Change and continuity' 7(1) *Criminology Australia* 19-16.

Kirk, B (1996) *Negative Images: a simple matter of black and white.* Aldershot: Avebury.

Konzhukov, V and Fields, C (1996) 'Measuring Cross-National Crime and Criminality: Methodological Considerations and Concerns' in Fields, C and Moore, R (eds) *Comparative Criminal Justice: Traditional and Nontraditional Systems of Law and Control.* Prospect Heights, Illinois: Waveland Press Inc, pp 15-29.

Krisberg, B and Austin, J (1993) *Reinventing juvenile justice.* Newbury Park, CA: Sage Publications.

Kucera, R (1993) 'Policing juveniles: an overseas and Western Australian perspective' in Atkinson, L and Gerull, S (eds) *National Conference on Juvenile Justice.* Canberra: Australian Institute of Criminology, pp 233-239.

LaFree, G (1989) *Rape and criminal justice: the social construction of sexual assault.* Belmont, California: Wadsworth Publishing Co.

LaPrairie, C (1997) 'Reconstructing theory: explaining Aboriginal over-representation in the criminal justice system in Canada' 30(1) *Australian and New Zealand Journal of Criminology* 39-54.

LaPrairie, C (1999) 'Some reflections on the new criminal justice policies in Canada: restorative justice, alternative measures and conditional sentences' 32(2) *Australian and New Zealand Journal of Criminology* 139-152.

Leacock, V (2000) Reviews of: *Understanding youth and crime: listening to youth?* (by Sheila Brown); and *Young people and youth justice* (by Kevin Haines and Mark Drakeford), 40 *British Journal of Criminology* 174-178.

Leadership Conference on Civil Rights (2000) *Justice on trial: racial disparities in the American criminal justice system.* See: <http://www.cnn.com/2000/LAW/05/ 04/civil.rights/index.html>.

Ledgerwood, I and Kendra, N (1997). *The Challenge of the Future: Towards the new millenium for the youth service.* Dorset: Russell House Publishing.

Lembert, E (1967) 'The Juvenile Court: Quest and Realities' in the President's Commission on Law Enforcement and Administration of Justice (ed) *Task force Report: Juvenile Delinquency and Youth Crime.* Washington DC: US Government Printing Office.

Leonard, K, Pope, C and Feyerherm, W (eds) (1995) *Minorities in juvenile justice.* London: Sage Publications.

Liddle, A and Gelsthorpe, L (1994) *Inter-agency crime prevention: organising local delivery.* London: Home Office.

Liebling, A, Elliot, C and Arnold, H (2001) 'Transforming the prison: romantic optimism or appreciative realism?' 1(2) *Criminal Justice: The International Journal of Policy and Practice* 161-180.

Lincoln, R and Wilson, P (2000) 'Aboriginal criminal justice: background and foreground' in Chappell, D and Wilson, P (eds) *Crime and the*

Criminal Justice System in Australia: 2000 and Beyond. Sydney: Butterworths, pp 205-221.

Lippmann, W (1922) *Public Opinion.* New York: Harcourt Brace.

Little, M (1990) *Young men in prison: the criminal identity explored through the rules of behaviour.* Aldershot: Dartmouth.

Louis Harris and Associates (1996) *Between Hope and Fear: Teens Speak Out on Crime and the Community.* Washington, DC: National Crime Prevention Council.

Lubow, B (1999) *Juvenile Detention Alternatives Initiative.* Available: <http://www.aecf.org/initiatives/juvenile/rising.htm>.

Luke, G and Cunneen, C (1995) *Aboriginal over-representation and discretionary decisions in the NSW juvenile justice system.* Sydney: Juvenile Justice Advisory Council of NSW.

Lumby, C (2000) 'The end is nigh, and other stories', in *Bulletin,* 118(6212) 22 February 2000, pp 34-35.

Mack, J (1909) 'The juvenile court' 22 *Harvard Law Review.*

Macko, S (1996) 'Kids With No Hope, No Fear, No Rules, And No Life Expectancy', *EmergencyNet NEWS Service,* Saturday, 18 May 1996, Vol 2 p 139.

Malcolm, D (1999) 'Young people, culture and the law' 18(4) *Youth Studies Australia* 29-35.

Mason, B (1990) 'US courts try children as adults: the prosecution of Nathaniel Abraham and the lessons of the James Bulger case in Britain'. Available: <http://www.wsws.org/news/1998/may1998/kidsm19.shtml>.

Mathiesen, T (1980) 'The future of control systems – the case of Norway' 8 *International Journal of Sociology of Law* 149-164.

Maxwell, G (1993) 'Family decision-making in youth justice: the New Zealand model' in Atkinson, L and Gerull, S (eds) *National Conference on Juvenile Justice.* Canberra: Australian Institute of Criminology, pp 113-126.

Maxwell, G, Kingi, V, Robertson, J and Morris, A (2002) *Achieving Effective Outcomes in Youth Justice: Draft Report to the Ministry of Social Development.* Wellington: The Crime and Justice Research Centre, Victoria University of Wellington.

McDonald, J (1992) 'Police initiatives in juvenile justice' in Vernon, J and McKillop, S (eds) *Preventing juvenile crime.* Canberra: Australian Institute of Criminology, pp 89-92.

McFadden, M (1993) 'Youth subcultures and resistance : desperately seeking solutions' in White, R (ed) *Youth subcultures : theory, history and the Australian experience.* Hobart: National Clearinghouse for Youth Studies, pp 151-156.

Meek, J (1992) 'Gangs in New Zealand Prisons' 25(3) *Australian and New Zealand Journal of Criminology* 255-277.

Memphis Shelby Crime Commission (1999) 'Best Practice Number Four: Community Courts –– An Alternative for Involving Citizens and the Community in the Justice Process'. Available: <http://www.memphiscrime.org/research/ bestpractices/bestpractices-4.html>.

Mickler, S (1998) *The myth of privilege: Aboriginal status, media visions, public ideas.* Fremantle: Fremantle Arts Centre Press.

Miller, J (1991) *Last one over the wall: the Massachusetts experiment in closing reform schools*. Columbus: Ohio State University.

Morris, A and Maxwell, G (1998) 'Restorative Justice in New Zealand: Family Group Conferences as a Case Study' 1(1) *Western Criminology Review* [Online]. Available: <http://wcr.sonoma.edu/v1n1/morris.html>.

Moore, L (1998) 'Focusing on the 'community' in community corrections: future directions in community safety and crime prevention', presented at the conference *Partnerships in Crime Prevention*, convened jointly by the Australian Institute of Criminology and the National Campaign Against Violence and Crime. Hobart, 25-27 February 1998.

Moore, M (1997) 'Legitimising criminal justice policies and practices'. Available: <www.FBI.gov/leb/oct973.htm>.

Muirhead, D (1996) *Solutions for Tomorrow's Communities*. Ottawa: Crime Prevention/Victim Services.

Mukherjee, S (1997) 'The Dimension of Juvenile Crime' in Borowski, A and O'Connor, I (eds) *Juvenile Crime, Justice, and Corrections*. Melbourne: Longman, pp 4-24.

Mukherjee, S (2000) 'Crime Trends: A National Perspective' in Chappell, D and Wilson, P (eds) *Crime and the Criminal Justice System in Australia: 2000 and Beyond*. Sydney: Butterworths, pp 45-62.

Mukherjee, S and Dagger, D (1990). *The Size of the Crime Problem in Australia*. Canberra: Australian Institute of Criminology.

Mukherjee, S and Graycar, A (1997). *Crime and Justice in Australia*. Sydney: Hawkins Press.

Muncie, J (1984) *The trouble with kids today*. London: Hutchinson.

Murphy, L (1996) *Statement before the Congressional Black Caucus Brain Trust On Juvenile Justice*. 14 May 1996. Available: <http://www.aclu.org/congress/juvtest.htm>.

Myers, L (1993) 'Detention as a last resort – end of the line or a new beginning?', paper presented at the Australian Institute of Criminology conference on *National Conference on Juvenile Detention*. Darwin, 10-13 August 1993.

NACRO (1999) *Establishing a youth offending team: a practical guide*. Available: <http://www.pentex.org.uk/pages/nacroyot.html>.

Naffine, N (1993) 'Philosophies of juvenile justice' in Gale, F, Naffine, N and Wundersitz, J (eds) *Juvenile Justice: Debating the issues*. Sydney: Allen & Unwin, pp 2-17.

Nash, N (1998) 'Establishing community safety projects: England and Australia', presented at the conference on Partnerships in Crime Prevention, convened jointly by the Australian Institute of Criminology and the National Campaign Against Violence and Crime. Hobart, Tasmania, 25-27 February 1998.

National Anti-Crime Strategy (1996): *Crime Prevention Compendium for Australian States and Territories*. Adelaide: South Australian Attorney-General's Department.

National Association of State Budget Officers (1999) *State juvenile justice expenditures and innovations*. Available: <http://www.cyc-net.org/Newsdesk/ newsdesk-000214-n.html>.

National Centre for Policy Analysis (1994) *Using the private sector to deter crime.* Available: <http://www.public-policy.org/~ncpa/w/w79.html>.

National Crime Prevention (1999) *Pathways to Prevention: Developmental and Early Intervention Approaches to Crime in Australia.* Canberra: Attorney General's Department.

National Crime Prevention Centre (1998) *Crime prevention partnership programme access guide.* Ottawa: National Crime Prevention Council.

Nelken, D (1985) 'Community involvement in crime control' *Current Legal Problems* 239-267.

New Zealand Ministerial Committee of Inquiry into Prisons System (1989) Part II: *The Future Prison System, Partnership and Te Ara Hou: The New Way (From Prison Review – Te Ara Hou: The New Way.* Wellington: New Zealand Government Printer.

New Zealand Ministry of Justice (1998) *Conviction and Sentencing of Offenders in New Zealand: 1987 – 1996.* Wellington: Ministry of Justice.

New Zealand Police (1986) *Police submissions to the Commission of Inquiry into Violence.* Wellington: New Zealand Police.

O'Connor, I (1992) 'Can the Children's Courts prevent further offending?' in Vernon, J and McKillop, S (eds) *Preventing juvenile crime.* Canberra: Australian Institute of Criminology, pp 131-139.

Omaji, P (1993) 'Schools and Juvenile Crime Prevention' in Atkinson, L and Sally-Anne, G (eds) *National Conference on Juvenile Justice: Conference Proceedings.* Canberra: Australian Institute of Criminology, pp 399-412.

Omaji, P (1995) Custodial sentencing in Australia's juvenile justice system' 37(4) *Indian Law Institute Journal* 483-495.

Omaji, P (1997) 'The violent juvenile offender' in Borowski, A and O'Connor, I (eds) *Juvenile Crime, Justice, and Corrections.* Melbourne: Longman, pp 206-224.

Omaji, P (1997b) Critical Issues in Managing Young Offenders: A Review of Western Australian Initiatives. *Juvenile Crime and Juvenile Justice: Toward 2000 and Beyond Conference Proceedings.* Canberra: Australian Institute of Criminology.

Omaji, P (1999) Crime Prevention Partnerships between Criminal Justice and Community Agencies, CRIMSA international conference, East London, South Africa. 25-28 May 1999.

Omaji, P (2001) 'The future of Africa: a crime and justice perspective' in Adesida, O and Oteh, A (eds) *African voices; African visions.* Stockholm: The Nordic African Institute, pp 161-176.

Omaji, P (2001b) 'The *Realcrime* of the State and Indigenous people's human rights' in Garkawe, S, Kelly, L and Fisher, W (eds) *Indigenous human rights.* Sydney: Sydney University Institute of Criminology, pp 228-247.

O'Malley, P (1997) 'The Politics of Crime Prevention' in O'Malley, P and Sutton, A (eds) *Crime Prevention in Australia: Issues in Policy and Research.* Sydney: Federation Press, pp 225-274.

O'Malley, P (2001) 'Risk, Crime and Prudentialism Revisited' in Stenson, K and Sullivan, R (eds) *Crime, Risk and Justice: The politics of crime control in liberal democracies.* Cullompton, Devon UK: Willan Publishing.

Owen, L and Carroll, M (1997) 'An Australian agenda for delinquency research' in Borowski, A and O'Connor, I (eds) *Juvenile Crime, Justice, and Corrections*. Melbourne: Longman, pp 440-464.

Page, B, Shapiro, R and Dempsey, G (1987) 'What moves public opinion?' 81 *American Political Science Review* 23-43.

Page, L (1950) *The young lag: A study in crime*. London: Faber and Faber Ltd.

Parker, H, Sumner, M and Jarvis, G (1989) *Unmasking the magistrates: the 'custody or not' decision in sentencing young offenders*. Philadelphia: Open University Press.

Pavarini, M (1997) 'Controlling social panic: questions and answers about security in Italy at the end of the millennium' in Bergalli, R and Sumner, C (eds) *Social control and political order*. London: Sage Publications.

Pearson, G (1983) *Hooligan: A history of respectable fears*. London: Macmillan.

Piliavin, I and Briar, S (1964) 'Police encounters with juveniles' 70 (September) *American Journal of Sociology* 206-214.

Pinnock, D (1997) *Piloting change for young people at risk: A Handbook*. Pretoria: Ministerial Committee on Young People at Risk.

Pitts, J (1999) *Working with young offenders*. London: Macmillan Press Ltd.

Pitts, J and Hope, T (1998) 'The Local Politics of Inclusion: the State and Community Safety' in Finer, C and Nellis, M (eds) *Crime & Social Exclusion*. Oxford: Blackwell Publishers, pp 37-58.

Police National Headquarters Youth at Risk of Offending Evaluation Team (1998) *Evaluation of the Mt Roskill Police Community Approach Trust*. Auckland: Police National Headquarters.

Polk, K (1997) 'The coming crisis of abandoned youth: a look at the future of juvenile justice in Australia' in Borowski, A and O'Connor, I (eds) *Juvenile crime, justice and corrections*. Melbourne: Longman, pp 489-501.

Polk, K and White, R (1999) 'Economic adversity and criminal behaviour : rethinking youth unemployment and crime' 32(3) *Australian and New Zealand Journal of Criminology* 284-302.

Potas, I, Vining, A and Wilson, P (1990) *Young people and crime: costs and prevention*. Canberra: Australian Institute of criminology.

Pratt, J (1993) 'Welfare and justice: incompatible philosophies' in Gale, F, Naffine, N and Wundersitz, J (eds) *Juvenile Justice: Debating the issues*. Sydney: Allen & Unwin, pp 38-51.

Pratt, J (1995) 'Dangerousness, risk and technologies of power' 28(1) *Australian and New Zealand Journal of Criminology* 3-31.

Presdee, M and Walters, R (1997) 'Policies, Politics, Practices: Crime Prevention in South Australia' in O'Malley, P and Sutton, A (eds) *Crime Prevention in Australia: Issues in Policy and Research*. Sydney: Federation Press, pp 200-216.

Puzzanchera, C (2000) Delinquency Cases Waived to Criminal Court, 1988-1997. Available: <http://www.ncjrs.org/txtfiles1/ojjdp/fs200002.txt>.

Queensland. Commission of Inquiry (1989) *Report of a Commission of Inquiry Into Possible Illegal Activities and Associated Police Misconduct pursuant to Orders in Council*. Brisbane: Government Printer.

Queensland Youth Advocacy Centre (1993) *Juvenile justice: Rhetoric or reality?* Brisbane: YAC.

Ranger, E and Hall, C (1999) 'Back to school for police officers' 173 (March) *Vedette* 14-15.

Rawlings, P (1999) *Crime and Power: A History of Criminal Justice 1688-1998*. London: Addison, Wesley, Longman Ltd.

Read, T and Tilley, N (2000) *Not Rocket Science? Problem-solving and Crime Reduction*. London: Home Office

Redding, R (1998) *National Trends in Juvenile Crime* [Online]. Available: <www.ness.sys.virginia.edu/juv/NatTrends.html>.

Reiss, A (1970) 'Police brutality: Answers to key questions' in Niederhoffer, A and Blumberg, A (eds) *The Ambivalent Force: Perspectives on the Police*. Massachusetts: Ginn and Co, pp 321-330.

Richards, L (1991) 'The appearance of youthful subculture: A theoretical perspective on deviance' in Thompson, W and Bynum, J (eds) *Juvenile Delinquency: Classic and contemporary readings*. Boston: Allyn and Bacon, pp 365-393.

Roscoe, M and Morton, R (1994) Disproportionate Minority Confinement. Available: <http://www.ncjrs.org/txtfiles/fs-9411.txt>.

Rutherford, A (1998) 'Criminal policy and the eliminative ideal' in Finer, C and Nellis, M (eds) *Crime & Social Exclusion*. Oxford: Blackwell Publishers, pp 116-135.

Sampson, A, Stubbs, P, Smith, D, Pearson, G and Blagg, H (1988) 'Crime localities and the multi-agency approach' 28 *British Journal of Criminology* 478-493.

Sampson, R and Lauritsen, J (1997) 'Racial and ethnic disparities in crime and criminal justice in the United States' in Tonry, M (ed) *Ethnicity, Crime, and Immigration: Comparative and Cross National Perspective*. Chicago: University of Chicago Press.

Samuelson, L (1993) *Aboriginal Policing Issues: a comparison of Canada and Australia*. Ottawa: Ministry of Solicitor General of Canada.

Sanderson, M (1998) 'Multiple agendas, one partnership: a case study of the navigator crime prevention project', paper presented at AIC conference on *Partnership in Crime Prevention*, convened jointly by AIC and National Campaign Against Violence and Crime. Hobart, 25-27 February 1998.

Sandor, D (1993) 'Visions for the Future' in Atkinson, L and Gerull, S (eds) *National Conference on Juvenile Justice: Conference Proceedings*. Canberra: Australian Institute of Criminology, pp 460-463.

Sarre, R (1997) 'Crime Prevention and Police' in O'Malley, P and Sutton, A (eds) *Crime Prevention in Australia: Issues in Policy and Research*. Sydney: Federation Press, pp 64-83.

Scarman, L (1982), *The Scarman Report: The Brixton Disorders*, London: HMSO

Schorr, L (1997) *Common Purpose: Strengthening families and neighbourhoods to rebuild America*. New York: Anchor Books.

Scotsman (1998) UK: 'Cheap Cigarettes Supplied By Drugs Gangs'. Available: <http://www.mapinc.org/drugnews/v98.n257.a06.html>.

Select Committee into Youth Affairs (1992) *Youth and the Law*. Perth: Western Australia Legislative Assembly.

Sercombe, H (1995) 'The face of the criminal is Aboriginal' in Bessant, J, Carrington, K and Cook, S (eds) *Cultures of crime and violence: the Australian experience*. Melbourne: La Trobe University Press, pp 76-95.

Sercombe, H, Omaji, P, Drew, N, Cooper, T and Love, T (2000) *Youth and the Future: Effective Youth Services for the year 2015*. Draft Report for the National Youth Affairs Research Committee. Canberra.

Settle, R (1990) *Police power: use and abuse*. Norcorthe, Australia: Muxworthy Press.

Seymour, J (1988) *Dealing with young offenders*. Sydney: Law Book Co.

Seymour, J (1993) 'Australia's juvenile justice systems: a comment' in Gale, F, Naffine, N and Wundersitz, J (eds) *Juvenile Justice: Debating the issues*. Sydney: Allen & Unwin, pp 52-56.

Seymour, J (1997) 'Children's Courts in Australia: the current role and functions' in Borowski, A and O'Connor, I (eds) *Juvenile crime, justice and corrections*. Melbourne: Longman, pp 292-306.

Shapland, J, Wiles, P and Wilcox, P (1994) *Targeted Crime Reduction for Local Areas: Principles and Methods*. London: Police Research Group.

Shearing, C and Ericson, R (1991) 'Culture as figurative action' 42 *British Journal of Sociology* 481-506.

Shepherd, R (1997) 'How the Media Misrepresents Juvenile Policies', Coalition for Juvenile Justice (1997) *False Images? the News Media and Juvenile Crime*. Annual Report. American Bar Association.

Shepherd, R (1999) *Doing justice to juvenile justice*. Available: <http://www.ncjfcj.unr.edu/homepage/da.html>.

Sherman, L, Gottfredson, D, Mackenzie, D, Eck, J, Reuter, P and Bushway, S (1998) *Preventing crime: what works, what doesn't, what's promising*. Washington: Office of Justice Programs, National Institute of Justice.

Sibley, D (1995) *Geographies of exclusion*. London: Routledge and Kegan Paul.

Sickmund, M, Snyder, H and Poe-Yamagata, E (1997) *Juvenile Offenders and Victims: 1997 Update on Violence*. Washington, DC: US Department of Justice, Office of Justice Programs, Office of Juvenile Justice and Delinquency Prevention.

Siegel, L and Senna, J (1988) *Juvenile Delinquency: theory, practice and law*. New York: West Publishing Co.

Simon, R (1982) *Gramsci's political thought: an introduction*. London: Lawrence and Wishart.

Skolnick, J (1975) *Justice without trial: Law enforcement in democratic society*. New York: John Wiley and Sons.

Snider, L (1998) 'Towards safer societies: punishment, masculinities and violence against women' 38(1) *British Journal of Criminology* 1-39.

Snyder, H, Sickmund, M and Poe-Yamagata, E (1996) *Juvenile offenders and victims: 1996 update on violence*. Washington DC: Department of Justice, Office of Juvenile Justice and Delinquency Prevention.

Snyder, H (1998) *Juvenile Arrests 1997*. Washington, DC: US Department of Justice, Office of Justice Programs, Office of Juvenile Justice and Delinquency Prevention.

Soler, M (1996) *The Treatment of Juveniles in the United States*. California: Youth Law Centre.

Springhall, J (1998) *Youth, Popular Culture and Moral Panics: Penny gaffs to Gangsta-Rap, 1830-1996.* New York: St Martins Press.

Stahl, A (1997) 'Delinquency Cases in Juvenile Courts'. Available: <http://www.ncjrs.org/txtfiles1/ojjdp/fs200004.txt>.

Sterner, P (1994) 'Delinquency Prevention'. Available: <http://www.ncjrs.org/txtfiles/fs9406.txt>.

Stevens, W (1957) *Opus Posthumous.* New York: Knopf.

Strang, H (2000) 'The future of restorative justice' in Chappell, D and Wilson, P (eds) *Crime and the criminal justice system in Australia: 2000 and beyond.* Canberra: Butterworths, pp 22-33.

Stratton, J (1992) *The Young Ones: Working class culture, consumption and the category of youth.* Brisbane: Black Swan Press.

Stroman, C and Seltzer, R (1985) 'Media use and perceptions of crime' 62 *Journalism Quarterly* 340-345.

Surette, R (1996) 'News from nowhere, policy to follow: Media and the social construction of Three-strikes and you're out' in Shichor, D and Sechrest, D (eds) *Three strikes and you're out: vengeance as public policy.* Thousand Oaks, California: Sage Publications.

Sutton, A (1997) 'Crime Prevention: Policy Dilemmas – A Personal Account' in O'Malley, P and Sutton, A (eds) *Crime Prevention in Australia: Issues in Policy and Research.* Sydney: Federation Press, pp 12-37.

Sutton, J (1992) 'Women in the job' in Moir, P and Fijkman, H (eds) *Policing Australia: Old issues, new perspectives.* Melbourne: Macmillan, pp 67-101.

Sviridoff, M, Rottman, D and Curtis, R (1997) *Dispensing Justice Locally: The Implementation and Effects of the Midtown Community Court.* Washington, DC: United States Department of Justice.

Szramka, Z (2001) 'The court's role in strengthening families', paper presented at the Australian Institute of Criminology conference on *Children, young people and communities – the future is in our hands.* Launceston, Tasmania, 27-28 March 2001.

Taylor, I (1999) *Crime in context: A critical criminology of market societies.* Cambridge: Polity Press.

Territo, L, Halsted, J and Bromley, M (1992) *Crime and justice in America.* St Paul, Minnesota: West Publishing.

The Onion (2000) NYPD Apologizes For Accidental Shooting-Clubbing-Stabbing-Firebombing Death. Available: <http://www.theonion.com>.

The President's Commission on Law Enforcement and Administration of Justice (1967) *Task Force Report: The Police.* Washington DC: US Government Printing Office.

Thornberry, T and Burch, J (1997) 'Gang Members and Delinquent Behavior', *Bulletin.* Washington, DC: US Department of Justice, Office of Justice Programs, Office of Juvenile Justice and Delinquency Prevention.

Tilley, N (1994) 'Crime prevention and the Safer Cities story' 32(1) *Howard Journal* 40-57.

Travis, J (1996) 'Lessons for the Criminal Justice System from Twenty Years of Policing Reform'. Keynote Address by at the *New Beginnings* – the First Annual Conference of the New York Campaign for Effective Crime Policy March 10, 1996, New York. Available: <http://www.ojp.gov/nij/speeches/lessons.htm>.

Travis, J (1998) 'Thinking about prevention: are we asking the right questions?', presented at the Conference on *Partnership in Crime Prevention*, convened jointly by AIC and National Campaign Against Violence and Crime. Hobart, 25-27 February 1998.

Tuck, M (1991) 'Community and the criminal justice system' 12(3) *Policy Studies* 22-37.

Turner, E (1998) 'Ecstasy in Britain: how Britannia got cool again'. Available: <http://www.ephidrina.org/ecstasy/britain.html>.

United Nations (1991) *The United Nations and Crime Prevention*. New York: UN.

van Dijk, J (1990) 'Crime prevention policy: current state and prospects' in Kaiser, G and Albrecht, H (eds) *Crime and criminal policy in Europe*. Criminological Research Report, vol 43. Freiburg: Max Planck Institute, pp 205-220.

van Dijk, J (1997) 'Towards Effective Public-Private Partnerships in Crime Control: Experiences in the Netherlands' in Felson, M and Clarke, R (eds) *Business and Crime Prevention*. Monsey, New York: Criminal Justice Press, pp 97-124.

Wakefield, W and Hirschel, J (1996) England, in Shoemaker, D (ed) *International Handbook on Juvenile Justice*. Westport, Connecticut: Greenwood Press, pp 90-109.

Walklate, S (1998) *Understanding criminology: current theoretical debates*. Buckingham: Open University Press.

Walker, J (1992) 'Estimates of the Costs of Crime in Australia', *Trends and Issues in Crime and Criminal Justice* No 39. Canberra: Australian Institute of Criminology.

Walker, J (1996) 'Estimates of the Costs of Crime in Australia in 1996', *Trends and Issues in crime and criminal justice*. No 72. Canberra: Australian Institute of Criminology.

Walker, J and Henderson, M (1991) 'Understanding crime trends in Australia' *Trends and Issues* No 28. Canberra: Australian Institute of Criminology.

Walker, S, Spohn, C and DeLone, M (1996) *The color of justice: race, ethnicity and crime in America*. Belmont, CA: Wadsworth Publishing Company.

Waller, L and Williams, C (1997) *Criminal Law: Text and Cases*. Sydney: Butterworths.

Warner, K (1987) 'Juveniles in the criminal justice system' in Zdenkowski, G, Ronalds, C and Richardson, M (eds) *The Criminal Injustice System*. Sydney: Pluto Press, pp 171-190.

Warner, K (1993) 'The courts, the judiciary and new directions: the limits of legislative change' in Atkinson, L and Gerull, S (eds) *National Conference on Juvenile Justice*. Canberra: Australian Institute of Criminology, pp 43-52.

Waters, R (1990) *Ethnic Minorities and the Criminal Justice System*. Aldershot: Avebury.

Welch, M, Fenwick, M and Roberts, M (1997) 'Primary definitions of crime and moral panic: A content analysis of experts' quotes in feature newspaper articles on crime' 34(4) *Journal of Research in Crime and Delinquency* 474-494.

White, R (1993) 'Young people and the policing of the community space' 26 *Australian and New Zealand Journal of Criminology* 207-218.

White, R (1997) 'Police practices, punishment and juvenile crime prevention' in Borowski, A and O'Connor, I (eds) *Juvenile crime, justice and corrections*. Melbourne: Longman, pp 254-269.

White, R, Perrone, S, Guerra, C and Lampugnani, R (1999) *Ethnic youth gangs in Australia : do they exist?*. Melbourne: Australian Multicultural Foundation.

Wiatrowski, M (1996) 'Three strikes and you're out: rethinking the police and crime control mandate' in Shichor, D and Sechrest, D (eds) *Three Strikes and You're Out: Vengeance as Public Policy*. London: Sage Publications, pp 117-134.

Wilber, S (1999) 'Can prevention programs stem the tide of delinquency?' Available: <http:www.juvenilejustice.com/prevention.html>.

Wilson, J (1968) 'The police and the delinquent in two cities', in Wheeler, S\ (ed) *Controlling delinquents*. New York: John Wiley and Sons, pp 9-30.

Wilson, J (1968) *Varieties of police behaviour: the management of law and order in eight communities*. Cambridge, Massachusetts: Harvard University Press.

Wilson, W (1987) *The Truly Disadvantaged: The Inner City, the Underclass, and Public Policy*. Chicago: University of Chicago Press.

Wilson, J and Herrnstein, R (1985) *Crime and Human Nature: The Definitive Study of the Causes of Crime*. London: Simon & Schuster.

Wolfgang, M, Thornberry, T and Figlio, R (1987) *From boy to man, from delinquency to crime*. Chicago: University of Chicago Press.

Worall, S (1996) *Evaluation of the Mt Roskill Police Youth At Risk of Offending Program*. Auckland: Mt Roskill Police Community Approach Trust.

Wordes, M and Bynum, T (1995) 'Policing juveniles: Is there bias against youths of color?' in Leonard, K, Pope, C and Feyerherm, W (eds) *Minorities in juvenile justice*. London: Sage Publications, pp 47-65.

Wundersitz, J (1993) 'Some statistics on youth offending: an inter-jurisdictional comparison' in Gale, F, Naffine, N and Wundersitz, J (eds) *Juvenile Justice: Debating the issues*. Sydney: Allen & Unwin, pp 18-36.

Wundersitz, J (2000) 'Juvenile justice in Australia: towards the new millenium' in Chappell, D and Wilson, P (eds) *Crime and the criminal justice system in Australia: 2000 and beyond*. Canberra: Butterworths, pp 102-118.

Yochelson, S and Samenow, S (1976) *The Criminal Personality*. New York: J. Aronson.

Youth Justice Coalition (1990) *Kids in Justice*. Sydney: Youth Justice Coalition (NSW)

Zdenkowski, G, Ronalds, C and Richardson, M (1987) *The criminal injustice system*. Sydney: Pluto Press

Zimring, F (1998) *American Youth Violence*. New York: Oxford University Press.

Zimring, F (2001) 'Crime, criminal justice and criminology for a smaller planet: some notes on the 21st century' 34(3) *Australian and New Zealand Journal of Criminology* 213-220.

Zimring, F (2001b) 'Imprisonment rates and the new politics of criminal punishment' 3(1) *Punishment and Society: The International Journal of Penology* 161-166.

Zimring, F and Hawkins, G (1995) *Incapacitation : penal confinement and the restraint of crime.* New York: Oxford University Press.

Index

Aboriginals *see* Black youth; Indigenous

Active citizenship
    signatories to the social contract, 192

Adams, Phillip, 3, 4

African-American juveniles, 96

American Revolution, 61

Appreciative Inquiry, 2
    research methodological tool, 2
    residual 'positives', 2

Australian Law Reform Commission, 24

Backcasting measures, 58

Beijing Rules, 10

Black youth, 44, 47, 71, 96, 116
    over-representation, 96, 99-102
    pervasive criminalisation of, 117

Borstal training, 63

British Parliament, *See* United Kingdom

Bulger, James, 38

Causes of crime, 34
    individual failings, 34
    social ills, 34
    unemployment, 29

Childsaving, 63, 64

Christianity
    Saviour's followers, 3

Community policing, 122, 133, 149, 175, 177

Community prosecution movement, 130

Corporal punishment, 59, 60

Corrections, 8,
    detention staff, 21, 30, 31
    Massachusetts experiment, 30
    pleasure-pain mechanism, 31
    rate of juveniles in, 102

Cost of youth crime and justice
    justice spending, 108-111
    methodological limitations, 108

Courts, 25-30, 79-81, 123-126, 148,
     differential processing, 29
     jurisprudence of the vulnerable, 29
     juvenile courts, 7
     Probate Court, Oakland County, Michigan, 27
     protecting private property, 29
     subculture of sentencing, 29
     therapeutic model, 123
     traditionally oriented judiciary, 26

Crime Concern, 127, 155, 156

Crime control, 5
     budget, 9, 108-111
     conservative ideology, 113

Crime prevention, 1, 38, 130-134, 169-171, 190-194
     new penology, 5, 190
     sociological fallacy, 6
     solidarity project, 190-191
     typology, 7

Criminal jurisprudence, 67

Criminal justice agencies, 1, 122-127, 165, 179, 194-200
     abuse of power and force, 32
     demonisation, 3, 17, 20
     extra-legal influences, 17
     incarceral mentalities, 3
     'normality' project, 40
     pro-active partners, 1
     radical role in crime prevention, 1, 6, 196
     unparalleled power position, 9

Criminal justice responses, 13-16, 57-59, 165
     criminogenic, 1, 7, 38, 46, 135, 190
     image and perceptions matter, 13
     reactive and retributive, 5, 57-59

Criminal justice system
     failing machine ticks on, 121
     incarceral archipelago, 113
     paralysis of pessimism, 198
     systemic malaise, 191

Criminal responsibility, 59

Criminal victimisation, 45, 122

Criminology, 34, 36
     classicist' thinking, 79, 81

Cross-national understanding, 11

Cultural hegemony, 41-44

Culture-neutral justice myth, 80

Custodial staff's perceptions
    authoritarian, 30
    inmates as rejectees, 30-31

Daily Telegraph (UK), 26

Daniel O'Connell's case, 1870, 65

Detention of youth, 81-82

Drug courts, 126

European Forum for Urban Security, 18
    Young People our Enemies, 18

European settlements, 61

Folk devils, 18, 20, 37
    everywhere young, 18

Garbathons (Canada), 134

Gault, In re 1967, 66

Gender analysis, 99

Giamoci, Antonio
    intellectual's error, 1, 2

Habeas corpus, 62, 65

Head Start intervention, 109

High impact partnerships
    ground rules, 179

High-speed car chases, 44

House of Refuge, 62, 65

Human rights instruments, international and regional, 14, 87

Ideology, 1, 14, 18, 26, 33
    huge swings, 14

Images of childhood
    the delinquent child, 19

Imaging of youth, 18
    gang warfare, 21
    hippy formula, 20
    mods and rockers, 20
    Shakespeare's The Winter's Tale, 19
    social constructions, 59
    Teddy Boys (UK), 26

Indigenous
    communities, 55, 178
    youth, 24, 38

Intensive wrap-around
    crime prevention, 15

Judges' perceptions, 25-30
    white middle-class standards, 26

Judicial response to youth crime
    not mechanical, 80

Judicial waiver, 70

Just deserts, 58

Justice model
    due process protections, 67, 69

Juvenile justice decalogue, 83

Juvenile justice system, 59-69, 115-120
    history cyclical, 9
    international standards, 59, 83-89

Keynesian welfare state, 117

Larry King Live Show, 36

Law and order, 5, 20, 46, 58, 121, 131
    neo-conservative politics, 5
    selective targeting, 5

Mandatory sentencing, 3, 69, 189

Maori, 31, 37

Media, 34-38, 72, 73, 79,
    community service, 159
    inflammatory, 3
    news coverage, 35
    portrayals of the police, 45
    preventative duty, 190
    sensationalising youth crime, 3, 188

Media construction, 20

Media news coverage
    benevolent paternalism, 37
    'if it bleeds, it leads', 35

Middle Ages, 60

Moral panics, 14, 20, 36, 43

Negroes, 25

New Zealand
    Inquiry into Violence, 1986, 24
    police, 24

Parens patriae, 62, 67, 118

Parkhurst Act of 1838, 62

Partnerships
    agency-initiated, 40
    community coalition, 10
    inter-agency, 127, 131-132, 138, 144
    inter-sectoral, 132, 184, 199
    multi-agency, 127, 128, 131
    resource-efficient, 114
    UN endorsement, 10

Partnership projects
  Baton Rouge Partnership, 138-142
  Cairns Community Safety Project, 157-163
  Juvenile Justice Teams, 144-145
  Maple Ridge Youth Conference, 143-144
  Midtown Community Court, New York, 148-151
  Mt Roskill Police Community Approach, 146-147
  Safer Slough Enterprise Partnership, 151-156

Paupers and criminals, 62

Penal colonies, 81

Police, 22-25, 32-33, 45-49
  abuse of power, 32, 46
  gatekeepers, 22
  masculinist orientation, 33
  police subculture, 23
  racism, 22, 23

Police Citizen's Youth Club, 160

Police self-perceptions
  front line troops, 22
  guardians of public morality, 22
  the 'thin blue line', 22

Police-Aboriginal relations, 77

Policing youth crime, 71-79
  bias-driven, 47
  interest of business, 33
  Peelian vision, 6
  selective enforcement, 72
  'vigilante' justice, 23
  zero tolerance, 58, 69, 189

Political opportunism, 1

Politicians
  election-driven, 3

Post-Fordist societies, 21, 55, 135
  turbo-charged capitalism, 55

Pre-sentence reports
  judges' perceptions, 26

Racial and ethnic minorities, 24

Racial and ethnic youth, 13
  feared 'Other', 18
  fight against inferiority, 13
  marginalised, 5, 13

Radical engagement
  criminal justice responses, 16

Recidivism, 7, 99, 141, 142

Reformatory movement, 64
    state industrial schools, 66

Research, 2, 9-13
    case study approach, 15
    critical discourses, 13
    cross-national perspective, 11
    eclectic methodology, 12
    inter-disciplinary, 13
    National Crime Victimization Survey, 103
    time series studies, 91

Restorative justice, 31, 126, 137, 190

Ryan, P, 22

Safer communities, 1

Social construction, 34
    exclusionary bias, 37
    experienced and symbolic realities, 34

Social exclusion, 104, 190

Sociology, 2, 13
    critical political economy, 56
    dialectical perspectives, 40

Stereotyping, 2, 22

Surveillance, 20

System-imposed inferiority, 44
    degradation ceremonies, 43, 73

Three strikes, 4, 121

Traditional police approach
    kerb-side justice, 72

Trappings of 'dangerousness
    clothing and hairstyles, 23

UK *see* United Kingdom

UNICEF, 18

United Kingdom
    anti-youth concern, 19
    British Parliament, 19
    Crime and Disorder Act 1998, 128, 138
    Home Office, 127, 131, 132
    images of 'childhood', 19
    Margate and Brighton beaches, 21
    Metropolitan Police, 6, 24
    Saxon and Norman kings, 60
    Tudor times, 60
    Victorian era, 19
    Youth Offending Teams, 125

United Nations, 10, 83-87

United States
    black kids in white neighbourhoods, 25
    House of Representatives, 4
    Judge Eugene A Moore, 27
    National Crime Prevention Council, 35
    President's Commission on Law Enforcement and the Administration
        of Justice, 22

Victims of crime, 47, 104,

Visible minority
    obvious scapegoat, 28

Vision, 1, 6, 15

Welfare model, 63, 68

Western world, 4
    adult imagination, 19
    ambivalence towards youth, 18
    anti-child spirit, 18
    collective neurosis, 21
    developed nations, 11
    industrialisation and urbanisation, 19
    infatuation with prisons, 114
    kindred settler societies, 11
    vengeful spirit is alive, 58

Young Aborigines, 23, 44, 79

Young offenders, 28
    'abnormal' minority, 40
    common denominators, 28

Young people
    create criminal images, 53
    'creators' of their own image, 41
    cultural muscles, 41
    disadvantaged segments, 54
    gregarious lifestyles, 197
    hanging-out-together, 55
    not passive objects, 40
    productive citizens, 1
    subcultural expressions, 13
    treasured asset, 4, 15
    'troubled' youth, 1
    victimisation, 47, 54, 103, 104

Youth
    active citizenship denied, 188
    adolescents, 18
    attitudes towards courts, 49
    constructed as delinquents, 20
    enduring scapegoat, 21
    generation with 'No Future', 197
    source of anxiety, 18

Youth (*cont*)
    stage in life course, 18
    teenagers, 37
    threat to be neutralised, 20

Youth action, 54
    broader context, 54

Youth and detention, 30-31, 50-52, 81-82, 100-103

Youth and the courts, 25-30, 49-50, 79-81, 96-100

Youth crime
    crime wave myth, 9
    demography is not destiny, 91
    drug factor, 107
    fear and concern, 9
    power contest, 44
    predator crime, 34
    risk and protective factors, 165
    status symbol, 44
    symptomatic, 2-3
    tyranny of 'small numbers, 92
    underlying social malady, 3, 188

Youth crime prevention
    future directions, 15, 187

Youth justice
    addressing offending behaviour, 128
    political enterprise, 58
    proportionality, 58
    reconfigured, 1

Youth responses
    rebel culturally, 41
    retreat into a cultural box, 41
    seeking societal approval, 41

Youth violence
    masculine honour contests, 54

Youth-adult tensions, 21
    inter-generational 'war', 41

Youthful subculture
    Hippie movement, 41, 43
    Teenspeak, 42